Contents

Contents

1 Being and belonging
- mp3-Audio und Transkript: *The Black Lives Matter Movement, Part I and II*
- Kopiervorlagen 1–4

2 Gran Torino
- mp3-Audio und Transkript: *My 'Oriental' father: On the words we use to describe ourselves*
- Kopiervorlage 1

3 Crooked Letter, Crooked Letter
- mp3-Audio und Transkript: *NPR Interview with Tom Franklin*
- Kopiervorlagen 1–4

Klausurvorschläge mit Erwartungshorizonten
- Being and belonging
- Gran Torino 1
- Gran Torino 2
- Crooked Letter, Crooked Letter 1
- Crooked Letter, Crooked Letter 2

Allgemeiner Teil

REIHENKONZEPT

Das vorliegende Heft zum zentralen Schwerpunktthema The ambiguity of belonging *(Baden-Württemberg ab 2019) ist ein speziell für die Abituranforderungen der Oberstufe in Baden-Württemberg entwickeltes Themenheft. Das Schülerheft bietet Materialien, die sowohl im Unterricht als auch zum Selbststudium verwendet werden können.*

LEHRERHEFT

*Im Lehrerheft wird der Inhalt des Schülerhefts methodisch-didaktisch aufbereitet sowie durch zahlreiche Hinweise ergänzt. Das Lehrerheft beinhaltet außerdem mögliche Lösungen für die Aufgaben im Schülerheft. Weitere themenrelevante Texte zu den USA finden sich in **Green Line Oberstufe Baden-Württemberg, Klettnummer 530402.***

Schülerheft

CHAPTERS

Das Schülerheft für die Kursstufe enthält drei Kapitel:
Chapter 1: Being and belonging
Chapter 2: Gran Torino
Chapter 3: Crooked Letter, Crooked Letter

TASKS

Die drei Kapitel bieten ein vielseitiges und abwechslungsreiches Aufgabenangebot mit dem Ziel, auf der einen Seite die Erarbeitung des zentralen Schwerpunktthemas zu ermöglichen und zu dokumentieren und auf der anderen Seite die Bewältigung der verschiedenen Lern- und Arbeitsbereiche der Oberstufe und die Anforderungen des Zentralabiturs zu erreichen.

OPERATOREN

Das Aufgabenangebot orientiert sich durchgehend an den Anforderungsbereichen der Einheitlichen Prüfungsanforderungen (EPA) – Comprehension, Analysis und Evaluation – und setzt auf die Verwendung der im Kerncurriculum definierten Operatoren. Dabei werden auch standardisierte Aufgabenformate eingesetzt.

KOMPETENZEN

Neben den textanalytischen Fragestellungen spielen Aufgaben zu verschiedenen Kompetenzen eine wichtige Rolle. Diese sind u. a. Discussing, Debating, Research, Presentation, Projects, Creative writing. Wortschatzarbeit und nachhaltiger Vokabelerwerb werden ebenso berücksichtigt wie die zentralen Fertigkeiten Lesen, Schreiben, Hörverstehen, Hörsehverstehen, Sprechen und Mediation.

SOZIALFORMEN

Die Aufgaben sind für unterschiedliche Sozialformen konzipiert, auf die in den jeweiligen methodisch-didaktischen Hinweisen näher eingegangen wird. Durch die sinnvolle Kombination der verschiedenen Aufgaben entsteht ein Angebot, das die zielgerichtete Vorbereitung auf die zentrale Abiturprüfung gewährleistet, gleichzeitig aber hinreichend Abwechslung bei den Aufgabenformaten bietet.

Lehrerheft

LEHRERHEFT

Das Lehrerheft setzt sich zum Ziel, einen wirksamen Beitrag zu einer effektiven und zeitsparenden Unterrichtsvorbereitung und -durchführung zu leisten. Die folgenden Elemente dienen in besonderer Weise zur Arbeitserleichterung:

DIDAKTISCHES INHALTSVERZEICHNIS

*Eine Erstinformation über die Inhalte des jeweiligen Kapitels bietet ein didaktisches Inhaltsverzeichnis, das in knapper und übersichtlicher Form über Titel, Textsorten und Themen sowie über Unterrichtsmethoden, Textproduktion und Kompetenzen informiert. Die Anmerkungen im Anschluss erläutern das Unterrichtskonzept und die Anbindung des zentralen Schwerpunktthemas an den Themenkreis des Kerncurriculums (**Green Line Oberstufe Baden-Württemberg**).*

**UNTERRICHTS-
KONZEPT**

Es folgen Hinweise zum Unterrichtsverlauf. Dazu gehören Verknüpfungen zu Inhalten in **Green Line Oberstufe Baden-Württemberg**, *Hintergrundinformationen, methodische Schritte, Unterrichtsergebnisse, Querverweise und Zusatzmaterialien.*

**ERGEBNIS-
SICHERUNG**

Besonderer Wert wurde auf die Sicherung der Unterrichtsergebnisse in Form von Lösungsvorschlägen gelegt. Bei zahlreichen Aufgaben gibt es ausführliche Vorschläge, insbesondere dann, wenn die Unterrichtsergebnisse für die Klausur- und Prüfungsvorbereitung relevant sind.

Servicematerial im Anhang und auf der CD-ROM

**KLAUSUR-
VORSCHLÄGE**

Im Anhang des Lehrerhefts befindet sich zu jedem Kapitel ein Klausurvorschlag (Seite 101–122). Zu den Kapiteln Gran Torino *und* Crooked Letter, Crooked Letter *stehen jeweils zwei Vorschläge zur Verfügung. Die Klausurvorschläge decken unterschiedliche Textsorten ab und enthalten u.a. auch einen Hörverstehens- und einen Mediationstext. Der notwendige Wortschatz ist jeweils unter dem Text annotiert. Die Klausurvorschläge werden, wie die aktuellen Aufgaben des zentralen schriftlichen Abiturs in Baden-Württemberg, in einen situativen Rahmen eingebettet.*

**ERWARTUNGS-
HORIZONTE**

Zu den Klausurvorschlägen gibt es Erwartungshorizonte für die Hand der Lehrkraft. Diese Lösungsvorschläge befinden sich direkt im Anschluss an die jeweiligen Klausurvorschläge. Die Transkripte der Hörverstehensaufgaben sind jeweils in den Erwartungshorizonten zu finden.

CD-ROM

Die CD-ROM enthält die Audiodateien samt Transkripten sowie zusätzliche Kopiervorlagen. Darüber hinaus stehen auf der CD-ROM die Klausurvorschläge in editierbarer Form zur Verfügung und für die Hand der Lehrkraft sind auch die Erwartungshorizonte zu den Klausurvorschlägen auf der CD-ROM zu finden.

AUDIOS ALS mp3

Systemvoraussetzung für die mp3-Dateien in den Kapiteln sind Computer oder mp3-abspielfähige CD-Player.

1 Being and belonging

Seite 4 – 23

Didaktisches Inhaltsverzeichnis

Titel	Textsorte	Thema	Unterrichtsmethoden	Kompetenzen Textproduktion
A Identity: Why are we who we are?				
Identity: Why are we who we are?	Combination of visuals *Kopiervorlage 1 (CD-ROM)*	Personal and social identity	*Unterrichtsgespräch Einzelarbeit Partnerarbeit* Think-Pair-Share	Describing and analysing pictures Brainstorming Sharing information Discussing aspects
Identity and belonging	Two cartoons	Identity and belonging	*Unterrichtsgespräch Einzelarbeit Partnerarbeit*	Describing and interpreting cartoons Comparing and contrasting aspects Writing personal letters Debating
Identity: Who are you	Word grid Diagram	Factors of identity	*Unterrichtsgespräch Einzelarbeit*	Working on vocabulary Ranking factors Making lists
Identity: What are your needs?	Pyramid	Hierarchy of needs	*Unterrichtsgespräch Einzelarbeit*	Describing and analysing graphs Making posters
B The push and pull of migration				
Belonging in an age of mass migration	Factual text	Mass migration	*Unterrichtsgespräch Einzelarbeit Leseverstehen*	Making mind maps Taking notes Comparing aspects
Migration on a global scale	Infographic	Global migration	*Unterrichtsgespräch Einzelarbeit Gruppenarbeit*	Interpreting statistics Designing posters Discussing aspects
Urbanisation: urban vs. rural living	Two line graphs Cartoon	Urbanisation	*Unterrichtsgespräch Einzelarbeit Partnerarbeit*	Brainstorming Discussing pros and cons Comparing graphs Interpreting cartoons Doing research
C Race in the United States				
The Black Lives Matter Movement	⊚ Podcast (Part One and Two) Transcripts *(CD-ROM)*	Race in the US	*Unterrichtsgespräch Einzelarbeit Hörverstehen*	Listening for gist / detail Writing a letter Preparing an interview Analysing rhetorical devices
Ethnicity in numbers	Graph Statistics	Unemployment rate and number of prisoners	*Unterrichtsgespräch Einzelarbeit*	Analysing graphs Comparing developments Debating
Thousands gather in tribute to five police officers killed at protest	Newspaper article	Violence against police officers	*Unterrichtsgespräch Einzelarbeit Partnerarbeit Leseverstehen*	Reading for detail Doing research Analysing emotions Discussing aspects

Titel	Textsorte	Thema	Unterrichtsmethoden	Kompetenzen Textproduktion
Guns in America: a controversial issue	Song lyrics	Private gun ownership in the US	*Unterrichtsgespräch* *Einzelarbeit* *Partnerarbeit*	Doing internet research Talking about songs Analysing song lyrics Presenting findings Writing song verses Collecting arguments
D Social class in the US				
Social class	Factual text	Social standing in the US	*Unterrichtsgespräch* *Einzelarbeit*	Making mind maps Completing a text
Factors influencing class	Graphs	Class by race and ethnicity	*Unterrichtsgespräch* *Einzelarbeit* *Gruppenarbeit*	Analysing graphs Discussing aspects
Do Americans still have a shared identity?	Newspaper article Two cartoons	American identity	*Unterrichtsgespräch* *Einzelarbeit* *Partnerarbeit*	Making lists Reading for detail Drawing graphs Interpreting cartoons
Jeder sechste in Deutschland von Armut bedroht	Visual German newspaper article	Social class and poverty in Germany	*Unterrichtsgespräch* *Einzelarbeit* *Mediation*	Describing and assessing pictures Writing personal letters Mediating
E Gender				
Gender	Cartoon	Female/Male gender stereotypes	*Unterrichtsgespräch* *Einzelarbeit* *Partnerarbeit* Think-Pair-Share	Describing and interpreting cartoons Making lists Discussing factors
Gender in cartoons and movies	Cartoon Movie *Zusatzmaterial: Klausurvorschlag mit Erwartungs- horizont (CD-ROM)*	Gender roles and stereotypes	*Unterrichtsgespräch* *Einzelarbeit* *Gruppenarbeit* *Hörsehverstehen*	Interpreting and creating cartoons Watching for gist Analysing films Writing reviews Doing research Making lists Speculating on aspects

Anmerkungen zur didaktischen Konzeption

**UNTERRICHTS-
KONZEPT**

Das Kapitel Being and belonging *dient der inhaltlichen Vorentlastung der späteren Arbeit mit dem Roman* Crooked Letter, Crooked Letter *(2010) sowie dem Film* Gran Torino *(2008). Beide zeitgenössischen Werke spielen an zwei sehr unterschiedlichen Handlungsorten und Regionen in den USA: Kleinstadt im Süden vs. Großstadt im Norden. Die Handlung von* Crooked Letter, Crooked Letter *ist dabei nicht nur im amerikanischen Süden angesiedelt, sondern rekurriert auch allenthalben auf gängige (reale wie literarische) Konzepte und Klischees bezüglich der Südstaaten. Der Handlungsort Mississippi steht einerseits – pars pro toto – stellvertretend für die Südstaaten und ist doch gleichzeitig unverwechselbarer, ja unersetzlicher Bestandteil der Erzählung. Der Film* Gran Torino *spielt in Detroit, Michigan, einer amerikanischen Großstadt, die – außer mit den herkömmlichen Problemen US-amerikanischer Metropolen – mit den Folgen des wirtschaftlichen Niedergangs zu kämpfen hat. Der eigentliche Handlungsort ist eine Vor- stadtsiedlung Detroits, die ihrerseits nicht unberührt von der ökonomischen Krise und deren Auswirkungen geblieben ist.*

Das Kapitel Being and belonging *thematisiert individuelle und soziale Identität und deren pro- minenteste konstituierende Faktoren, nämlich Herkunft, Rasse, soziale Schicht und Geschlecht.*

Hierbei wird nicht nur die Wechselwirkung zwischen individueller und sozialer Identität beleuchtet, sondern auch das (soziale) Spannungsfeld zwischen einerseits Selbstbestimmung und Fremdbestimmung sowie andererseits Zugehörigkeit(-sgefühl) und (sozialer) Isolation thematisiert. Das Kapitel Being and belonging *umfasst damit fünf zentrale Themenbereiche, die für die unterrichtliche Behandlung des Romans und des Films von zentraler Bedeutung sind:*
Identity, Migration, Race, Class *und* Gender.

Das Kapitel Being and belonging *liefert weiterhin Hintergrundwissen zum Thema Schusswaffen, welches sich als wiederkehrendes Motiv durch beide Werke zieht. In* Crooked Letter, Crooked Letter *wird gleich im ersten Kapitel einer der beiden Hauptcharaktere, Larry Ott, angeschossen und schwer verletzt. Bezeichnenderweise darf Larry Ott selbst keine Schusswaffe besitzen. In* Gran Torino *beginnt die Beziehung und spätere Freundschaft zwischen Walter und Thao (und dessen Familie) mit Walters erstem Waffengebrauch gegen die Hmong-Gang; ein Zwischenfall der Walter zum (unfreiwilligen) Helden der Nachbarschaft macht. Beim finalen Showdown am Ende des Films führt Walter – in einem ultimativen Akt der Selbstlosigkeit – die Mitglieder der Hmong-Gang ihrer gerechten Strafe zu. Er tut dies eben nicht, indem er selbst von der Waffe Gebrauch macht, sondern in voller Absicht nur vortäuscht, eine Waffe zu ziehen. Dadurch bringt er die Gangmitglieder dazu, ihn (einen Unbewaffneten) vor Zeugen zu erschießen.*

Nachfolgend wird anhand der oben genannten Themenbereiche jeweils konkret Bezug auf beide Werke genommen.

Identity: *Sowohl in* Crooked Letter, Crooked Letter *als auch in* Gran Torino *wird die Frage nach Identität und Zugehörigkeit gestellt. In* Crooked Letter, Crooked Letter *erfahren die beiden Hauptfiguren, Silas „32" Jones und Larry Ott, erst am Ende der Geschichte die Wahrheit über ihre eigene Identität sowie über das Verhältnis, in dem sie zueinander stehen. Weiterhin sind beide mit Brüchen und Bruchstellen in ihrer Identität konfrontiert und müssen lernen mit diesen umzugehen und zu leben.*
Auch in Gran Torino *ergeht es Walt und Thao – unter völlig anderen Vorzeichen – ganz ähnlich. Walt fühlt sich zunehmend als Fremder in einer (Um-)Welt, die er nicht mehr versteht / verstehen will: seine geliebte Frau Dorothy stirbt, er hat kein gutes Verhältnis zu seinen beiden Söhnen sowie seinen Enkelkindern, er ahnt, dass er sehr krank ist (er hustet Blut); außerdem sieht er „sein Amerika" vor seinen Augen verschwinden, z.B. die Autofabrik, in der er ein Leben lang gearbeitet hat oder seine Wohngegend, in der er sein Leben lang gewohnt hat. Thao, als Kind einer Einwandererfamilie, muss erst lernen, in einer (Um-)Welt zurecht zu kommen, die er (noch) nicht versteht, was ihm aber mit Walts Hilfe zunehmend gelingt. Thao steht zwischen mehreren Gruppen: zwei Kulturen (Hmong-Kultur vs. American way of life) und zwei Familien (seine biologische Familie und die Hmong-Gang, die für ihre Mitglieder eine Art Ersatzfamilie ist).*

Migration: *Im Falle von Silas „32" Jones verhält es sich so, dass er im Alter von 14 Jahren zusammen mit seiner Mutter aus Chicago in die (fiktive) Südstaatenkleinstadt Chabot kommt, diese später verlässt (Studium an der „Ole Miss" in Oxford, Mississippi und Dienst in der US Navy) und dann schließlich wieder dorthin zurückkehrt, um als Polizist zu arbeiten. Das bedeutet, seine Biografie ist in einem gewissen Sinn auch von Migration geprägt.*
Thao und seine Familie sind (klassische) Einwanderer aus Asien. Auch Walt Kowalski, ehemaliger Ford-Mitarbeiter und Veteran des Koreakrieges, wird im Film mit seinen polnischen Wurzeln konfrontiert. Im Rahmen seiner Friseurbesuche beschimpfen er und sein Frisör (und Freund) Martin sich, u.a. indem sie sich über die (polnische / italienische) Abstammung des anderen lustig machen. Ein weiterer Aspekt, nämlich urbane Migration, findet sich ebenfalls in Gran Torino: *viele von Walts Nachbarn haben die Vorstadtsiedlung verlassen, in die wiederum nach und nach Einwandererfamilien gezogen sind.*

Race: *Offener und latenter Rassismus sowie die Frage bezüglich der (Un-)Möglichkeit eines friedlichen Zusammenlebens verschiedener Ethnien und Rassen sind in beide Werken sehr prominent. Die Protagonisten in* Crooked Letter, Crooked Letter *sind der afroamerikanische Polizist Silas „32" Jones und der weiße Automechaniker Larry Ott.*
Die Hauptfiguren in Gran Torino *sind der Einwandererjunge Thao (aus der Volksgruppe der Hmong) sowie der polnischstämmige Walt Kowalski, der (anfänglich) seine rassistische Einstel-*

lung klar zum Ausdruck bringt. Er bezeichnet Asiaten u.a. als „swamp rats", „damn barbarians", „gooks", „egg rolls", etc. und ist außerdem offensichtlich sehr unglücklich darüber, dass seine neue Hausärztin Asiatin ist. Konflikte zwischen verschiedenen Rassen werden in Gran Torino *außerdem dargestellt anhand der Auseinandersetzung zwischen verschiedenen Straßengangs (mexikanische Gang vs. Hmong-Gang) sowie anhand der (sexuellen) Belästigung von Thaos Schwester Sue durch Mitglieder einer afroamerikanischen Straßengang.*

Class: *In* Crooked Letter, Crooked Letter *spielen Herkunft und soziale Schicht eine prägende Rolle. Die Romanfiguren werden jeweils vor dem Hintergrund ihrer Zugehörigkeit zu einer bestimmten sozio-ökonomischen Klasse und deren (stereo-)typischen Merkmalen und Verhaltensweisen charakterisiert. Auch die Mitglieder der armen, weißen Unterschicht („white trash") in Mississippi (z.B. Irina Mott und Wallace Stringfellow) werden dabei nicht ausgelassen. Nichtsdestotrotz besteht ein klarer, sogar reziproker, Zusammenhang zwischen der Zugehörigkeit zu einer sozialen Schicht und Rasse. Silas ist zwar der Polizist („constable") der Kleinstadt Chabot, aber seine Vorgesetzten, z.B. Chief French, sind weiß. Auch der reichste Mann in Chabot, Sägewerkbetreiber Rutherford, ist ein Weißer. In* Gran Torino *lässt sich der Einfluss, den Herkunft und Zugehörigkeit zu einer bestimmten sozialen Schicht auf individuelle Verhaltensmuster haben, besonders deutlich am Beispiel Walt Kowalskis erkennen, der als typischer Vertreter der Arbeiterschicht auch deren Weltsicht teilt.*

Gender: *In* Crooked Letter, Crooked Letter *sind es zwei junge Frauen, Cindy Walker und Tina Rutherford, die Opfer von Verbrechen werden, welche von Männern begangen werden. Das Konfliktpotenzial traditioneller Geschlechterrollen zeigt sich ebenso deutlich in* Gran Torino. *Die Gangmitglieder einer mexikanischen Straßengang beschimpfen Thao und bezeichnen ihn als „Mädchen", weil er ein Buch liest. Thaos Cousin behandelt ihn herablassend und wirft ihm vor, er mache Frauenarbeit („woman's work"), weil er im Garten arbeitet. Ein weiteres Beispiel ist Thaos Großmutter, die sich über ihn beklagt und prophezeit, dass er nie „der Mann im Haus" („the man of the house") werden würde, weil er tut, was seine Schwester ihm sagt und z.B. das Geschirr abwäscht. Unterstützung erfährt Thao hingegen von Walt und dessen Freund, dem Frisör Martin, die ihn darin unterrichten, zu „reden wie ein Mann" („learn how guys talk"). Ein weiteres geschlechtsspezifisches Stereotyp wird thematisiert als Thaos Schwester Sue dem staunenden Walt erklärt, dass die Hmong-Mädchen sich in Amerika besser anpassen als die Jungen. Die Mädchen schaffen es bis an die Uni und die Jungen landen im Gefängnis.*

ZUSATZMATERIAL *Zu dem Kapitel liegt ein Klausurvorschlag mit Erwartungshorizont im Anhang vor. Er steht zusätzlich in editierbarer Form auf der CD-ROM zur Verfügung.*

CD-ROM → **Klausurvorschlag mit Erwartungshorizont (White, working-class and angry: Ohio's left-behind help Trump to stunning win)**

Unterrichtsverlauf

A Identity: Why are we who we are?

INTRODUCTION **1** 👥 **Look at the images above. Take turns describing and analysing …** → S28.1

UNTERRICHTS-KONZEPT *Die SuS beschreiben die Fotos abwechselnd. Sie verwenden dazu* Skill 28.1 Working with visuals: Pictures *(Green Line Oberstufe Baden-Württemberg) und die* Useful phrases: Talking about identity. *Die Lehrkraft macht die SuS auch auf das* Fact file *zu* Identity *aufmerksam.*

METHODISCHE TIPPS *Bevor die SuS abwechselnd die Bilder beschreiben, kann die Lehrkraft am Beispiel eines der Bilder auf der Seite bzw. eines anderen Fotos (mit ähnlichem Inhalt) die für die Beschreibung notwendigen* phrases *(inklusive Präpositionen) mit den SuS wiederholen:* in the photo, in the foreground / background, on the left / right, at the top / bottom, in the top right-hand corner.

LÖSUNGSVORSCHLAG Individual answers expected.

BRAINSTORMING **2** **Make a list of the components and factors that shape your identity ...**

**UNTERRICHTS-
KONZEPT** *Die Lehrkraft fordert die SuS auf, in Einzelarbeit eine Liste der Bestandteile und Faktoren anzu-
fertigen, welche die menschliche Identität formen / beeinflussen, und zwar in Bezug auf:*
- *Menschsein an sich*
- *Mensch als einzigartiges Individuum*
- *Mensch als Mitglied einer sozialen Gruppe / Gesellschaft*

LÖSUNGSVORSCHLAG Individual answers expected.

THINK-PAIR-SHARE **3** **a) – d)** 👥 **Make a mind map of the most important factors that ...**

CD-ROM → Kopiervorlage 1 (Two cartoons)

**UNTERRICHTS-
KONZEPT** *Die SuS erstellen in Teilaufgabe a) in Einzelarbeit eine Mindmap der wichtigsten identitätskons-
tituierenden Faktoren. Sie einigen sich danach mit dem Partner auf die drei wichtigsten Faktoren (Teilaufgabe b). Die Klasse diskutiert und identifiziert danach diejenigen Faktoren, die nicht
beeinflusst oder verändert werden können (Teilaufgabe c). Schließlich überlegen die SuS, ob
unveränderliche (identitätskonstituierende) Faktoren eine wichtigere Rolle spielen als solche, die
beeinflusst oder verändert werden können (Teilaufgabe d).*

LÖSUNGSVORSCHLAG a) **Make a mind map of the most important factors that shape our identity.**
   Individual answers expected.

   b) 👥 **Discuss with your partner and agree on the three most important factors.**
   Individual answers expected.

   c) **As a class, identify those factors that cannot be influenced or changed.**
   gender, race, age, physical traits (height, build / physique, etc.), intelligence, etc.

   d) **Some identity-forming factors cannot be changed. Discuss whether they play ...**
   factors that cannot be changed are more important

EVALUATION **4** **Assess whether there is a correlation between changeability and ...**

**UNTERRICHTS-
KONZEPT** *Diese Aufgabe kann schriftlich oder mündlich durchgeführt werden.*

LÖSUNGSVORSCHLAG Individual answers expected.

ANALYSIS **5** 👥 **Make a list of the different social groups we live in. Describe how ...**

LÖSUNGSVORSCHLAG
- Different social groups we live in: e.g. immediate family, extended family, neighbourhood,
  (close) friends, classmates, team mates (sports), colleagues at work, etc.
- (Social) Identity is defined in relation to the social groups we live in; there is a mutual
  interdependence. The social group exerts influence on the individual and the individual
  exerts influence on the social group.
- People have a (social) identity (as a member of a social group) and an (individual) identity.
- As a member of a social group/society, it is important to find the right balance between
  conformity and individuality: group membership requires a (certain) degree of (social)
  conformity; yet individuals long for (a certain degree of) individuality.

SPEAKING **6** **Discuss how our idiolect (our very own individual and unique language) ...**

**UNTERRICHTS-
KONZEPT** *Die Aufgabe kann in Partner- oder Gruppenarbeit erledigt werden. Es ist anzunehmen, dass die
(meisten) SuS den Begriff „Idiolekt" und dessen Bedeutung nicht kennen. Es empfiehlt sich daher, diesen Begriff in einem kurzen Lehrervortrag zu erklären.*

LÖSUNGSVORSCHLAG
- Many social groups have a language of their own that distinguishes them from other social
  groups. Some examples include:
  - the (official) language of a country, regional dialects (within a country),
  - certain professions that have their own language, a so-called professional jargon,

- sociolects,
  - young people (in general) have their own language varieties,
  - members of certain youth cultures have their own slang.
- An individual who wants to be a member of a social group will use the language of that social group as a sign of belonging. A person's idiolect is therefore influenced by the language of the social group he / she is part of.
- An individual who does not / cannot speak the language of a certain social group (e. g. on account of a certain accent) might not be fully accepted as a member. His/Her idiolect separates him / her from the social group in which he / she lives.

EVALUATION

7 Discuss whether one's identity is shaped more by genetic predisposition …

UNTERRICHTS-KONZEPT

Die Aufgabe kann in Partner- oder Gruppenarbeit erledigt werden. Die SuS berücksichtigen das Fact file *zu den Begriffen* nature vs. nurture.

LÖSUNGSVORSCHLAG

Nature is more important:
- People very often inherit physical traits from their parents.
- Some physical traits are very important, e. g. gender.
- People also inherit character traits.
- Some people behave like their parents, etc.

Nurture is more important:
- People certainly change when they grow up / grow older due to various learning processes.
- People definitely change when they come in contact with other people.
- The bigger the input (impressions of any kind, external influences, experiences), the higher the degree of change.

ERWEITERUNG

Research: Dystopian novels and movies

a) There are a number of dystopian novels and movies that deal with the topic of society exerting influence on either nature or nurture in order to control people's identities and personalities. Conduct a webquest and find several such novels or movies.

b) Make a list: What do these dystopias have in common? Could taking such steps to exert influence on nature or nurture be desirable or even justified? Why (not)?

c) Explain whether you would like to live in a society like that.

UNTERRICHTS-KONZEPT

Die SuS arbeiten in Gruppen und recherchieren dystopische Romane und Filme. Da die SuS erfahrungsgemäß eher dystopische Filme als dystopische Romane kennen, lohnt hier der Hinweis, sie mögen bei der Recherche in Teilaufgabe a) mit den Romanen beginnen; auch weil diese ja sehr oft die literarische Vorlage für spätere Verfilmungen liefern. Die SuS finden Gemeinsamkeiten und erstellen eine Liste. Die Lehrkraft kann hier – nach Klärung der Gemeinsamkeiten und gattungsspezifischen Charakteristika – auch auf die Entstehungsgeschichte und den Zeitgeist zur Zeit der Entstehung einiger Werke eingehen. Hier bieten sich u. a. an:

- Brave New World, Aldous Huxley, 1932 *als Reaktion auf die Weltwirtschaftskrise in den 1930er Jahren und den zunehmenden Faschismus in Europa;*
- 1984, George Orwell, 1949 *als Reaktion auf die Nachkriegszeit in Europa und den Kalten Krieg;*
- Fahrenheit 451, Ray Bradbury, 1953 *als Reaktion auf den eskalierenden Kalten Krieg.*

Es lohnt die Beschäftigung mit folgenden Fragen: Gibt es bestimmte Epochen, die der Entstehung von Dystopien zuträglicher sind als andere? Warum gibt es seit den frühen 2000er Jahren eine so große Anzahl an neuen Werken des Genres / eine Renaissance des Genres?

LÖSUNGSVORSCHLAG

a) **Dystopian novels**
- The Time Machine, H.G. Wells, 1895
- Brave New World, Aldous Huxley, 1932
- 1984, George Orwell, 1949
- I, Robot, Isaac Asimov, 1950

- Fahrenheit 451, Ray Bradbury, 1953
- Lord of the Flies, William Golding, 1954
- I Am Legend, Richard Matheson, 1954
- The Chrysalids, John Wyndham, 1955
- Planet of the Apes, Pierre Boulle, 1963
- The Running Man, Richard Bachman a.k.a. Stephen King, 1982
- Neuromancer, William Gibson, 1984
- The Handmaid's Tale, Margaret Atwood, 1985
- The Children of Men, P.D. James, 1992
- Uglies, Scott Westerfeld, 2005
- Pretties, Scott Westerfeld, 2005
- Specials, Scott Westerfeld, 2006
- The Road, Cormac McCarthy, 2006
- The Hunger Games, Suzanne Collins, 2008
- Catching Fire, Suzanne Collins, 2009
- Mockingjay, Suzanne Collins, 2010
- The Maze Runner, James Dashner, 2009
- The Scorch Trials, James Dashner, 2010
- The Death Cure, James Dashner, 2011
- The Kill Order, James Dashner, 2012
- The Fever Code, James Dashner, 2016
- Matched, Ally Condie, 2010
- Crossed, Ally Condie, 2011
- Reached, Ally Condie, 2012
- Divergent, Veronica Roth, 2011
- Insurgent, Veronica Roth, 2012
- Allegiant, Veronica Roth, 2013

Comic book series
- The Surrogates, Robert Venditti & Brett Weldele, 2005 – 2006

Dystopian movies
various movie adaptations of the novels above
original movies
- Mad Max trilogy, 1979 – 1985
- (remake) Mad Max: Fury Road, 2015
- Total Recall, 1990
- (remake) Total Recall, 2012
- Rise of the Planet of the Apes, 2011
- Dawn of the Planet of the Apes, 2014
- plus numerous movies that make up part of the Zombie genre

Original TV series
- The Walking Dead, 2011–present
- Z Nation, 2015 – present

b) **Make a list: What do these dystopias have in common?**
- set in the (near) future
- very often set in a post-apocalyptic world / after the earth has (nearly) been destroyed
- living conditions in general are very dangerous, very bad
- (organisation of) society and state:
  - no state, no government, no laws, no public order → (absolute) chaos and anarchy
  - no civilisation, no moral values
  - or a totalitarian, repressive, inhumane dictatorship (to uphold order); no freedom, no human rights, no democracy, etc. and, likewise, no moral values
- (often) a group of survivors fights to stay alive, fights for the last (scarce) resources

- often critical / sceptical of advanced technology and science → often both factors have contributed to / brought about the dire living conditions
- partly overlap with science fiction genre

Could taking such steps to exert influence on nature or nurture be desirable ...?
- taking steps to exert influence on nature or nurture are neither desirable nor justified; it's a form of physical and psychological manipulation of the individual
- influence on nature: manipulation of (tampering with) genomes / genetic material might lead to diseases, congenital disorder; and is ethically / morally questionable
- influence on nurture: manipulation and ideological indoctrination run counter the formation of an individual's free will and the capacity of independent thought

c) Individual answers expected.

Identity and belonging

VISUALS

1 👥 **Describe and interpret the cartoons, using the steps provided ...**   → S28.2

UNTERRICHTS-KONZEPT

*Die SuS beschreiben und interpretieren die beiden Cartoons mit Hilfe von Skill 28.2 Working with visuals: Cartoons (**Green Line Oberstufe Baden-Württemberg**) sowie der vier Schritte im Tipp zu Commenting on cartoons.*

LÖSUNGSVORSCHLAG

Cartoon 1
- a middle-aged / older, (partly) bald man, with a moustache and glasses, wearing a pink bra and a pink skirt is looking at himself in the mirror
- the man's thought bubble reads ...
- message: when people get older, they tend to become like their parents
- humour: the fact that the man is wearing women's undergarments and admits that he is turning into his mother (as opposed to his father or grandfather) creates the humorous punch line

Cartoon 2
- a man is looking at a baby lying in a cradle / children's bed and is talking to the baby
- the caption under the cartoon represents the man's speech bubble and reads ...
- message: nature and nurture both play a role in a child's development
- humour: the fact that a) the man presents the process of human growth and development as a personal choice of factors and b) the man involves the baby in the decision creates the absurd twist

ANALYSIS

2 **Compare and contrast the difference between your generation and that ...**

UNTERRICHTS-KONZEPT

Die Aufgabe kann nach der Methode Think-Pair-Share bearbeitet werden. Die SuS verwenden die Useful phrases: Talking about youth cultures.

LÖSUNGSVORSCHLAG

Differences between generations:
- young people today: many single-parent families; many single-child families; parents are (often) not as strict as previous generations; more (pocket) money; access to / in possession of electronic devices & mobile devices (computer, laptop, smartphone, cell phone, etc.) and thus a wealth of information at their fingertips
- parents: (much more often) two-parent families; often more than one child per family; their parents were stricter than parents are today; bigger difference between ideas / values /
- lifestyle / fashion of different generations; less (pocket) money; electronic devices & mobile devices were virtually unknown

Today there are adults who dress/look like teenagers. Is that your impression as well? ...
Individual answers expected

Possible reasons why adults dress and look like teenagers:
- today the boundaries between generations are less clearly set and visible than in the past

- many features of the 'wild' 60s (and 70s) are still around, such as wearing sneakers, jeans, T-shirts, etc. and listening to pop / rock (youth) music
- some well-adjusted adults have yet to live out their rebellious years and do so when they are grown up; others may be trying to get close to their children by dressing similarly; yet others might never have outgrown their rebellious teenage years

DISCUSSION   **3 a) – b) Growing up, teenagers often want to distinguish themselves ...**   → S24

UNTERRICHTS-KONZEPT   *Man kann dieser Aufgabe ein Unterrichtsgespräch vorschalten, bei dem man den SuS Gelegenheit gibt, sich zu äußern und ihre Meinungen und Erfahrungen zu teilen. Da das Thema Jugendkultur die Lebenswelt der SuS unmittelbar betrifft, können sich alle SuS dazu äußern und sind – so steht zu erwarten – auch intrinsisch motiviert an einem Unterrichtsgespräch teilzunehmen. In Aufgabe a) machen sich die SuS in Einzelarbeit Notizen. Aufgabe b) kann mündlich bearbeitet werden. Die Lehrkraft verweist auf Skill 24 Discussion and debate (Green Line Oberstufe Baden-Württemberg).*

LÖSUNGSVORSCHLAG   **a) Characterise some youth subcultures you know and identify the clothing, slang and ...**
   - youth subcultures: bro, emo, goth, geek / nerd, metal head, punk, weeaboo, etc.
   - affiliation shown by a certain / distinct style of clothes / fashion / dress code, hairdo, make-up, music, language

   b) Have you ever been a member of a youth subculture?
   Individual answers expected.

SPEAKING   **4 Growing up, many teenagers go through different phases: sometimes ...**

LÖSUNGSVORSCHLAG   Individual answers expected.

DISCUSSION   **5 a) – c) Human beings have an innate need and desire to belong to social ...**

UNTERRICHTS-KONZEPT   *Die SuS machen sich in Einzelarbeit schriftlich Notizen. Sie verwenden die* Useful phrases: Talking about peer groups.

LÖSUNGSVORSCHLAG   Individual answers expected.

WRITING   **6 Think of a situation that would throw you off balance. Write a ...**   → S18.4

UNTERRICHTS-KONZEPT   *Die SuS müssen hier nicht mit dem Banknachbarn zusammenarbeiten. Es sollte ihnen vielmehr die Gelegenheit gegeben werden, den Partner in der Klasse frei zu wählen. Die Lehrkraft verweist auf* Skill 18.4 Personal letter or email (Green Line Oberstufe Baden-Württemberg).

LÖSUNGSVORSCHLAG   Individual answers expected.

Identity: Who are you?

VOCABULARY   **1 In the grid below, circle all the terms that refer to the notion of identity, ...**

UNTERRICHTS-KONZEPT   *Die Lösungswörter aus mehreren Bestandteilen sind im Wörterrätsel ohne Abstände angelegt.*

LÖSUNG   → city, classmates, dialect, education, ethnicity, extended family, friends, immediate family, nationality, parents, part of town, place of residence, political affiliation, upbringing
   ← children, colleagues, country, degree, free-time activities, gender, income, neighbourhood, occupation, peer group, place of birth, religion, school, siblings, teachers
   ↑ age, creed, language, role models
   ↓ faith, hobbies, race, social class
   ↗ experience
   ↘ personal interests
   ↙ spouse

Across: line = l. / Down: column = c.

→ UPBRINGING – l.1 / c.4
↘ PERSONALINTERESTS – l.1 / c.5
→ DIALECT – l.1 / c.14
↓ HOBBIES – l.1 / c.21
→ IMMEDIATEFAMILY – l.2 / c.3
↑ AGE – l.3 / c.1
← PLACEOFBIRTH – l.3 / c.16
→ FRIENDS – l.4 / c.2
↓ RACE – l.4 / c.3
→ EDUCATION – l.4 / 9
→ PARTOFTOWN – l.5 / c.2
← OCCUPATION – l.5 / c.20
→ EXTENDEDFAMILY – l.6 / c.6   →
→ ETHNICITY – l.7 / c.12
← TEACHERS – l.7 / c.13
→ CITY – l.7 / c.17   →
↙ SPOUSE – l.7 / c.21
↓ SOCIALCLASS – l.7 / c.21
↑ LANGUAGE – l.8 / c.1
← SCHOOL – l.8 / c.6
← RELIGION – l.8 / c.14
← GENDER – l.8 / c.19

→ POLITICALAFFILIATION – l.9 / c.1
← NEIGHBOURHOOD – l.10 / c.14
→ NATIONALITY – l.11 / c.6
→ PLACEOFRESIDENCE – l.12 / c.1
← FREETIMEACTIVITIES – l.13 / c.18
↓ FAITH – l.13 / c.20
← CHILDREN – l.14 / c.8
→ CLASSMATES – l.14 / c.8
↑ CREED – l.14 / c.19
← INCOME – l.15 / c.6
← PEERGROUP – l.15 / c.15
↑ ROLEMODELS – l.15 / c.22
← COUNTRY – l.16 / c.7
← DEGREE – l.16 / c.13
→ PARENTS – l.16 / c.15
← SIBLINGS – l.17 / c.8
↗ EXPERIENCE – l.17 / c.13
← COLLEAGUES – l.17 / c.17

EVALUATION **2 a) Rate how important the different ... b) Evaluate how much ...**

LÖSUNGSVORSCHLAG a)/b) Individual answers expected.

EVALUATION **3 Make a list of factors that will play a role in shaping your identity ...**

LÖSUNGSVORSCHLAG experience, professional ambition, new hobbies, spouse, children, occupation, colleagues, income, political affiliation, etc.

Identity: What are your needs?

RESEARCH **1** 👥 **Using various sources, research and find out more about Maslow's ...**

LÖSUNGSVORSCHLAG Individual answers expected.

RESEARCH **2 Find concrete examples of how Maslow's five needs are met and ...**

LÖSUNGSVORSCHLAG Individual answers expected.

B The push and pull of migration

BEFORE YOU READ **1 Can you think of reasons why people leave their native countries? ...**

UNTERRICHTS-KONZEPT *In Einzelarbeit erstellen die SuS eine Mindmap, auf der mögliche Gründe für Migration bzw. Fluchtursachen aufgelistet werden. Diese Mindmap wird später weiterverwendet und ergänzt.*

LÖSUNGSVORSCHLAG Individual answers expected.

ANALYSIS **2 Using the table below, match the push factors mentioned in ...**   → S4.2

UNTERRICHTS-KONZEPT *Die Lehrkraft weist die SuS auf das* Fact file *zu NAFTA und den Tipp zu* Talking about migration *hin. Die SuS verwenden außerdem* Skill 4.2 Analysing non-fictional texts *(**Green Line Oberstufe Baden-Württemberg**).*

LÖSUNGSVORSCHLAG

PUSH factors	PULL factors	PUSH factors	PULL factors
1. economic problems, unemployment, poverty, hunger	high(er) standard of living, better jobs, better chances for a good life	5. social friction, persecution, oppression	social peace, freedom, civil liberties
2. dysfunctional political and other institutions, ineffective governments, deficient or non-existent health system	rule of law, well-functioning institutions, effective administration and functioning governments, good health system	6. political unrest instability, armed conflicts	peace, stability, security
3. corruption, crime	less corruption, less crime	7. child labour	no child labour
4. lack of infrastructure	good infrastructure	8. natural disasters	no natural disasters

ERWEITERUNG   *Nach Erledigung der Aufgabe kann die Lehrkraft in einem Unterrichtsgespräch das Thema* trade agreements *vertiefen. Hier lassen sich aktuelle Bezüge herstellen: CETA (Kanada und EU; ratifiziert am 15. Februar 2017 durch das Europäische Parlament) sowie TTIP (USA und EU; Verhandlungen noch nicht abgeschlossen).*

ANALYSIS   **3 Compare the difficulties of internal vs. international migration.**

LÖSUNGSVORSCHLAG   **Internal migration:**
people stay in their native countries where they speak the language, know the culture, but often these countries are very poor, dangerous, they don't get help / support

International migration:
people migrate to other countries where they get help / support, but the trip can be dangerous, they have many problems: different language, culture, customs

EVALUATION   **4 Assess the role that globalisation has played within the context of mass …**

LÖSUNGSVORSCHLAG   **Globalisation has played a very important role:**
- technology → global communication
- economy → global travel, transport, trade
- politics → sanctions, embargoes, interventions
- result: greater economic disparity between rich and poor countries, growing (global) injustice; there are more people who want to improve their standard of living to match what they see on TV

Migration on a global scale

VISUALS   **1 Interpret the infographic.**   → S27

UNTERRICHTS-
KONZEPT   *Die SuS verwenden* Skill 27 Statistics, diagrams and maps *(Green Line Oberstufe Baden-Württemberg) sowie die* Useful phrases: Talking about diagrams.

LÖSUNGSVORSCHLAG
- Migration between countries on the same continent has been higher than migration between different continents; in Asia: 62 million, in Europe: 40 million, in America: 26 million, in Africa: 18 million; exception: Asia to Europe: 20 million.
- Migration between continents: Asia to Europe: 20 million, Asia to North America: 17 million, Africa to Europe: 9 million, Europe to Asia & Europe to North America: 8 million; global net migration: losing: Asia: –29 million, Africa: –9 million; gaining: North America: +51 million Europe: +13 million.

ANALYSIS **2 Relate the international movement of migrants to the push and pull …**

LÖSUNGSVORSCHLAG **Asia to Europe & Asia to North America & Africa to Europe:**
- push factors: wars, terror, poverty, hunger
- pull factors: security, better life

Latin America and the Caribbean to North America:
- push factors: poverty, very high crime rate → drug cartels, bleak future prospects
- pull factors: jobs, better life

Europe to Asia:
- push factors: expectations not met
- pull factors: desire to return home

Europe to North America:
- push factors: (youth) unemployment
- pull factors: hope for a better life, better job/career opportunities

SPEAKING **3 Discuss what could be done to reduce the number of international …**

LÖSUNGSVORSCHLAG **In the native countries:**
- support people in their native countries
- implement fair international trade deals
- create better living conditions and better working conditions

On the way from the native countries to the host countries:
- fight human trafficking
- secure national borders

In the host countries:
- communicate to migrants that economic hardship is not a reason to apply for political asylum
- communicate to migrants that not every applicant will be granted political asylum
- communicate to migrants that a turned-down application results in being sent back home

CREATIVE TASK **4 ☺☺☺ Outline what should be done to support people a) in their native …**

UNTERRICHTS-KONZEPT *Die SuS sollten dazu ermutigt werden, ihre Poster vielfältig und interessant zu gestalten, mit Texten, Bildern, Fotos und auch Grafiken.*

LÖSUNGSVORSCHLAG **a) Support in native countries:**
- rich countries should not just give more money / developmental aid, but help poor countries to help themselves, i. e. give effective and sustainable support
- rich countries should not force developing countries to sign unfavourable economic deals or trade agreements

b) Support in host countries: host countries should offer
- language courses
- courses to learn about the laws, the moral principles and values, the culture, the customs and traditions of the host country in order to be able to adapt to the new surroundings and integrate into the host society
- opportunities for vocational training / apprenticeships
- grants (to study at university)

RESEARCH **5 ☺☺☺ Using the internet and other sources, find out how today's migration …**

UNTERRICHTS-KONZEPT *Die SuS recherchieren selbstständig – wahlweise in Partner- oder Gruppenarbeit – und verwenden dabei verschiedene Quellen. Im Rahmen der Bearbeitung dieser Aufgabe kann ein Abstecher in die Schulbibliothek oder die örtliche Bibliothek angeregt werden.*

LÖSUNGSVORSCHLAG Individual answers expected.

EVALUATION   **6** **Discuss what immigrants can do to better adapt to their new ...**

LÖSUNGSVORSCHLAG
- learning the language of the host country
- abiding by the laws of the host country
- accepting the moral principles and values of the host country
- adapting to the culture, the customs and traditions of the host country

DISCUSSION   **7** **Comment on how Germany has dealt with the current refugee crisis.**

LÖSUNGSVORSCHLAG   Individual answers expected.

Urbanisation: urban vs. rural living

BRAINSTORMING   **1** 👥 **Where would you like to live – in a big city or in a small town / in the ...?**

UNTERRICHTS-
KONZEPT   *Hier kann die Lehrkraft auf das* Fact file *zu* Urbanisation *hinweisen und die SuS zuerst über die Vorzüge bzw. Nachteile ihrer eigenen Wohnorte sprechen lassen. Damit stellt man eine sehr organische Verknüpfung mit der Lebenswelt der SuS her.*

LÖSUNGSVORSCHLAG   Individual answers expected.

SPEAKING   **2** **Discuss the pros and cons of growing up in the city vs. growing up in ...**

LÖSUNGSVORSCHLAG

Pro small town / country	Pro (big) city
• life / rent / housing is cheaper • life is less hectic / more relaxed / less stressful • more space / you are in touch with nature • less social pressure to be successful or up-to-date • people / neighbours know each other • (strong) sense of community / no feeling of alienation • less crime and violence • less traffic and less air pollution / smog • less noise and less garbage • a great place for children to grow up	• more (well-paid) jobs, better jobs, a wider variety of jobs • more shops, specialised shops • more leisure / recreational activities: arts and culture (opera, museums, etc.) • more doctors and hospitals • more schools / better schools (supported by a higher tax base) • better infrastructure: public transport • no need to own a car / shorter commutes • fewer social norms to follow / more privacy • dating is easier • a great place for teenagers to hang out

Preferences:
- older people seem to prefer the country: more peace and quiet
- younger people seem to prefer the city: more action and opportunities

VISUALS   **3** **Interpret and compare the two line graphs.**   → S27

UNTERRICHTS-
KONZEPT   *Die SuS verwenden* Skill 27 Statistics, diagrams and maps *(Green Line Oberstufe Baden-Würt-temberg).*

LÖSUNGSVORSCHLAG   Line graph 1:
- between 1950 and today:
  the proportion of the urban population has steadily increased
- between today and 2050:
  the proportion of the urban population is projected to increase further
- between 1950 and today:
  the proportion of the rural population has steadily decreased
- between today and 2050:
  the proportion of the rural population will decrease further

Line graph 2:
over the past 40 years (1970 – 2010) the measured level of happiness of residents
in the US has been:
- highest in small towns / in the country
- second highest in suburbs
- third highest in small and medium-sized cities
- lowest in (very) big cities
- all numbers are relatively stable, indicating a steady overall decrease of happiness for all residents; biggest decrease of happiness: residents of small and medium-sized cities; exception: residents of (very) big cities: here, apart from some ups and downs, the level of happiness did not change much between the early 1970s and 2010

EVALUATION   **4   Assess the long-term consequences of urbanisation on US society, …**

LÖSUNGSVORSCHLAG   **Consequences: American way of life**
- the rural (American) way of life might become less prominent
- the urban (American) way of life might become more prominent

Consequences: US politics
- the political weight of less populous states might decline further
- the political 'gap' between East and West coast (Democratic states) on the one hand and 'America's Heartland' / 'Middle America' / 'Fly-over country' (Republican states) on the other hand might become even bigger

VISUALS   **5   Interpret the cartoon below and comment on how successful …   → S28.2**

UNTERRICHTS-
KONZEPT   *Die SuS werden auf Skill 28.2 Working with visuals: Cartoons (**Green Line Oberstufe Baden-Württemberg**) und das Fact file zu Derogatory terms aufmerksam gemacht.*

LÖSUNGSVORSCHLAG
- A man in a KKK outfit, holding a report card in his hands, is talking to his son.
- The boy, wearing sneakers, jeans, and a T-shirt, is looking at his father.
- The caption that represents the speech bubble spoken by the father reads …

Message:
The father doesn't mind / can tolerate his son's – obviously – bad grades because …
- he believes that ultimately skin colour is more important than education,
- he believes that people are primarily defined by their skin colour,
- he believes that success in life depends only on skin colour.

RESEARCH   **6   The terms "America's Heartland", "Middle America", and …   → S32**

UNTERRICHTS-
KONZEPT   *Diese Aufgabe dient speziell der Vorentlastung der Romanlektüre. Die SuS lernen hierbei den Handlungsort und dessen besondere Gegebenheiten kennen. Sie recherchieren mit Hilfe des Internets und weiterer Medien – wahlweise in Einzel-, Partner- oder Gruppenarbeit – und sammeln Fakten über Mississippi und bilden sich eine eigene Meinung, inwieweit dieser Bundesstaat als typisches Beispiel für die in der Aufgabenstellung benannte Gruppe von US Staaten betrachtet werden kann. Die Lehrkraft verweist auf Skill 32 Doing research (**Green Line Oberstufe Baden-Württemberg**).*

LÖSUNGSVORSCHLAG
- Mississippi lies in the American South; during the time of the American Civil War (1860 – 1865) it belonged to the Confederate States
- Mississippi is part of the so-called Bible Belt where conservative evangelical Protestantism is a dominant factor in society and politics
- 3 million inhabitants
- white: 59 %, black: 37 % (highest percentage of all states) → USA: white: 80 %, black: 13 %
- 125,443 km² (= Bavaria + Baden-Württemberg + Rheinland-Pfalz) → Germany: 357,168 km²
- population: rank 32 / 50
- size: rank 32 / 50
- capital: Jackson (175,000 inhabitants)

- flag: the only state flag that includes the Confederate battle flag
- political affiliation: Republican
- unemployment rate: 5,9 % (October 2016) → USA: 4,9 % (October 2016)
- murder rate: 2nd highest murder rate in the USA = MS: 0.09 (per 1,000) → USA: 0.04 (per 1,000)
- prison population: 3rd highest adult incarceration rate in the USA
- capital punishment: lethal injection, last execution: 2012
- same sex marriage: legalised in 2015
- most famous Mississippians: William Faulkner (1897–1962), Tennessee Williams (1911–1983), Elvis Presley (1937–1977)

C Race in the United States

PRE-LISTENING

1 Brainstorm what you know about race issues and racism in the US today.

UNTERRICHTS-KONZEPT

Die SuS sammeln beim Brainstorming erste Ideen. Die Lehrkraft kann sie hier ggfs. zuerst Notizen machen lassen – wahlweise in Einzel-, Partner- oder Gruppenarbeit – und die Ideen / Stichwörter dann hinterher im Unterrichtsgespräch sammeln und auswerten. Es erfolgt ein Hinweis auf den Tipp zu Working with listening texts.

METHODISCHE TIPPS

Das Wecken von Neugier und das Erzeugen von Aha-Effekten dient dazu, die SuS für ein Thema zu motivieren. Eine Möglichkeit dies hier beim Thema Race zu tun besteht darin, die SuS den Anteil (in Prozent) der Afroamerikaner an der Gesamtbevölkerung der USA erraten zu lassen. Die SuS schätzen diesen – sehr verlässlich – stets viel zu hoch ein und machen Vorschläge zwischen 25 % und 50 %. Die Antwort – 13 % – erstaunt / überrascht die SuS erfahrungsgemäß. Weiterhin lohnenswert ist es, die Ursachen für die viel zu hoch geschätzten Prozentangaben zu eruieren und zu thematisieren. Die Frage danach kann die Lehrkraft den SuS direkt im Anschluss stellen. Gründe: Die SuS sind durch US-amerikanische TV-Serien und Spielfilme geprägt, die sehr oft in US Großstädten spielen, in denen der Anteil der Afroamerikaner überdurchschnittlich hoch ist. Die SuS kennen i.d.R. sehr viele afroamerikanische Sportler, Sänger, Schauspieler, etc., wobei auch hier – besonders bei den in Deutschland populären US Sportarten – der Anteil der Afroamerikaner überdurchschnittlich hoch ist; Basketball: fast 75 %, American Football: 68 %.

LÖSUNGSVORSCHLAG

Individual answers expected.

WHILE-LISTENING

2 a) ◉ **Listen to two excerpts from … b)** ◉ **Listen to Part Two and …**   → S21

CD-ROM

→ Podcast, Part One and Two (The Black Lives Matter Movement) • Transcripts

UNTERRICHTS-KONZEPT

Die SuS hören die beiden Textauszüge und bearbeiten die Aufgaben. Die Lehrkraft verweist dazu auf Skill 21 Listening comprehension *(**Green Line Oberstufe Baden-Württemberg**). In der Regel werden Hörtexte für Hörverstehensaufgaben zweimal gehört. Beim ersten Vorspielen hören die SuS nur zu, danach lesen sie die Aufgaben im Schülerheft. Beim zweiten Vorspielen machen sich die SuS während des Hörens Notizen zu den Aufgaben. Dies bedeutet im konkreten Beispiel hier, die SuS hören zwei Mal* Part One, *danach zwei Mal* Part Two. *Vor dem zweiten Hören lesen die SuS zusätzlich die* Fact files *zu* The Black Lives Matter Movement, Racial profiling, The Civil Rights Movement (1954–1968).

LÖSUNGSVORSCHLAG

a) Part One
1. d)
2. d)
3. mistreated, yelled at, and talked down to
4. c)
5. false
6. Because he thinks that society / the police doesn't do enough to protect the lives of black people; e.g. there is police brutality, lack of appreciation of black lives, lack of fairness.

7. false
8. true

b) **Part Two**
1. c)
2. It was started by young (black) people who were frustrated about the contradiction between having civil rights (in theory) and being treated badly (in reality).
3. false
4. better organisation, better leadership, more cohesion, better communication
5. a)
6. end the war on black people; reparations; invest – divest; economic justice; community control; political power

POST-LISTENING   **3** a) – d) Creative task: Write a letter to Russell Simmons OR Dr. ...   → S18.1

UNTERRICHTS-KONZEPT   *Die Lehrkraft macht die SuS bei Aufgabe a) auf* Skill 18.1 Writing a formal letter / letter to the editor *(**Green Line Oberstufe Baden-Württemberg**) aufmerksam. Den Fragenkatalog für das Interview in Aufgabe b) kann in Einzel- oder in Partnerarbeit erstellt werden. Für die Analyse-Aufgabe c) verwenden die SuS als Unterstützung das Transkript des Hörtextes. Der abschließende Comment in Aufgabe d) kann als schriftliche Hausaufgabe aufgegeben werden.*

LÖSUNGSVORSCHLAG   a) **Creative task: Write a letter to Russell Simmons OR Dr. Carson to comment on ...**
Individual answers expected.

b) **Creative task: Imagine you are going to conduct an interview with one or both of them. ...**
Individual answers expected.

c) **Analysis: Work with the transcript of the listening text. Analyse and compare the way ...**
Russell Simmons
03:16 – 07:38, "Here with me now ... I'm gonna be scared."
- fun: "I have a big mouth", "I'm a hundred" → effect: he comes across as likeable
- talks about his personal experiences → effect: makes his standpoint believable, convincing
- provides numbers and examples: "kids shot in Chicago", "girl missing in Brooklyn" → effect: he comes across as well-informed
- re-phrases the name of the organisation: "Black lives don't matter" → effect: makes his story more interesting

Dr. Clayborne Carson
07:39 – 12:55 (*nicht Bestandteil der* Listening task)
- makes historical references: Germany, Rwanda → effect: makes his points convincing
- explains that he once was a good friend of Donald Trump's, but that they're not friends anymore → makes his criticism of Trump convincing

15:15 – 20:07, "Now let's turn to ... Speaking as a scholar of ...", (fade out)
- provides a lot of information in a very orderly way (talks like a professor) → makes his standpoint very convincing
- provides dates, names of laws → makes his standpoint very convincing
- refers to MLK (a famous personality / an authority) → makes his standpoint very convincing
- refers to books he read or wrote → makes his standpoint very convincing

20:08 – 28:17
- same: provides facts, refers to historical events, etc. → makes his standpoint very convincing

d) **Evaluation: Comment on whether this is a disparaging detraction or a deliberate ...**
Disparaging detraction:
- people might feel that the slogan creates a (unnecessary) distinction between black lives and non-black lives

Deliberate distraction:
- it's stating the obvious, namely that "All Lives Matter"
- a distraction from the idea behind the motto
- people who rally behind the slogan "Black Lives Matter" don't intend to express that other lives don't matter

Ethnicity in numbers

ANALYSIS **1 Analyse the line graph, comparing the developments of the three ...**   → S27

UNTERRICHTS-KONZEPT *Die SuS berücksichtigen Skill 27 Statistics, diagrams and maps (Green Line Oberstufe Baden-Württemberg) und die Useful phrases: Talking about line graphs.*

LÖSUNGSVORSCHLAG
- 2007 – 2009 recession: real estate bubble, subprime mortgage crisis
- over 45 years (1970 – 2015): unemployment rate: blacks higher than Hispanics, Hispanics higher than whites; whites always ca. 1/2 of blacks; Hispanics always ca. 3/4 of blacks; the numbers of all three groups significantly rose during/after recessions and fell afterwards; parallel movement/development for all three groups

ANALYSIS **2 First, analyse the pie chart; second, relate your findings to the line ...**   → S27

UNTERRICHTS-KONZEPT *Es wird auf Skill 27 Statistics, diagrams and maps (Green Line Oberstufe Baden-Württemberg), die Useful phrases: Talking about pie charts sowie das Fact file zu Affirmative Action verwiesen.*

LÖSUNGSVORSCHLAG
- highest percentage: male black, second: male white, third: male Hispanic
- all races: male prisoners are in the majority; blacks: highest unemployment rate and highest incarceration rate
- blacks and whites: almost same percentages for imprisonment and death row, despite huge difference in percentage of population
- Hispanics: number of jobless people and inmates is higher than for whites, but situation for Hispanics is better than for blacks

DEBATE **3 "Only affirmative action can solve the many current race-related ..."**   → S24.1

UNTERRICHTS-KONZEPT *Die SuS organisieren eine Debatte. Dazu erfolgt ein Hinweis auf Skill 24.1 Debate (Green Line Oberstufe Baden-Württemberg).*

LÖSUNGSVORSCHLAG
Pro affirmative action:
- affirmative action aims at preventing discrimination against minorities
- affirmative action aims at helping integrate minorities
- affirmative action aims at making sure everybody gets a fair chance, regardless of their ethnic background, etc.

Contra affirmative action:
- many people consider affirmative action as unconstitutional as it is a form of (reverse) discrimination
- leads to discrimination against white men
- defeats the very concept of competition, which is one of the core principles of every market economy
- runs counter to the very purpose of an application: the most highly qualified person should get the job
- applicants (for university or the workplace) should be chosen/hired on grounds of their aptitude, not other criteria like political conviction or ethnic background
- prevents any society from harnessing the full potential of its human resources
- another 'politically correct' measure to interfere in people's lives

RESEARCH **4 Conduct a webquest and find out about these race-related numbers ...** → S32

UNTERRICHTS-
KONZEPT *Die SuS recherchieren selbstständig im Internet. Sie verwenden dazu Skill 32 Doing research
(Green Line Oberstufe Baden-Württemberg).*

LÖSUNGSVORSCHLAG

Germany	United States
population: 81 million ethnicity German: 91,5% Turkish: 2,5% others: 6%	population: 324 million race & ethnicity white: 80% black: 13% Asian: 4% others & two or more races: 3% Hispanic (of any race): 15%
no death penalty	has the death penalty in some states

BEFORE YOU READ **5 What do you know about deadly violence against police officers in the US?**

UNTERRICHTS-
KONZEPT *Es ist zu erwarten, dass die SuS aus den Medien mehr über die Fälle wissen, bei denen Afro-
amerikaner die Opfer von Gewalt waren, z. B. Trayvon Martin (Miami, 2013), Michael Brown
(Ferguson, 2014) und Eric Garner (New York City, 2014). Der vorliegende Text, der tödliche Gewalt
gegen Polizeibeamte thematisiert, stellt für die SuS deshalb wahrscheinlich eine inhaltliche
Überraschung dar.*

LÖSUNGSVORSCHLAG Individual answers expected.

RESEARCH **6 ⚇ Using various sources, find out more about what happened in Dallas ...**

UNTERRICHTS-
KONZEPT *Die SuS recherchieren selbstständig und verwenden dabei verschiedene Quellen. Es bietet sich
an, diese Aufgabe – vor der Unterrichtsstunde, in der der Text behandelt wird – als Hausaufgabe
aufzugeben. Sie verwenden Skill 32 Doing research (Green Line Oberstufe Baden-Württemberg)
und berücksichtigen die Fact files zu The Second Amendment, National Rifle Association (NRA)
und Gun violence in the US.*

LÖSUNGSVORSCHLAG **Events in Dallas, Texas, July 8, 2016**
- 5 police officers were murdered in Dallas, Texas, by Micah Xavier Johnson, a 25-year-old African American Army veteran
- 7 other policemen were wounded in the shooting rampage
- this was the deadliest assault on law enforcement in the US in decades
- the killing was carried out in a sniper-style ambush: the gunman fired an assault rifle shooting at police officers who were on duty during a protest march
- during the following standoff, Johnson told the police that he was upset about police violence against blacks and "wanted to kill white people, especially white police officers"
- Johnson was later killed by a bomb disposal remote control vehicle
- President Obama ordered all flags on government buildings across the US to be lowered to half-staff in order to honour the police officers who were murdered

a) An atypical crime:
- (hired) snipers / assassins usually shoot (at) famous people: John F. Kennedy, Dr. Martin Luther King, John Lennon, Ronald Reagan, Pope John Paul II, Olof Palme, etc.
- the killer was an ex-soldier: soldiers – like policemen – usually protect the state and its citizens
- policemen are usually shot (at) by armed gangsters

b) A menace to society as a whole:
- the police represents the state, protects its citizens, upholds public order
- if the police is attacked, the state / society / the citizens / public order is attacked
- it was a kind of terror attack

ANALYSIS

7 **a)–c) Explain the effect created by the quotes from the Bible.** → S4.2

UNTERRICHTS-
KONZEPT

Die Lehrkraft verweist auf Skill 4.2 Analysing non-fictional texts (Green Line Oberstufe Baden-Württemberg).

LÖSUNGSVORSCHLAG

a) **The effect created by the quotes from the Bible.**
  • makes the text resemble a sermon
  • sounds solemn; is moving; gives people hope and consolation

b) **Explain why police chief Brown lists the names of the murdered police officers …**
  • Brown quotes lines from the Superman TV series
  • he does it to compare the dead police officers to Superman / super heroes
  • he wants to express that the murdered police officers were real-life heroes

c) **What does the last sentence reveal about the people in Dallas, …?**
  • the people in Dallas have great respect and admiration for their police department
  • the people in Dallas wanted to express their sincere condolences by covering the police cars in flowers

ERWEITERUNG

1. Are there other passages in the text that express similar sentiments? Possible solution:
  • at the vigil people lit candles
  • after the vigil people took "pictures with the [dead] officers' oversized photographs" and met "officers who were injured during Thursday's attack"

2. Creative writing: Write an obituary for either one of the dead police officers mentioned in the text or a famous person who has recently died. In either case, you need to do some research on your own in order to write a serious obituary. Possible solution: Individual answers expected.

EVALUATION

8 **Taking into consideration the information provided on this page, …**

LÖSUNGSVORSCHLAG

Against the right to bear arms:
• because of guns there is / are
• school shootings / high school massacres
• mass shootings or killing sprees in shopping malls, discos, movie theatres / public places (by people running amok)
• deadly violence against police officers
• drive-by shootings
• gang-related gun violence
• many crime-related gun victims
• (small) children (find and) play with guns and shoot each other / their siblings / other family members
• every year 600 women are shot to death by their husbands, boyfriends, etc.
• (higher) suicide rate / guns make suicide (too) easy
• gun violence is very expensive for US taxpayers and US society
• high medical costs for gunshot-related injuries
• costs of the criminal justice system
• costs of security measures (metal detectors, security guards, etc.)

In favour of the right to bear arms:
• the Second Amendment guarantees the right to bear arms (which makes sense because)
• ordinary / law-abiding citizens need guns for their protection / security because (all the) criminals are (heavily) armed
• guns are an effective deterrence against burglars, muggers, rapists, etc.
• guns (in private possession) guarantee democracy / are a safeguard against oppressive
• government / dictatorship
• unlike some European / other countries – Germany, Italy, the Soviet Union, etc. – the US has never been ruled by a dictator
• some people need guns because they live in remote places
• some people have guns for hunting and other sports

- the right to bear arms is part of the American way of life
- the right to bear arms was introduced at the time of the American War of Independence (1775–1783) when ordinary American citizens (a.k.a. Minutemen) fought against the British army (and won the war and America's independence)

SPEAKING **9** 👥 **In an increasingly insecure world, many people call for stricter …**

LÖSUNGSVORSCHLAG **In favour of (more) security:**
- terrorism has become a clear and present danger for the US and European countries
- the internet is used for committing crimes
- the internet is used for dangerous propaganda
- people are radicalised and recruited via the internet
- surveillance cameras in public places are a deterrent for criminals
- with the help of surveillance cameras, criminals can be identified, arrested, tried, convicted and locked up

In favour of (more) freedom:
- too many security measures might limit (personal) freedom
- we should not compromise (ignore) our (moral) values in order to defend our values

Guns in America: a controversial issue

RESEARCH **1** **Many songs criticise the all too easy accessibility of guns in the US. …**

UNTERRICHTS-
KONZEPT *Die Aufgabe ermöglicht den SuS einen motivierenden Zugang zum Themenkomplex guns. Sie können hier einerseits auf Interpreten zurückgreifen, die sie kennen/mögen sowie andererseits gezielt nach Songs zum Thema suchen. Je nach Klasse ist es nicht ausgeschlossen, dass hier – durchaus auch unabsichtlich – mitunter gewaltverherrlichende Songs vorgeschlagen werden. Ein genauer Blick auf die Textinhalte ist daher empfehlenswert. Es erfolgt ein Hinweis auf die* Useful phrases *zu* Talking about songs. *Mögliche Songs:*
- Put Out The Fire (Queen)
- Gun God (Freak Kitchen)
- 1000 Points of Light (Bruce Dickinson)

LÖSUNGSVORSCHLAG Individual answers expected.

ANALYSIS **2** 👥 **a) Listen to the songs on your … b) Examine the emotions evoked …**

LÖSUNGSVORSCHLAG **a)/b)** Individual answers expected.

EVALUATION **3** 👥 **a)–c) Analyse the lyrics of your song, paying attention to imagery …**

LÖSUNGSVORSCHLAG Individual answers expected.

SPEAKING **4** **Present your song and its lyrics as well as your findings to the class.**

LÖSUNGSVORSCHLAG Individual answers expected.

EVALUATION **5** **In class, agree on the song you like best (for its music or lyrics or both).**

LÖSUNGSVORSCHLAG Individual answers expected.

CREATIVE TASK **6** **a)–c) Think of an alternative title for your song. Explain your choice.**

UNTERRICHTS-
KONZEPT *Die Lehrkraft macht die SuS auf den Tipp zu* Stylistic devices *aufmerksam. Sie können sich hier auf kreative Art und Weise mit dem Thema auseinandersetzen und dabei die* Stylistic devices *aktiv verwenden.*

LÖSUNGSVORSCHLAG **a)–c)** Individual answers expected.

RESEARCH **7** 👥 **Using the information that you got from dealing with your song . . .**

LÖSUNGSVORSCHLAG

Guns should be allowed	Guns should be banned
the Second Amendment guarantees the right to bear arms (which makes sense because): • ordinary/law-abiding citizens need guns for their protection/security because (all the) criminals are (heavily) armed • guns are an effective deterrence against burglars, muggers, rapists, etc. • guns (in private possession) guarantee democracy/are a safeguard against oppressive government/dictatorship • unlike some European/other countries – Germany, Italy, the Soviet Union, etc. – the US has never been ruled by a dictator • some people need guns because they live in remote places • some people have guns for hunting and other sports • the right to bear arms is part of the American way of life • the right to bear arms was introduced at the time of the American War of Independence (1775–1783) when ordinary American citizens (a.k.a. Minutemen) fought against the British army (and won the war and America's independence)	because of guns there is/are: • school shootings/high school massacres • mass shootings or killing sprees in shopping malls, dance clubs, movie theatres/public places (by people running amok) • deadly violence against police officers • drive-by shootings • gang-related gun violence • many crime-related gun victims • (small) children (find and) play with guns and shoot each other/their siblings/other family members • every year 600 women are shot to death by their husbands, boyfriends, etc. • (higher) suicide rate/guns make suicide (too) easy • gun violence is very expensive for US taxpayers and US society • high medical costs for gunshot-related injuries • costs of the criminal justice system • costs of security measures (metal detectors, security guards, etc.)

D Social class in the US

BEFORE YOU READ **1** **What do you know about social class in the United States? Make a mind map.**

UNTERRICHTS-
KONZEPT

Die SuS verwenden die Useful phrases: Talking about social standing in the US *und erstellen eine Mindmap, die im Laufe des Unterrichts weiter ergänzt wird.*

LÖSUNGSVORSCHLAG Individual answers expected.

COMPREHENSION **2** **Use these 12 terms to fill the gaps in the text on the previous page.**

UNTERRICHTS-
KONZEPT

Die in den Useful phrases *eingeführten Begriffe* Medicaid, Medicare, trailer park, top one percent *sind u. U. nicht allen SuS geläufig. Es empfiehlt sich hier, nachzufragen und die Begriffe zu (er)klären. Dies kann auch durch eine/n SuS geschehen.*

LÖSUNG 1. classless society, 2. meritocracy, 3. American Dream, 4. recession, 5. social disparity, 6. social gap, 7. inequality, 8. working poo, 9. social mobility, 10. fractured society, 11. race, 12. gender

WRITING **3** **Summarise the text in your own words and use all of the 12 terms above.**

LÖSUNGSVORSCHLAG Individual answers expected.

RESEARCH **4** 👥 **There are several quotations in the text. Find the sources, and . . .**   → S32

UNTERRICHTS-
KONZEPT

Die SuS recherchieren selbstständig und verwenden dabei verschiedene Quellen. Es erfolgt ein Hinweis auf Skill 32 Doing research (***Green Line Oberstufe Baden-Württemberg***).

LÖSUNGSVORSCHLAG   Quotations in the text:
- "land of the free" → US national anthem "The Star-Spangled Banner"
- "tired … poor … huddled masses" → poem "The New Colossus" by Emma Lazarus on the Statue of Liberty
- "liberty and justice for all" → "The Pledge of Allegiance"
- "all men are created equal" → US Declaration of Independence
- "certain inalienable rights" → US Declaration of Independence
- "life, liberty and the pursuit of happiness" → US Declaration of Independence
- "yearning to breathe free" → poem "The New Colossus" / Statue of Liberty
- "from rags to riches" → prominently used by American writer Horatio Alger (1832 – 1899)
- "from the log cabin to the White House" → used to refer to US Presidents who came from modest family backgrounds, e.g. Andrew Jackson, Abraham Lincoln

Created effect:
- makes the text sound more authentic, reliable
- connects the text to American history, culture, traditions

ANALYSIS   **5 Fill in the key words for the graph: Asian, Black, Hispanic, White. Discuss . . .**

UNTERRICHTS-KONZEPT   *Die SuS verwenden* Skill 27 Statistics, diagrams and maps *(Green Line Oberstufe Baden-Württemberg) und die* Useful phrases: Talking about bar charts.

LÖSUNGSVORSCHLAG   All adults – White – Hispanic – Black – Asian

ANALYSIS   **6 Fill in the following countries as you imagine they would appear in the . . .**

UNTERRICHTS-KONZEPT   *Die Lehrkraft verweist auf das* Fact file *zu* The Great Gatsby Curve.

LÖSUNGSVORSCHLAG   From top to bottom: China, UK, USA, Germany, Denmark.

ANALYSIS   **7 Find out which social class your parents / grandparents belong(ed) to. . . .**

UNTERRICHTS-KONZEPT   *Diese Aufgabe sollte als Hausaufgabe aufgegeben werden. Dann haben die SuS die Gelegenheit, zu Hause nachzufragen. Es ist hierbei allerdings unabdingbar, die SuS darauf hinzuweisen, dass die Auskunft absolut freiwillig erfolgt.*

LÖSUNGSVORSCHLAG   Individual answers expected.

EVALUATION   **8 Based on your experience in everyday life, discuss whether Germany is a . . .**

LÖSUNGSVORSCHLAG   **Germany is a class society:**
- the gap between rich and poor has become bigger in recent years and is increasing
- many people eat at soup kitchens / meal centres
- many children grow up in poverty

Germany is not a class society:
- parents don't have to pay school fees → everybody can (and must) go to school
- there are no fees for universities and colleges → everybody may study
- unlike in some other (European) countries, Germany's political and economic élites are not recruited from one or two renowned élite universities
- unlike in some other (Western) countries, people who run for political office do not have to be multi-millionaires or multi-billionaires: e.g.
  - German chancellor Gerhard Schröder grew up in a very poor family
  - Bavarian Minister President Horst Seehofer comes from a working-class family

ERWEITERUNG   1. In GB language is a marker / an indicator of social class. To what extent is this also the case in Germany / the US / other countries with which you are familiar?

2. Did the end of the Soviet Union / the end of communism influence how we regard class? Did it make the traditional concept of class obsolete?

3. In today's post-industrial societies, does the term 'worker' still bear any meaning?

4. Sometimes journalists/analysts use the term 'German dream'. Do you believe that it is justified to establish this analogy to the 'American dream'? Explain why (not).

American identity

BEFORE YOU READ

1 Make a list of what you believe are the core components of American ...

LÖSUNGSVORSCHLAG Individual answers expected.

COMPREHENSION

2 👥 According to the text, how many "Americas" can be identified today? ...

UNTERRICHTS-KONZEPT *Die Lehrkraft verweist auf das* Fact file *zu* Social class in the US. *Die SuS sollten für den im Text verwendeten Begriff* working class *sensibilisiert werden. Die Lehrkraft stellt die Frage, wo die SuS die* working class *in der Definition im* Fact file *verorten würden. Als Hinweis wird angemerkt, dass aktuelle soziologische (Klassen-)Modelle den Begriff* working class *nicht mehr verwenden. Je nach Klasse/Leitungsstand/Vorwissen kann vor der Lektüre des Textes erneut der Unterschied zwischen den beiden Konzepten* salad bowl *und* melting pot *thematisiert werden.*

LÖSUNGSVORSCHLAG **How many "Americas" can be identified today?**
*   the text mentions two "Americas", but more groups can be indentified (cf. l. 5 "… two groups – among many others …")
*   the two (big) groups are: rural, white, conservative vs. urban, liberal

Parameters and criteria defining different "Americas":
*   place of residence (rural vs. urban; East coast/West coast vs. "middle America"), race, political affiliation, income, education, profession, class, creed/religion, (moral) values/norms/ideals

ANALYSIS

3 Explain how these different "Americas" have come into existence.

LÖSUNGSVORSCHLAG
*   (increasing) tendency towards individualisation/fragmentation within all modern (Western) societies
*   growing cultural differences between rural and urban America
*   members of different groups "share information only with each other, consuming news sources … increasingly tailored to them" (ll. 38–39) ➡ this fact reinforces the differences between the different groups

EVALUATION

4 Discuss the extent to which a shared American identity is a prerequisite ...

LÖSUNGSVORSCHLAG Individual answers expected.

SPEAKING

5 👥 Choose one of the cartoons and interpret it for your partner. ...   ➡ S28.2

UNTERRICHTS-KONZEPT *Die SuS interpretieren die beiden Cartoons mit Hilfe der vier Schritte im Tipp auf Seite 9 im Schülerheft. Sie verwenden zusätzlich Skill 28.2 Workings with visuals: Cartoons (Green Line Oberstufe Baden-Württemberg).*

LÖSUNGSVORSCHLAG **Cartoon 1:**
*   on the left: a rich man (wearing a stylish suit, expensive shoes, and a tie) is sitting on the sidewalk; to his left there is his funny-looking dog (wearing some kind of poncho); next to him there is an expensive-looking bottle and a wine glass; in front of him there is his top hat (upside down) filled with bundles of money (oversized bank notes); the top hat is overflowing with money
*   on the right: a poor man (wearing old clothes: a pullover, a scarf, a pair of trousers with a patch, fingerless gloves) is sitting on the sidewalk; his dog (an ordinary breed) is lying on the ground next to him (to his right); next to him there is a bottle of cheap wine; in front of him there is an old hat (upside down) with some coins in it

- the rich man (with a snobbish facial expression) looks at - and looks down upon – the poor man; the poor man looks at the rich man and his wealth and is shocked / very surprised (→ bulging eyes) by the obvious disparity/inequality/injustice he sees
- message: (sometimes) rich and poor people live astonishingly close to one another (especially in big cities), but still they live in separate worlds and lead entirely different lives; the growing disparity between rich and poor is a serious social problem

Cartoon 2:
- the heading reads: US infrastructure deteriorating
- a crumbling bridge spans the gap across a canyon between two sides
- on the left it says "haves", on the right it says "have nots"
- on the left there are big, expensive houses (→ wealth), on the right there are small houses/ huts (→ poverty)
- message: the gap between rich and poor has become bigger / is still increasing; the collapsing bridge indicates that it is becoming increasingly difficult to move easily from one side to the other (→ i.e. that it is becoming increasingly difficult to climb the social ladder)

Social class and poverty in Germany

BRAINSTORMING   **1 Describe what you know about poverty in Germany.**

LÖSUNGSVORSCHLAG   Individual answers expected.

MEDIATION   **2 Your 16-year-old pen pal in the US is working on a presentation on social ...**

LÖSUNGSVORSCHLAG   Dear ...,

How are you doing? I hope that you are well! What have you been up to lately?
Have you been working on that presentation for your history class?
I have come across an online newspaper article that I found on the website of the German news magazine FOCUS. The article deals with the situation of poor people in Germany. I thought I should not only send you the link, but also summarise the most important information for you.
In Germany in 2015 every 6th person (15.7%) ran the risk of becoming poor. In Western Germany more people were threatened by poverty than 10 years ago, whereas things have developed differently in Eastern Germany. Between 2005 and 2015, the percentage of people who run the risk of becoming poor increased by 1.5% and reached 14.7% for people in Western Germany. This was the case for all federal states in Western Germany apart from Hamburg (which is a city and at the same time a federal state). Over the same period of time the percentage dropped from 20.4% to 19.7% for people in Eastern Germany. So the situation is still worse in Eastern Germany.
In 2015 the highest risk of falling into poverty existed for the people in Bremen (24.8%), followed by those in Berlin (22.4%) and those in Mecklenburg-Vorpommern (21.7%). People with the lowest risk live in Bavaria (11.6%), Baden-Württemberg (11.8%), and Hessia (14.4%).
In 2015 the sharpest rise in the number of people who run the risk of falling into poverty took place in North Rhine-Westphalia. There was an increase of 3.1% to 17.5%.
The official statistics are based on the number of people who earn so little that they run the risk of falling into poverty. The official threshold is set at 60 percent of the median net income (compared to the population as a whole). In 2014 that threshold was 2072 euros per month for a family of four (two adults and two children under 14) and 986 euros per month for a single adult.
The opposition parties criticise the government and hold it responsible for the high number of poor people in Germany. The opposition demands a raise of the minimum wage to 12 euros per hour and the monthly payment of 1050 euros to every eligible (unemployed, etc.) adult.
I hope this information will help you with your presentation.
Take care and take it easy

...

P.S. Don't forget to say "hi" to your parents for me.

E Gender

VISUALS

1 Describe and interpret the cartoon and comment on its message.   → S28.2

UNTERRICHTS-
KONZEPT

Die SuS beschreiben und interpretieren den Cartoon mit Hilfe des Tipps auf Seite 9 im Schüler-heft und der Useful phrases: Talking about cartoons. *Die Lehrkraft verweist zusätzlich auf* Skill 28.2 Workings with visuals: Cartoons *(Green Line Oberstufe Baden-Württemberg).*

LÖSUNGSVORSCHLAG

Description:
- a man on the left and a woman on the right – both are portrayed as black silhouettes – are each looking at an emergency box
- above the man's box there is a sign that reads: "HIS – IN CASE OF EMERGENCY BREAK GLASS"
- next to the man's box there is a hammer with a blue head (= male)
- inside the man's box there is a bottle of beer (with a blue label on it)
- above the woman's box there is a sign that reads: "HERS – IN CASE OF EMERGENCY BREAK GLASS"; on the glass pane there is a sign that says "free hugs"
- next to the woman's box there is a hammer with a red head (= female)
- inside the woman's box there is a teddy bear wearing a red ribbon

Message:
- women and men are very different, have different (emotional) needs, resort to different means if they have problems / need consolation / want to find comfort

THINK-PAIR-SHARE

2 a) – c) Make a list of what traits you think belong to the female / male ...

LÖSUNGSVORSCHLAG

a) **Traits that belong to the female / male gender stereotype:**

Girls / Women	Boys / Men
• beautiful handwriting	• bad handwriting
• diligent, orderly, tidy, organised	• lazy, sloppy, untidy, disorganised
• good at languages	• good at natural sciences
• are ahead of boys, faster development	• lag behind girls, slower development
• care a lot about clothes and appearance	• don't care about what they wear
• always need hours to get dressed	• have good motor skills
• have good language skills	• don't like shopping, hate window shopping
• are crazy about shoes and handbags	• don't cry (at least not in public)
• love shopping and window shopping	• want to become: firefighter, astronaut, football player
• cry quickly and often	• like football, motor sports, martial arts
• want to become: doctor, veterinarian, model, actress	• (often) work in physically demanding jobs
• like to read and have other quiet hobbies	• are more aggressive: more men are in jail
• like ballet and dancing	• are whiny and oversensitive to pain: almost seem to "die" every time they get a cold
• work as secretaries, teachers, nurses, etc.	• good drivers, park their car "anywhere", have a good sense of orientation
• are more peaceful / peace-loving	• can only do one thing at a time
• are physically resilient: after all, they give birth to children	• don't think / worry so much, don't feel the need to talk all the time
• bad drivers: can't back into a parking space, have no sense of orientation	• are childish at any age
• are capable of multi-tasking	• like to watch horror and adventure films
• think / worry too much, always talk about everything	
• are not childish; are reasonable	
• like to watch romantic films	

b) **Discuss how much truth is contained in female / male stereotypes as well as ...?**
- there is probably a grain of truth in every (kind of) stereotype, also in female / male stereotypes
- example: "All Germans eat Sauerkraut and wear Lederhosen." Well, not all Germans do it all the time, but many Germans (especially in Bavaria) do it more or less regularly.
- stereotypes help (the human brain) to categorise and simplify new information; new information can be processed faster

c) **Explain whether there are different gender roles / stereotypes in different countries ...**
- a country's culture, customs and traditions, and predominant moral values heavily influence / coin the gender roles and gender stereotypes in that country
- that means: in different countries (with different cultures, etc.) there are different gender roles and gender stereotypes

SPEAKING **3 Describe the last time you encountered any of these stereotypes in ...**

LÖSUNGSVORSCHLAG
- Encountered stereotypes in real life: Individual answers expected.
- One's behaviour: being conscious of stereotypes helps one be conscious of one's own behaviour towards other people in general; regarding gender, but also race, age, etc.

ANALYSIS **4 Examine why progress regarding (full) gender equality is made at a ...**

LÖSUNGSVORSCHLAG
- the level of gender equality (in a country) seems to be related to factors like education and standard of living
- differences in education and standard of living lead to differences in gender equality

EVALUATION **5 Assess the degree to which gender roles have changed in Germany in ...**

UNTERRICHTS-KONZEPT
Diese Aufgabe kann als Hausaufgabe aufgegeben werden. Damit gibt die Lehrkraft den SuS die Gelegenheit, ihre Eltern nach deren Erfahrungen zu fragen.

LÖSUNGSVORSCHLAG
Change of gender roles in Germany (in comparison to 50 years ago):
- today more women work (full time)
- today more women work in formerly male-only professions: bus drivers, truck drivers, etc.
- today more women get a university diploma
- today more women hold leading positions in the business world or in politics
- today women are paid higher wages than in the past → but: still income equality is rare
- fewer couples / people have (fewer) children → women have more time to go to work
- fewer people get married: more one-person households → women have to go to work
- more people get divorced: more single-parent households → women have to go to work
- fewer women stay home as full-time housewives and mothers
- today sometimes men stay home to take care of the children

Acceleration of change in the future:
- through technological advances, digitalisation, internet, social media
- through robots that can do hard manual / physical work → human physical strength becomes less important

Gender in cartoons and movies

VISUALS **1 a) Discuss the message of the ... b) Create your own cartoon ...** → S28.2

UNTERRICHTS-KONZEPT
Die SuS interpretieren den Cartoon mit Hilfe des Tipps auf Seite 9 im Schülerheft und Skill 28.2 Workings with visuals: Cartoons *(Green Line Oberstufe Baden-Württemberg).*

LÖSUNGSVORSCHLAG **a) / b)** Individual answers expected.

PRE-WATCHING	**2 Gender identity, gender roles, and gender stereotypes are a popular and ...**
UNTERRICHTS-KONZEPT	*Die Aufgabe kann wahlweise in Einzel- oder in Partnerarbeit erledigt werden. Die Lehrkraft verweist auf den Tipp zu Criteria for talking about films.*
LÖSUNGSVORSCHLAG	Individual answers expected.

WHILE-WATCHING	**3 a) – c) Get together in groups of 4 – 5, choose one of the movies ...** → S29
UNTERRICHTS-KONZEPT	*Die Wahlfreiheit bezüglich der Auswahl des Films ist der Motivation der SuS zuträglich. So können sich z.B. auch Gruppen auf Basis der Wahl des gleichen Films konstituieren. Es erfolgt ein Hinweis auf Skill 29 Workings with films (**Green Line Oberstufe Baden-Württemberg**).*
LÖSUNGSVORSCHLAG	a) – c) Individual answers expected.

POST-WATCHING	**4 a) – c) Assess whether humour is universal or related to a specific ...**
LÖSUNGSVORSCHLAG	**a) Evaluation: Assess whether humour is universal or related to a specific ...**

- there might be some universal features of humour
- on the whole, humour seems to be related to a specific cultural context
- many jokes only work in a certain language
- that's why jokes cannot be translated

b) Creative task: Write a movie review for your movie.
Individual answers expected.

c) Research: Find out which other movies the director of your movie has made. ...
Individual answers expected.

DISCUSSION	**5 Make a list of the stereotypes you have seen in the media and ...**
UNTERRICHTS-KONZEPT	*Hier kann die Lehrkraft die SuS echte Beispiele aus Zeitungen und Zeitschriften sammeln und analysieren lassen. Weiterhin bietet es sich an, gemeinsam Beispiele von Werbeclips im Unterricht anzuschauen und zu analysieren. Die SuS verwenden die Useful phrases: Talking about gender stereotypes.*
ERWEITERUNG	What kinds of products are advertised in what way? Are there advertisements for certain products that exploit female / male gender roles and stereotypes more than others? Why?

- *Erweiterung 1: Bei der Analyse der Werbeclips kann man schon erste Aspekte der Filmanalyse behandeln; Werbeclips (für TV und Kino) sind (auch) auf Grund ihrer Kürze dafür gut geeignet.*
- *Erweiterung 2: Analyse von Musikclips.*

LÖSUNGSVORSCHLAG

Stereotypes in the media and advertising:
- (ideal) men are portrayed as: strong, brave, active, love cars, love tools, love outdoor activities
- (ideal) women are portrayed as: beautiful, attractive, romantic, love fashion and shoes, love cooking, love handicrafts

Stereotypes (still) used because ...
- stereotypes still seem to work for advertising / are obviously still a successful strategy,
- people (= consumers) seem to respond on a subconscious level,
- it's a kind of self-perpetuating cycle: stereotypes are prevalent → that's why: stereotypes are used in advertising, people watch / read ads → that way: stereotypes are re-enforced.

EVALUATION	**6 Comment on the relationship between a country's standard of living and ...**
LÖSUNGSVORSCHLAG	• a higher standard of living leads to more gender equality
	• there is more gender equality in countries where the standard of living is higher

SPEAKING **7** **Speculate about how our personal perception of gender changes over …**

LÖSUNGSVORSCHLAG **Perception of gender:**
- very personal matter
- individual perception might differ greatly

Importance of gender:
- younger: more important
- older: less important

ZUSATZMATERIAL *Zu diesem Kapitel gibt es im Anhang einen Klausurvorschlag mit Erwartungshorizont. Der Klausurvorschlag steht zusätzlich editierbar auf der CD-ROM zur Verfügung.*

CD-ROM → Klausurvorschlag mit Erwartungshorizont (White, working-class and angry: Ohio's left-behind help Trump to stunning win)

2 Gran Torino

Seite 24 – 45

Didaktisches Inhaltsverzeichnis

Titel	Textsorte	Thema	Unterrichtsmethoden	Kompetenzen Textproduktion
A Detroit: Introduction				
Some myths about Detroit	Visuals Newspaper article	Detroit from 1910 to now	*Unterrichtsgespräch* *Einzelarbeit* *Partnerarbeit*	Describing and assessing pictures Reading for detail Finding subheadings Doing internet research
B Gran Torino: The film				
Sequence 1 (00:17 – 10:36)	Film, opening scene	Out of touch	*Unterrichtsgespräch* *Einzelarbeit* *Partnerarbeit* *Hörsehverstehen*	Viewing for detail Working with a dictionary Comparing results Analysing relationships Writing an e-mail
Sequence 2 (10:36 – 17:19)	Film scenes	Out of place	*Unterrichtsgespräch* *Einzelarbeit* *Partnerarbeit* *Hörsehverstehen*	Viewing for detail Analysing characters Writing an interior monologue
Sequence 3 (17:20 – 38:39)	Film scenes	Building bridges	*Unterrichtsgespräch* *Einzelarbeit* *Partnerarbeit* *Hörsehverstehen*	Viewing for detail Analysing a character's behaviour Writing a conversation Discussing aspects
Sequence 4 (38:40 – 50:04) (50:05 – 1:07:52)	Film scenes	New alliances	*Unterrichtsgespräch* *Einzelarbeit* *Partnerarbeit* *Hörsehverstehen*	Viewing for detail Analysing relationships Comparing speculations Taking notes Writing an analytical essay Revising essays
Sequence 5 (1:07:53 – 1:17:07)	Film scenes	Manning up Thao	*Unterrichtsgespräch* *Einzelarbeit* *Partnerarbeit* *Hörsehverstehen*	Viewing for detail Working with a dictionary Writing a comment
Sequence 6 (1:17:08 – 1:26:13) (1:27:13 – 1:29:58) (1:32:44 – 1:34:40) (1:34:41 – 1:43:35)	Film scenes	Dealing with the gang	*Unterrichtsgespräch* *Einzelarbeit* *Partnerarbeit* *Hörsehverstehen*	Viewing for detail Speculating on further events Writing an interior monologue Taking notes Analysing cinematic devices Analysing atmosphere Collecting pro and con arguments Writing a comment

Titel	Textsorte	Thema	Unterrichtsmethoden	Kompetenzen Textproduktion
Sequence 7 (1:43:36 – 1:46:00) (1:46:01 – the end)	Film, final scenes	Ultimate belonging	*Unterrichtsgespräch Einzelarbeit Partnerarbeit Hörsehverstehen*	Speculating on similarities and differences Comparing ideas Writing a eulogy Writing a will Taking notes
C Wrapping up the film				
The science behind why some people embrace uncertainty, and others don't	Book excerpt/ Newspaper article *Kopiervorlage 1 (CD-ROM)*	Uncertainty	*Unterrichtsgespräch Einzelarbeit*	Reading for detail Analysing character traits
D Further activities				
Concepts of assimilation	Newspaper article *Zusatzmaterial: Klausurvorschläge 1, 2 mit Erwartungshorizonten (CD-ROM)*	Assimilation of immigrants	*Unterrichtsgespräch Einzelarbeit*	Analysing relationships Reading for detail Commenting on quotes Writing a story Describing scenes

Anmerkungen zur didaktischen Konzeption

UNTERRICHTS-KONZEPT

Der 2008 produzierte und vielfach ausgezeichnete Film Gran Torino *mit Clint Eastwood als Walt Kowalski in der Hauptrolle ist sein bislang größter kommerzieller Erfolg. Eastwood führte gleichzeitig Regie und singt auch das Lied, komponiert von seinem Sohn Kyle Eastwood, am Ende des Films.*

Der Film ist für die SuS nicht nur sprachlich, sondern auch der linearen Erzählstruktur wegen insgesamt gut verständlich. Er bietet als Mikrokosmos einen nachdrücklichen Einblick in die Bruchstellen eines früheren und aktuellen Selbstverständnisses der USA. Walt Kowalski, selbst Kind polnischer Immigranten, ist Sinnbild des assimilierten Einwanderers der zweiten oder dritten Generation. Er ist Patriot durch und durch – die amerikanische Flagge hängt demonstrativ am Haus – und der Gran Torino, sein ganzer Stolz, ist ein rein amerikanisches Produkt, das er selbst gebaut hat. Er selbst war 50 Jahre lang loyaler Mitarbeiter einer ureigentlich amerikanischen Firma – der Ford Car Company. Er erwartet von allen Mitbürgern und in diesem Fall von seinen Hmong Nachbarn, sich in gleicher Weise zu assimilieren und dem amerikanischen Mainstream, wie er ihn definiert, der aber längst nicht mehr gilt, anzugehören. Da sie dies in seinen Augen nicht tun, belegt er sie mit rassistischen und diffamierenden Begriffen wie „zipper head" und „gook". So sehr er auf seinem Territorium beharrt und sogar bereit ist, dieses mit der Waffe zu verteidigen, so sehr fühlt er sich fremd in der Nachbarschaft, in der er wahrscheinlich fast schon so lange lebt, wie er für Ford gearbeitet hat. Insofern stellt seine Situation den Zwiespalt des – wie seine Söhnen sagen – nach wie vor in den 1950er Jahren lebenden Fließbandarbeiters dar, der sich der modernen Vorstellung einer multikulturellen Gesellschaft widersetzt. In diesem Kontext bietet es sich an, den Text Do Americans still have a shared identity? *(Kapitel 1, Seite 19) unmittelbar vor der Behandlung des Films zu besprechen. Damit erfährt der Film eine Einbettung in das Schwerpunktthema* The Ambiguity of Belonging, *denn es zeigt sich im Film, dass sich Walt der Entwicklung und den Herausforderungen der amerikanischen Neuzeit letztlich nicht ganz verschließen kann, auch wenn er die Ambiguität am Ende in seinem Sinne auflöst.*

Diese Unterrichtseinheit ist so aufgebaut, dass die S den Film sukzessive in Abschnitten sehen und analysieren, um die Entwicklung der Hauptfiguren besser beleuchten und nachvollziehen zu können. Teil A gibt einen Einblick in die Geschichte und derzeitige Situation Detroits, die wichtig ist für das Verständnis des Kontextes. Im Teil B werden die S sukzessive durch den Film geführt. Jede der sieben Sequenzen enthält eine Überschrift, die auf das Schwerpunktthema Bezug nimmt. Auch wenn es in den Arbeitsaufträgen nicht explizit gesagt wird, sollten Szenen je nach Länge, Komplexität bzw. Leistungsstand des Kurses zweimal gesehen werden – beim ersten Mal zum Verständnis, beim zweiten Mal mit Blick auf die analytische Aufgabe. Teil C betrachtet den Film als Ganzes nochmals mit Blick auf das Schwerpunktthema The Ambiguity of Belonging. Die abschließenden Aufgaben (Teil D) sind als Schreibaufgaben gedacht. Sie können aber auch arbeitsteilig in Gruppen bearbeitet und dann im Plenum vorgestellt werden. Auch diese Aufgaben behandeln vorrangig Aspekte des Schwerpunktthemas.

ZUSATZMATERIAL   *Zu dem Kapitel liegen zwei Klausurvorschläge mit Erwartungshorizonten im Anhang vor. Sie stehen zusätzlich in editierbarer Form auf der CD-ROM zur Verfügung.*

CD-ROM   → **Klausurvorschlag 1 mit Erwartungshorizont (Mediation: Große Mehrheit der Zuwanderer liebt Deutschland)** • **Klausurvorschlag 2 mit Erwartungshorizont (Listening: My 'Oriental' father: On the words we use to describe ourselves)**

Unterrichtsverlauf

A Detroit: Introduction

SPEAKING   **1** 👥 **The film *Gran Torino* is set in Detroit. Look at the pictures . . .** → S28.1

UNTERRICHTS-KONZEPT   *Einen Einblick in den historischen und ökonomischen Kontext, vor dem der Film spielt, auch wenn der Niedergang der Stadt Detroit nur anklingt, ist für das Gesamtverständnis des Films förderlich. Walt als „übrig gebliebener" weißer Mann in einer Nachbarschaft von jüngst eingewanderten Asiaten verweist auf die schlechte sozioökonomische Situation der Stadt. Es ist unklar, wo Walts erwachsene Kinder wohnen, aber es ist anzunehmen, dass auch sie Teil der „white flight" aus der Stadt an einen Ort sind, an dem die Wirtschaft besser aufgestellt ist. Angesichts ihrer Autos, der Größe ihres Hauses oder der Collegeambitionen von Walts Enkelin haben sie es offensichtlich zu einigem Wohlstand gebracht und sind in die Mittelschicht aufgestiegen. Die SuS berücksichtigen für die Bildbeschreibung Skill 28.1 Working with visuals: Pictures (Green Line Oberstufe Baden-Württemberg).*

LÖSUNGSVORSCHLAG
1. (most recent) Today Detroit is rebounding from decades of high unemployment, urban flight and a recent municipal bankruptcy. The city's infrastructure is adjusting to the changes.
2. (1950s) Men work on the Buick assembly line in the 1950s. This was Detroit's heyday when it was one of the richest cities on earth.
3. (July 1967) During the 1967 riots in Detroit 43 people died and over a thousand were injured as more than 2,000 buildings were destroyed. The riots were a result of the increased unemployment in the city due to increased automation and consolidation in the auto industry.
4. (ca. 2009) The Packard Factory 6 has been abandoned since the end of the 1950s when the automobile manufacturer closed its doors.

READING   **2 a) Read the following text in . . . b) Reread the article and fill in . . .** → S5, S32

UNTERRICHTS-KONZEPT   *Die Lehrkraft verweist bei Teilaufgabe a) auf Skill 5 Dealing with narrative texts (Green Line Oberstufe Baden-Württemberg). Nach einer ersten sorgfältigen Lektüre des Textes Some myths about Detroit notieren die SuS in Einzelarbeit eine Überschrift zu jedem Paragrafen. In Vierergruppen tauschen sie sich aus und einigen sich auf die jeweils beste Lösung. Anschließend werden die Vorschläge im Plenum besprochen und mit den Originalüberschriften verglichen (siehe Lösungsvorschlag). Im zweiten Lesedurchgang scannen die SuS den Artikel und erstellen eine Timeline, wobei sie für die Anfänge der Autoindustrie in Detroit über den Text hinaus recherchieren müssen. Einen sehr guten Überblick bietet der knapp siebenminütige Filmclip mit Erläuterungen und historischen Aufnahmen (https://www.youtube.com/watch?v=KNYfVPWP4mY), mit dessen Hilfe die SuS den Werdegang der Stadt vertiefen und die beiden ersten Zeilen für das frühe 20. Jahrhundert ausfüllen können. Ein weiterer Filmclip gibt eine Einführung in den Doku-*

mentarfilm Detropia *aus dem Jahr 2012 über den Untergang von Detroit (http://www.bbc.com/ news/entertainment-arts-19578766). Die SuS sollten in b) nur Notizen machen, wobei es für den Spracherwerb förderlich ist, wenn sie Wörter und Phrasen aus dem Text aufgreifen und die wesentlichen Informationen nicht in eigenen Worten festhalten. Zu Teilaufgabe b) erfolgt ein Hinweis auf* Skill 32 Doing research *(Green Line Oberstufe Baden-Württemberg).*

LÖSUNGSVORSCHLAG

a) **Summarise the message of each part and write a concise subheading.**
1. The auto industry is back, so Detroit should be, too.
2. Unions destroyed the auto industry – and Detroit.
3. The city began declining after the 1967 riots.
4. Public pensions sank the city's budget.

b) **Fill in the most important information for each period in the timeline below. . . .**

1910s	• the 4th largest city in the US • automotive manufacturing centre in the US • Ford Model "T" first car to be produced on the assembly line → first mass production of an affordable car
1930s	• Great Depression in 1929: beginning of the decline of the city
1950/60s	• 1950s: population peaked; rise of the middle class • but: plants being built in other parts of the country; whites leave the city ("white flight") and Southern blacks move to Detroit → racial proportion shifts • in 1967 racial tensions lead to bloody riots between a nearly all-white police force and black residents → exodus of small businesses, loss of 110,000 jobs, whites leave the city
21st century	• only two of the 16 auto plants left; • 16% unemployment, city files for bankruptcy in 2013 • modest recovery since then
Reasons for the decline	• white flight, economic decline → shrinking tax revenue • racial conflicts • lack of diversification in industry • globalisation and loss of jobs in the 1990s due to free-trade agreements (see NAFTA) • scandals and political corruption • pensions chewing up much of the city's budget

RESEARCH

3 **Search the internet for the "Ford English School" and find out how . . .** → S22

UNTERRICHTS-KONZEPT

Die Lehrkraft verweist zum Einstieg auf Skill 22 Presentaton *(Green Line Oberstufe Baden-Württemberg). Da die Wirtschaft zu Beginn des 20. Jahrhunderts in Detroit boomte, gab es einen hohen Bedarf an Arbeitskräften, der vielfach durch neue Einwanderer, besonders aus den osteuropäischen Ländern gedeckt wurde. Die* Ford English School *ist ein bemerkenswertes Beispiel, wie die amerikanische Industrie, hier die* Ford Car Company, *die Amerikanisierung ihrer neuen Arbeiter betrieb. Die Neuankömmlinge gingen, nach erfolgreich abgeschlossenen Integrations- und Sprachkursen buchstäblich durch einen* melting pot, *in dem sie die Kleidung ihres Herkunftslandes ablegten und als Amerikaner wieder erschienen. Die Kurse waren so angesehen, dass die Einwanderungsbehörde diese als Voraussetzung für den* Citizenship test *anerkannten. Die SuS sollen selbst die Bedeutung dieser Schule im Internet erforschen und über eine Kurzpräsentation diese darstellen; ein Bild des* melting pots *als Illustration wäre eindrücklich. Geeignete Quellen: http://www.autolife.umd.umich.edu/Labor/L_Overview/FordEnglishSchool. htm (der Artikel stammt aus dem Jahr 1915), https://www.thehenryford.org/collections-and-research/digital-resources/popular-topics/sociological-department, https://detroitdecadence. wordpress.com/2012/10/10/tester-123/.*

LÖSUNGSVORSCHLAG
• established in 1914 at Ford Car Company
• target group: new immigrant workers, primarily from East European countries

- goal: English language classes to make sure safety regulations are understood, assimilation made possible through culture and history classes and classes on proper American behaviour
- final ceremony: going through the "melting pot" by discarding one's clothes i. e. former cultural identity and emerging as a true American
- qualification helped them to pass the citizenship test

EVALUATION   **4 Can you think of another region, potentially in Germany, which has . . .**

UNTERRICHTS-KONZEPT   *Die SuS sollen die historische Dimension des Niedergangs von Detroit und mögliche Lösungsansätze für die Revitalisierung der Stadt erfassen, indem sie eine Region oder Stadt aus ihrem näheren bzw. europäischen Umfeld kennenlernen, die eine ähnliche Wirtschaftskrise erlebt und Wege aus der Krise gefunden hat. Die SuS können Recherchen zu folgenden Städten oder Regionen/Ländern anstellen: Dresden, Leipzig, das Ruhrgebiet, Dublin, Irland. Für das Ruhrgebiet zum Beispiel empfiehlt sich:*
http://www.germany.travel/en/towns-cities-culture/towns-cities/ruhrgebiet.htm.
Wie auch Detroit versucht, wieder auf die Füße zu kommen, können die SuS z. B. auf folgenden Internetseiten erfahren:
https://www.thestar.com/life/travel/2016/09/10/detroit-is-americas-great-comeback-story.html
http://elitedaily.com/life/detroit-next-american-success/1145067/
https://www.theguardian.com/travel/2014/mar/02/detroit-michigan-first-steps-urban-renewal
(für sehr gute S).
Oder die SuS definieren Recherchebegriffe selbst, z. B. Detroit revival, Detroit comeback, Detroit renewal und finden somit entsprechende Internetseiten. Lektüreaufträge zu den Internetseiten könnten lauten:
a) **What are indicators of Detroit's renewal?** Possible answers:
   decrease in crime, growth in population downtown, increase in occupied buildings, more big sports events again, improvement of public transport etc.
b) **What has helped Detroit to revive?** Possible answers:
   attracting tourists and therefore businesses through
   1. culture (i. e. theatre district = second largest after Broadway in New York, Detroit Institute of Arts)
   2. renovation of historic parts of the city (i. e. Corktown = city's oldest neighbourhood, used to house Irish immigrants from Cork)
   3. restaurants (quite similar to the Ruhrgebiet, for instance, which was the European Capital of Culture in 2010)

LÖSUNGSVORSCHLAG   Individual answers expected.

B Gran Torino: The film

Sequence 1: Out of touch (00:17 – 10:36)

UNTERRICHTS-KONZEPT   *In dieser ersten Sequenz lernen die SuS die Familienverhältnisse der Protagonisten Walt und Thao kennen und analysieren diese eingehend. Beide stehen ihrer jeweiligen Familie fremd gegenüber. Sie kommunizieren nur sehr eingeschränkt mit ihren Angehörigen und somit wird hier bereits angedeutet, dass sie, auch wenn sie sich als Nachbarn zunächst argwöhnisch und ablehnend beäugen, doch einiges gemeinsam haben. Dass Letzteres nur nahe gelegt und nicht explizit von den Protagonisten angesprochen wird, sollen die SuS in dieser Sequenz ebenfalls erkennen. Dies deutet die Distanz und gleichzeitig die Abhängigkeit und damit die Ambiguität der Beziehung zwischen den Nachbarn Walt und den Hmongs an.*

COMPREHENSION   **1 Watch the beginning of the film (0:17 – 3:13) without sound. What . . . ?**   → S29.2

UNTERRICHTS-KONZEPT   *Die SuS werden auf Skill 29.2 Analysing films (**Green Line Oberstufe Baden-Württemberg**) hingewiesen. Den Film zunächst ohne Ton zu sehen soll die SuS darauf einstimmen, dass sie neben den Äußerungen der Figuren auch immer die Sprache des Films im Auge behalten sollten, denn* *darüber erschließen sich maßgeblich die Aspekte des Schwerpunktthemas, insbesondere die Ambiguität. Es erfolgt ein Verweis auf den Tipp zu Watching films.*

LÖSUNGSVORSCHLAG
- Walt: static, disconnected from everyone; first above the congregation and then separate from his sons/daughters-in-law; piercing look at his family; looks grim, motionless and mistrustful rather than sad when looking at his family and listening to the priest
- Grandchildren: dressed differently and not up to the occasion (their grandmother's funeral); detached from their parents and grandfather; not paying attention to the priest called Father Janovich; granddaughter comes across as irreverent because she is preoccupied with her phone
- Congregation: all dressed alike, all from the same section of society

COMPREHENSION   **2 Watch the scene again, this time with sound. Explain how the words ...**

LÖSUNGSVORSCHLAG
- Walt: disconnected from the church; he curses in church, does not take Father Janovich seriously
- Sons: detached from their father; they say he is disconnected from modern times, still lives in the 1950s, has no sympathy for his grandchildren; he can never be pleased; no more Thanksgiving with their father; they don't want him near them

ANALYSIS   **3 a)–d) 🧑‍🤝‍🧑 Explain Walt's situation in terms of belonging as ...   → S3**

UNTERRICHTS-KONZEPT   *Die SuS sollen ihre ersten Beobachtungen mit Bezug auf das Schwerpunktthema nun bündeln. Die folgende Wortschatzarbeit erweitert ihr themenrelevantes Vokabular und sensibilisiert sie in der Überarbeitung für eine erste stilistische Verbesserung. Im Verlauf der folgenden Unterrichtseinheit sollte die Lehrkraft immer wieder auf einen variantenreichen Gebrauch dieses Vokabulars achten bzw. ihn einfordern. Die SuS werden auf den Tipp zu* Thesaurus *und auf* Skill 3 Working with a dictionary *(**Green Line Oberstufe Baden-Württemberg**) hingewiesen. Grundsätzlich sollten die SuS immer wieder dazu angeregt werden, anhand eines Online-Thesaurus Wörter mit synonymer oder ähnlicher Bedeutung zu ermitteln (www.thesaurus.com). Im einsprachigen Wörterbuch (www.dictionary.cambridge.org/, www.oxfordlearnersdictionaries.com/ oder https://www.merriam-webster.com/) finden die SuS die Bedeutungsunterschiede und die Verwendung heraus, was sich arbeitsteilig ggf. als Hausaufgabe lösen lässt.*

LÖSUNGSVORSCHLAG   **a) Explain Walt's situation in terms of belonging as presented in this opening scene.**
- isolated, not comforted by his children, disconnected from his immediate family
- unclear whether he is sad about the death of his wife or rather upset about the behaviour of his family
- he does not seem to belong neither to his family nor to his church and fellow Catholics.

b) Spot on vocabulary: Group the following terms into the respective column.

to belong	not belonging
• to be attached to sb/sth	• to be estranged/alienated from sb
• to bond with sb, to develop a bond with sb	• to be disconnected from sb/sth
• to perceive sb as one's own	• to be detached from sb
• to feel connected with sb/sth	• to be separated from sb
• to feel an affinity with sb	• to distance yourself from sb, to keep sb at a distance
• to find common ground with sb	• to be out of step with sb/sth
• to identify with sb	• to be an outsider
• to form an in-group	• to be a misfit
• to fit in with sb	• to emphasise the differences between oneself and others
• to be part of a community	• to be banished from a place

c)/d) Individual answers expected.

VIEWING   **4** **Watch 3:14 – 10:36. a) Comprehension … b) Analysis … c) Creative …**   → S12.2

UNTERRICHTS-
KONZEPT

Erstmalig wird das Thema der Ambiguität durch die Verknüpfung der Szenen (zwei parallel ablaufende, aber in der Stimmung sehr unterschiedlich geartete Familienfeiern der Nachbarn) deutlich. Teilaufgabe c) bereitet die nächste Sequenz vor, in der das Verhältnis der Nachbarn beleuchtet wird. Dazu erfolgt ein Verweis auf Skill 12.2 Material-based writing (Green Line Oberstufe Baden-Württemberg) hingewiesen.

LÖSUNGSVORSCHLAG

a) **Comprehension: Complete the sentences.**
1. Walt rejects Father Janovich when the latter wants him to go to confession.
2. Walt's granddaughter is in a bad mood because:
   her mobile does not work in the "ghetto",
   she is asked to help Walt with the chairs,
   Walt does not give her the furniture.
3. The grandsons secretly go through Walt's chest in the basement and find black and white photographs of Walt in Korea dated 1952 and a medal.
4. Walt is angry with his sons when they depart because they drive a foreign car instead of an American car.
5. Cars are important to him because he worked for Ford for many years.
6. The Hmong family has come together in order to welcome a newborn family member in a celebration.
7. Not everyone is happy in the Hmong family because a man is missing in the household.

b) **Analysis: Compare the relations within the Kowalski family and the Hmong family. …**
Both families come together but for different reasons – the Kowalskis for a funeral and the Hmong family for a birth celebration. Whereas all the generations of the Hmong family unite in a circle for the welcome ritual, the Kowalskis float around separately and only the members within a generation bond. Intergenerationally, they are not on good terms. Whereas the Kowalskis are presented as very materialistic and the person, Dorothy Kowalski, whose death brings them together, is not even mentioned, the Hmong family unites in a spiritual ceremony making the baby the center of attention and wishing the newborn well. The family situations are reversed mirror images of each other.
However, there are also similarities beyond the mere fact that their families gather. Both men, Walt and Thao do not fit in with their respective family: they are outsiders, detached from their families and barely communicate with them. They avoid family members as best illustrated in their heads bowed down when around family members; neither of them meets their family's eyes and in fact both leave the reunion to go outside; they also do not meet their family's expectations for that matter: Walt does not give up his furniture, car and house and does not allow himself to be pushed around, unlike Thao who does not assume a manly role as demanded by Hmong culture. Instead he is blamed for acting like a woman, being ordered around by his sister, washing the dishes and doing other household chores. Their sense of belonging is ambiguous as they are related to their family by blood yet are out of touch with their respective family members.

c) **Creative writing: Write the dialogue based on the first 10 minutes of the film.**   → S12.2
Individual answers expected.

Sequence 2: Out of place (10:36 – 17:19)

UNTERRICHTS-
KONZEPT

In dieser Sequenz öffnet sich der Blick auf die Nachbarschaft und das Verhältnis der Anwohner untereinander. Was sich angedeutet hat über das Setting der beiden benachbarten Häuser, wird nun auch inhaltlich deutlich: Auch wenn Walt und die Hmong Familie sich spinnefeind und sehr unterschiedlich sind, verbindet sie mehr, als sie wahrhaben bzw. zulassen wollen, und sei es nur, dass sie sich in gleicher Weise ihre gegenseitige Missachtung kundtun (beide, Walt und die Hmong Großmutter spucken, um ihren mangelnden Respekt für den anderen deutlich zu machen).

COMPREHENSION   **1 Write one word to make true statements.**

UNTERRICHTS-
KONZEPT
Nur ein Wort einsetzen zu können, mag eine Herausforderung für die SuS sein. Darum können als Differenzierungsangebot die korrekten Wörter und drei weitere (personality, disrespect, drive) bereit gestellt werden. Alternativ können die korrekten Sätze gemischt und dann von den SuS in die richtige Reihenfolge gebracht werden. Die Lehrkraft verweist auf das Fact file zu Clint Eastwood.

LÖSUNGSVORSCHLAG
1. Walt and his old neighbour are both/equally upset about the others living in the neighbourhood.
2. Walt refuses to talk to Father Janovich because of the latter's youth/inexperience.
3. When the Latino gang approaches Thao, he ignores them.
4. The Hmong gang wants Thao to join them because they helped/saved him.
5. Sue tells the Hmong gang members that she is superior to them.
6. The Hmong gang members offer to protect Thao.
7. One Hmong gang member says that he was beaten/harassed in the past.
8. Thao's cousin wants him to be a real man and steal the Gran Torino.

ANALYSIS   **2 Walt stands at the plot boundary when he looks at or talks to his ...**

UNTERRICHTS-
KONZEPT
Erneut wird hier über die Montage der Szenen bzw. den Schauplatz darauf aufmerksam ge-macht, dass Walt und die Hmong Familie zwar nicht zueinander gehören (wollen), aber mehr gemeinsam haben, als sie bislang wahrgenommen haben. Die Abgrenzung gegenüber den Nachbarn macht Walt eindeutig über seinen territorialen Anspruch (sie sollen sich von seinem Grundstück fernhalten), dem er mit seinem Gewehr Nachdruck verleiht. Weitere Informationen zu der Rolle der Hmong als Laienschauspieler in diesem Film sind folgendem viereinhalbminüti-gen Hörbeitrag zu entnehmen: http://www.mprnews.org/story/2008/12/19/grantorino.

LÖSUNGSVORSCHLAG   **Belong together:**
- same style of the houses (front yard, porch, two floors, layout), situation is mirrored: family get-together in both houses
- both Walt and Grandmother Phong like to sit on the porch and both complain about the other's residence in this neighbourhood
- they both treat each other disrespectfully (both spitting and calling each other names)

Different:
- proper house and garden on Walt's lot versus run-down house and garden on the Hmong side
- death vs. birth
- single resident vs. family
- male vs. mostly female
- European background (Polish) vs. first-generation Asian immigrants
- pride in America (see the flag) vs. pride in Hmong culture (see their clothing)
- Walt with two cars vs. Hmongs without a vehicle
→ Walt economically better off than the Hmong family

ANALYSIS   **3 Analyse Walt's reaction to his neighbours. Use the phrases from the box ...**

UNTERRICHTS-
KONZEPT
Bevor die S mit der Analyse beginnen, sollten sie die Useful phrases durchlesen und dann mög-lichst viele davon auch benutzen. Wichtig für den Spracherwerb ist, dass bei der Ausarbeitung auch auf der Verwendung insistiert wird, u. U. mit dem Hörauftrag, wie viele bzw. welche Phrases von den Mitschüler(inne)n eingesetzt wurden.

LÖSUNGSVORSCHLAG
- acts defensively toward his territory
- different culture which he objects to, portrayed as arrogant when calling them "barbarians"
- growls at everyone
- full of disdain but at the same time blames Thao for being disrespectful himself when he rings his doorbell during the funeral celebration
- he comes across as a racist when addressing or talking about them

COMPREHENSION/
ANALYSIS

4 Describe Thao's encounter with the Hmong gang members and analyse . . .

LÖSUNGSVORSCHLAG
- he is a misfit in this crime-ridden part of town
- he reads even when walking down the street in a wasteland and is more interested in ideas than in material things
- he is easy prey for gang members who are interested in cars and positioning themselves in a community even if it means using violence
- the Latino gang members refuse to accept Asians on what they claim as their territory
- Thao ignores the Latino gang, even smiling when they insult him
- when the Hmong gang rescues him, he refuses to communicate with them or to get into their car
- they want him to join the gang to strengthen their position in the neighbourhood
- he does not even react to his cousin's call to join the gang

ANALYSIS

5 Explain the significance of the Gran Torino for Walt, Thao and the Hmong . . .

UNTERRICHTS-
KONZEPT

Die SuS lesen zunächst das Fact file *zum Modell Gran Torino. Unter* Special features *befindet sich auf der DVD der vierminütige Beitrag* Gran Torino: More than a Car, *der darüber hinaus einen guten Einblick gibt, welchen Stellenwert Autos bzw. Oldtimer für das Selbstverständnis von amerikanischen Männern haben können, besonders in Detroit, der (früheren) Autostadt schlechthin. Die SuS betrachten dann die beiden Standbilder (17:03 die Gang sieht mit Thao in Richtung Garage, 17:04 Gran Torino in der offenen Garage) und beantworten die Fragen. Das andere Feature auf der DVD* Manning the Wheel *zeigt in den ersten zwei Minuten die Bedeutung des Autos für Walt auf. Dieser Teil könnte präsentiert werden, nachdem die SuS sich Gedanken zu Walts Einstellung zum Gran Torino gemacht haben. Um den Filmclip auch sprachlich zu nutzen, hören die S zwei bis drei* Phrases *heraus, die sie selbst in diesem Zusammenhang verwenden können. In den weiteren sieben Minuten kommen auch spätere Szenen zum Einsatz, so dass Szenen des Films vorweggenommen würden.*

LÖSUNGSVORSCHLAG
a) Walt:
- it is his whole pride and he wants everyone to see it (open garage), more devoted to the vehicle than to any person, keeps it in perfect shape
- it is of sentimental value: connects him with a time gone by when his wife was alive and Detroit was still going strong
- it reflects his hard work and his pride in the USA (as opposed to his sons who sell and drive Japanese cars)

b) Thao:
- the car is of no value whatsoever to him
- it is not clear whether he wants to get his cousin and his friends off his back or himself to get accepted into the gang after all
- he is reluctant to steal it but it is not clear why he gives in

c) Hmong gang members:
- as an American car it is a status symbol and, on a symbolic level, owning it would be a means of showing that they have moved up and made it in America
- it is in stark contrast to their Honda which they have modified but is not as prestigious and valuable as the Gran Torino

CREATIVE WRITING

6 Choose between one of the following tasks: a) – b) Thao does not . . .   → S12

UNTERRICHTS-
KONZEPT

Je nach Neigung können sich die SuS für eine kreative oder analytische Aufgabe entscheiden. Die Lehrkraft erinnert an Skill 12 Creative writing (**Green Line Oberstufe Baden-Württemberg**). *Zu Teilaufgabe a) erfolgt ein Hinweis auf den Tipp zum* Interior monologue. *In beiden Aufgaben wird die Hin- und Hergerissenheit von Thao angesichts der Forderungen der Hmong Gang thematisiert. In Partnerarbeit können jeweils zwei S, die sich für die kreative und für die analytische Aufgabe entschieden haben, zusammenkommen und sich darüber austauschen, inwieweit Analyse und kreative „Lösung" zum gleichen Schluss kommen.*

LÖSUNGSVORSCHLAG a) **Write an interior monologue in which he contemplates whether or not he should give …**
Individual answers expected.

b) **Analyse to what degree Thao's sense of belonging can be called ambiguous up to …**
- his sense of belonging to the gang members: he belongs due to familial ties and they rescued him from the Hispanic gang
- he does not belong: lack of aggressiveness, car, gun; more interested in books yet wants to belong; when stealing the car he wants to be initiated into the gang but he is very reluctant and fails
- his sense of belonging to the family: he belongs as a son, does what the older family members/women tell him to do
- he does not belong because he does not fulfil the role of a male and is the only male and therefore an outsider, no male bonding possible

Sequence 3: Building bridges (17:20 – 38:39)

UNTERRICHTS-
KONZEPT

In dieser dritten Sequenz erleben wir Walt zum ersten Mal von seiner gelösteren und zugewandteren Seite. Dies ist der Fall, wenn er unter seinesgleichen ist, in diesem Fall in der Bar mit seinen Freunden, die ebenso patriotisch sind wie er und, so ist zu vermuten, dieselben Werte hochhalten. In der richtigen Umgebung kann er sich sogar öffnen für das hartnäckige Interesse des Pastors Janovich. Gleiches gilt, wenn er von Sue, Thaos Schwester, angesichts seines Biermangels, in deren Haus „gelockt" wird. Er grenzt sich nicht länger vollkommen ab, sobald Personen seiner unmittelbaren Umgebung auf ihn eingehen und ihn in seinen Bedürfnissen erreichen bzw. etwas finden, das sie mit ihm gemeinsam haben. Es obliegt aber den „Fremden", auf ihn zuzugehen, von sich aus tut es Walt bislang nicht.

COMPREHENSION/
ANALYSIS

1 Describe and analyse Walt's behaviour in the bar before his …

LÖSUNGSVORSCHLAG

This is the first time we see him mingle, crack jokes (though still racist in nature) and laugh. He seems to be familiar with and belong in this bar, frequented by men his age and background. The decoration (American flags on the walls and on the glasses) suggests that this is where he belongs; he feels at ease with his two elderly friends. This sets a positive atmosphere for the encounter with Father Janovich in which he can open up to him. Consequently, it is the first time he allows Father Janovich to address him by his first name.

CREATIVE WRITING

2 Write the conversation between the two soldiers in the picture above.

UNTERRICHTS-
KONZEPT

Während das Fact file *die* Hard facts *des Korea Krieges nennt, gilt es in dieser Aufgabe die SuS für die emotionale Situation der Soldaten im Krieg zu sensibilisieren und damit die möglichen Beweggründe für Walts Verhalten besser verstehen zu lernen. Als Vorbereitung bzw. zur Anregung kann die Lehrkraft den SuS folgenden Link empfehlen:* http://www.thememoryproject. com/stories/Korea. *Hier können sie den Erlebnissen einzelner Veteranen zuhören. Letztere sind zwar Kanadier, aber in der Sache macht dies keinen Unterschied. Alternativ kann sich jeder SuS einen Veteranen aussuchen und die S erzählen sich gegenseitig im Unterricht „ihre" Geschichte in einer* milling around activity.

LÖSUNGSVORSCHLAG

Individual answers expected.

COMPREHENSION

3 a) Listen the the conversation between … b) What do you learn about …?

LÖSUNGSVORSCHLAG

a) **Tick the correct answer (18:10 – 19:50). If the statement is false, correct it …**
1. False. … to make him come to confession.
2. False. … she asked the priest to talk Walt into confessing his sins.
3. True.
4. True.
5. False. … he started a family after the war.
6. True.

b) What do you learn about Walt's experience in the Korean War?
- He spent three years in the Korean War.
- He is responsible for shooting and stabbing men and butchering teenagers.
- These experiences have haunted him ever since so death would mean salvation.

ANALYSIS **4** a) **Explain to what degree this ...** b) **Describe and analyse Walt's ...**   → S29.2

UNTERRICHTS-KONZEPT *Die SuS werden bei Teilaufgabe b) auf Skill 29.2 Analysing films (Green Line Oberstufe Baden-Württemberg) aufmerksam gemacht.*

LÖSUNGSVORSCHLAG **a) Explain to what degree this encounter is a turning point and compare it with Thao's ...**
Walt still does not come across as very approachable in his tone of voice and he does not seem comfortable interacting with Father Janovich who has put pressure on him to open up even if he does not confess. But it is the first time that he does talk about his past and grants one of his community members and thus the audience some insight into his psyche. Ironically he, just like Thao, deviates from his previous behaviour in that both of them act in a way that is out of line with their character as far we have experienced them. Both give up their stubbornness and yield to the pressure that has been exerted from the outside, be it by Father Janovich or the gang members.

b) Describe and analyse Walt's behaviour during and after the attempted theft. Explain ...
During the theft, he resorts to means acquired in the war – he uses a weapon to chase away the thief. The drama that, for Walt, is linked to this incident is underlined by the handheld camera which makes the imagery less stable and involves the viewer far more than a static shot would do. Even though Walt manages to scare the thief (Thao) off, he himself falls down and lies with his back on the floor of the garage. He coughs up blood which makes him look less victorious and rather vulnerable. First the camera looks down at him, conveying the humiliation that he must feel, but then it goes down to him at eye level as if to identify with him. On the day after the incident he publicly shows his resilience by parking his car not in the open garage but even more prominently in the driveway. His attachment to the car comes across as endearing, given the soft music that is played when he sentimentally looks at his newly polished car from his porch. The eye-level shot on the Gran Torino with him bending down to clean the car with almost carressing moves makes the viewer perceive car and person as one and inseparable. "Ain't she sweet", he says when looking at the car. It seems that in hard times the car is the only thing that he can rely on. It is him, the car, the flag and Daisy, the dog. At the same time he seems to feel reconfirmed that he belongs where he is, even though he cannot feel safe.

COMPREHENSION **5** (22:50 – 29:17): **Complete the following sentences.**

LÖSUNGSVORSCHLAG
1. Walt is belligerent because he wants to be left alone and nobody should trespass.
2. When pointing his gun at the gang members, he refers to how he treated the enemy in Korea.
3. The episode with the Hmong family and the gang members bears a certain amount of irony because Walt saves Thao, who wanted to steal his car.
4. Walt calls all the presents from Thao's family garbage.
5. Father Janovich accuses Walt of not calling the police to solve the conflict.
6. Walt makes fun of Father Janovich when he says that he prayed the police would show up but nothing happened.
7. Father Janovich suggests that Walt get rid of the burden of the bad war memories and alleviate his guilt.

EVALUATION **6 Choose between one of the following tasks: a) – b)** 👥 **Speaking: ...**   → S12.2

UNTERRICHTS-KONZEPT *In dieser Aufgabe sollen die SuS darüber nachdenken, warum eine Tat, die nicht angeordnet wurde, unter Umständen schwerer auf dem Gewissen lastet. Damit wird die Frage nach der Eigenverantwortung aufgeworfen, die sich selbst dann im Nachhinein stellt, wenn ein Soldat im Krieg als Mitglied des Militärs Befehlsempfänger ist. Auch hier erhält der Zuschauer einen Ein-*

blick in die Psyche und Gedankenwelt Walts, die sein abweisendes Verhalten ein Stück weit verständlicher macht. Diese Gedanken deuten an, dass er sich in der Armee, in der das Zugehörigkeitsgefühl in der Regel zunächst sehr hoch ist, nur bedingt zugehörig gefühlt haben mag. Die Lehrkraft erinnert die SuS bei Teilaufgabe b) an Skill 12.2 Material-based writing *(Green Line Oberstufe Baden-Württemberg).*

LÖSUNGSVORSCHLAG

a) The thing that bothers a man the most is what he is not ordered to do. What could he …?
Individual answers expected.

b) Creative writing: Finish the conversation.
Individual answers expected.

ANALYSIS

7 Watch the next scene where the African American gang encounters Sue …

LÖSUNGSVORSCHLAG

This is the second time Walt has saved somebody that he claims he despises. Even though he does not talk about it explicitly, this time he might do something that he was not ordered to do. It turns out to be a good thing unlike in the Korean War. As he alluded to earlier vis à vis the priest he became personally guilty. So saving Sue might also be motivated by making up for his personal guilt.

COMPREHENSION

8 The Hmong: a) – c) 👥 Listen to what Sue says about the Hmong …   → S29.2

UNTERRICHTS-
KONZEPT

Bei Teilaufgabe c) erfolgt ein Hinweis auf Skill 29.2 Analysing films *(Green Line Oberstufe Baden-Württemberg).*

LÖSUNGSVORSCHLAG

a) Comprehension: Listen to what Sue says about the Hmong people and use her …
place – people – hills – Laos, Thailand and China – Americans – communists – 1975 – Thailand – Vietnam War

b) 👥 Evaluation: Walt may have had other reasons to help Sue. Speculate on them …
Another reason why he saves Sue might be his protective instinct towards females. In addition, he seems to have more respect for her than for her brother ("you are alright") because she stands up for herself, whereas he is pushed around by the female members of the family. This is shown, for example, when they urge him to confess the attempted theft and apologise for it.

c) Analysis: Outline how Walt starts connecting with the Hmong family.   → S29.2
His interest in the Hmong neighbours might be triggered by the fact that their war histories are, even though not directly, intertwined. Through Sue he starts taking an interest in Thao as well. Again Walt and Thao act alike as seen when a female neighbour has problems with her groceries and three juveniles walk by without helping her. Just as Walt is ready to get up and help the woman, Thao steps in and gives her a hand. This is a sign that there is a certain affinity between Thao and a member of the white community and it is telling that Walt's Hmong neigbour, Thao's grandmother, nods in approval just as Walt is slightly impressed or at least surprised.

Sequence 4: New alliances (38:40 – 50:04)

UNTERRICHTS-
KONZEPT

Die erste Szene dieser Sequenz, in der Walt erneut seiner Familie begegnet, steht in krassem Gegensatz zu den folgenden Szenen, in denen Walt mit seinen Hmong Nachbarn interagiert. Der abschätzige Umgang des Sohns und der Schwiegertochter, als sie ihm den Einzug in ein Altersheim nahelegen, untergräbt erneut Walts Zugehörigkeitsgefühl zu seiner eigenen Familie und zeigt gleichzeitig auf, wie ambig und konfus sein generelles Zugehörigkeitsgefühl ist. Auf der einen Seite fühlt er sich aufgrund der neuen Nachbarn seiner unmittelbaren Umgebung entfremdet, auf der anderen Seite ist er nicht bereit, seine gewohnte Umgebung zu verlassen und auf den Vorschlag seines Sohns einzugehen. Das, wie er findet, despektierliche Verhalten seines Sohnes und seiner Schwiegertochter steht aber nicht nur im Kontrast zu der genuin fürsorglichen Zuwendung von Sue und ihrer Mutter. Dieses im Konflikt endende Aufeinandertreffen von Walt und seinen Verwandten macht, wenn auch unausgesprochen, verständlich, warum Walt sich trotz anfänglicher Abwehr auf Sue und ihre Mutter einlässt.

ANALYSIS

1 Watch the scenes and compare Walt's family and the Hmong family.

UNTERRICHTS-
KONZEPT

Die SuS werden auf die Useful phrases *zu* Talking about relationships *aufmerksam gemacht.*

LÖSUNGSVORSCHLAG

Walt's sons suggest he move from the neighbourhood into a residence for elderly people. They belittle him by making him feel old and dependent. Walt rejects their ideas and they take back all the gadgets for old people that they have bought him for his birthday. There is no sense of belonging to his family.

The extended Hmong family, on the other hand, all gather and seem to get along across the generations. The only black sheep that does not belong is Thao's cousin, the gang member.

ANALYSIS

2 Describe how Sue connects Walt with her family and culture and analyse …

LÖSUNGSVORSCHLAG

It is the first time that Walt crosses the "border" to his next-door Hmong neighbours. He does not explicitly say why he does so, but it becomes clear that Sue talks him into it. She simply does not give him any choice. She repeatedly explains and insists that honour and the social code are what guide her family. This puts pressure on Walt to accept their wishes.
During the party at the Hmong family's house Walt follows Sue wherever she goes. She mediates between him and the family members and explains their customs such as not patting anyone on the head because that is where the soul resides. It seems that she makes him feel less insecure and she is the only one who takes a genuine interest in him. Consequently, he starts feeling closer to her and her family than to his own children, who are only interested in material things. He opens up, asks questions and even allows the shaman, called Kor Khue, to read him. The latter gives Walt a grim reading: he has made mistakes in the past, he is not at peace with himself, and he is not respected. His words are quite similar to Father Janovich's earlier confrontation. Walt comes across as very perturbed and stares into the void. Coughing up more blood seems to be worrisome and embarrassing for him at the same time. Sue, on the other hand, is truly concerned about him. In the bathroom he comes to the conclusion that he has more in common "with these goddamned gooks than my own spoiled-rotten family". It is the first time we don't see him isolated but rather mingling and trying to belong. Later on he reluctantly accepts being showered with gifts.

PRE-VIEWING

3 Thao and Walt: male bonding (50:05–1:07:52): a) – d) 👥 Before …   → S29.2

UNTERRICHTS-
KONZEPT

Die SuS sollen zunächst die Bilder eingehender betrachten und visuell erfassen, dass sich die Beziehung ändert. Die Gründe hierfür erschließen sie sich dann während der Präsentation dieses Filmabschnittes. Auch erkennen sie, mit welchen Mitteln ein Regisseur den Betrachter lenkt und über formale Mittel – in diesem Fall das Zugehörigkeitsgefühl, das sich allmählich zwischen den beiden Protagonisten entwickelt – unterstreicht. Es bietet sich ein Verweis auf Skill 29.2 Analysing films (Green Line Oberstufe Baden-Württemberg) an.

LÖSUNGSVORSCHLAG

a) **Pre-viewing: Before you watch the next sequence, you will study 5 stills from …**
1. **(50:10 – Thao and Walt are in the basement)**
   This scene might be in Thao's house. Walt seems to approach Thao but he does not respond. Thao might be ashamed of trying to steal Walt's car. Walt might confront Thao about him stealing the Gran Torino.

2. **(52:47 – Walt is talking to Sue and her mother)**
   Thao's mother and sister get involved. Thao is still ashamed as he looks down and does not look anybody in the eye. Walt has eye contact only with Thao's sister so she seems to be important. The camera angle suggests that the two women are in charge as the camera looks down on Walt and the scene takes place on the Hmong territory.

3. **(55:53 – Walt is looking across the street)**
   Thao and Walt, without the women, are left to themselves. They do not have any eye contact i. e. do not connect. They look in opposite directions and it is not clear if they communicate. Both seem to refuse to connect (see Thao's arms folded).

4. **(1:03:28 – Walt and Thao are in the garage)**
   Thao and Walt stand side by side and seem to interact. They are both preoccupied with the same things i.e. tools. Walt being talller signifies that he is teaching Thao something and is thus in a position of authority.

5. **(1:05:59 – Thao and Walt are outside with the fridge)**
   Even though both are opposite each other they are in the same situation: they face each other, they both have aches (Thao: his neck, Walt: his back); they look each other in the eye as opposed to all the previous pictures.

→ **Development of the relationship:**
   They become closer, thanks to/despite the help of the Hmong women; they find something they can share (tools, physical work).

b) 🧑‍🤝‍🧑 **Comprehension: Watch the scenes and, together with a partner, compare your ...**
   Individual answers expected.

c) **Analysis: Now go back to the beginning of this sequence and outline how ...   → S29.2**
   Down in the basement with the young Hmong family members, Walt first observes Thao but Thao avoids eye contact with him because he feels guilty. Then Walt approaches him but humiliates him wrongly calling him "toad" (= *Kröte*) and deriding him about his lack of confidence with girls. When Thao stands up for himself for the first time by insisting on his correct name, Walt starts scolding him for being shy about the girl he likes and not making an effort. He keeps insulting and provoking him by using disrespectful labels.

d) **Analysis: Describe how the relationship between Walt and Thao develops. Take notes ...**

	Thao	**Walt**
Scenes	1. in the Hmong's basement 2. last day of work 3. asking for help (faucet)	1. in the Hmong's basement 2. after his visit to the doctor 3. asking for help (freezer)
Appearance and effect	**scene 1** shoulders low, slow, = no self-confidence ↓ **scene 2** shoulders straight, eye contact, energetic	**scene 1** upright, self-assured posture ↓ **scene 2** down, depressed, staring into the void when by himself ↓ **scene 3** in charge, but down on the floor with Thao standing above him = suggests reversal of roles ↓ **scene 4** bent, goes down = giving in, coming across as inactive and vulnerable
Way of communicating	**scene 1** barely speaking ↓ **scene 2** addressing and asking Walt directly, outspoken ↓ **scene 4** telling Walt how to bring up the	**scene 1** commands ↓ **scene 2** slow speech, speechless ↓ **scene 4** subdued, very short answer to signal agreement, growling

	freezer, saying who is in charge, even interrupts Walt to stand his ground and calls him "old man" to indicate his authority; once Walt has given way, he calls him "pal", indicating that they are on equal terms	
Things to be learnt	how to use tools how to work hard (physically) how to use (bad) language how to deal with women = how to be a man (according to Walt; "you have no balls")	empathy: "this kid does not have a chance" to be protective and to care = how to be a mentor/father

→   In the end they become teacher and student, father and son for each other with their roles also reversed when necessary.

WRITING

4 Use your notes to write an analytical essay in which you also …   → S14, S29.2

UNTERRICHTS-KONZEPT

Ein erstes Mal sollen die SuS in größerem Umfang die Beziehung zwischen den beiden männlichen Hauptfiguren und deren Entwicklung zusammenhängend darstellen und damit eine Zwischenbilanz ziehen. Sie verwenden dazu die Useful phrases *zu* Giving evidence from the film. *Die SuS werden auf* Skill 14 Essay *und* Skill 29.2 Analysing films *(**Green Line Oberstufe Baden-Württemberg**) hingewiesen. Weitere längere Schreibaufgaben finden sich am Ende dieses Kapitels im Abschnitt* D Writing tasks. *Der Lösungsvorschlag weist auf die wesentlichen inhaltlichen Punkte hin.*

LÖSUNGSVORSCHLAG

Thao is pushed by his sister and mother to make amends for his attempted car theft and Walt reluctantly accepts. It is clear that Walt does not take Thao seriously when he makes him count the birds in the tree across the street. Next he gives him a more purposeful task, namely painting and fixing the house across the street.

It becomes evident that both benefit from each other: With Thao lacking a father, Walt becomes his teacher for how to act like a man. This involves how to use tools and fix things, how to deal with women, how to use language "properly", and how to take pride in oneself which is, according to the traditional American work ethic, based on hard work. Thao, on the other hand, ironically helps Walt feel a sense of belonging in the neighbourhood again when he fixes the houses around him to their old familiar appearance. And using time lapse underlines how effective Thao is and how much he gets done.

The dynamics actually change when Thao comes by, head high and shoulders up for the first time on his last day, implying that he has gained self-confidence. His eagerness to see Walt is suggested by the repeated and impatient ringing of the bell. Yet the camera presents this scene still from slightly above i. e. from Walt's perspective. This implies that he can still be annoyed at him and the relationship is still not on equal terms. He ironically orders him to take the day off, which clearly disappoints Thao, as suggested by his facial expression. Walt, on the other hand, is rather down in the next two scenes after he has seen the doctor and his son has no time to listen to his father and is too insensitive to realise that his father needs him at that moment. As a result he barely speaks, stares into the void and comes across as quite helpless. The roughness that Thao is still confronted with in this scene results from Walt's illness and worry rather than from what Thao does. They have started to take an interest in each other, which is more than they can expect from their own family members. So it becomes obvious that Walt and Thao's relationship develops in a positive way and when they ask each other for help with the faucet and the freezer it is an indication that they are now on equal terms.

PEER CORRECTION
5 Give your analysis to your partner, who will circle the phrases you have ...

UNTERRICHTS-
KONZEPT
Diese Aufgabe leitet die bewusste Spracharbeit und Verbesserung des Ausdrucksvermögens der SuS an. Ein besonders gelungener Text, der die sprachlichen Mittel auch variantenreich einsetzt, sollte den S am Ende vorgelegt werden, damit sie am Modell lernen.

LÖSUNGSVORSCHLAG
Individual answers expected.

Sequence 5: Manning up Thao (1:07:53 – 1:17:07)

UNTERRICHTS-
KONZEPT
Thao und Walt haben sich nun zwar aufeinander eingelassen, ihre Beziehung ist aber nach wie vor ambig, wie es das letzte Standbild ausdrückt: sie haben zusammen den Gefrierschrank bewegt, stehen sich aber immer noch gegenüber. Auch in der folgenden Szene, in der Thao Gartenarbeit verrichtet, wird dieses Ungleichgewicht zunächst noch deutlich, als Thao sich am Boden bewegt und Walt über ihm steht. Diese Sequenz thematisiert nun den letzten Schritt, diese Ambiguität aufzulösen, indem Walt Thao in seine Welt „initiiert". Was der Gang nicht gelungen ist, wird Walt bewerkstelligen, nämlich ihn „rhetorisch" und gesellschaftlich in seine (Werte) welt einzuführen und ihn somit zu seinem und damit zu einem assimilitierten amerikanischen „Kind" macht, das ihm näher stehen wird, als seine eigenen Kinder bzw. Enkel und die selben Werte leben und vertreten wird: harte und körperliche Arbeit, Familie und ein sicheres, wenn auch bescheidenes Einkommen. Für eine nähere Betrachtung von blue collar ethics siehe: http://www.bluecollarcrossing.com/article/650079/Blue-Collar-Ethics/.

PRE-VIEWING
1 👥 Discuss the following issues with a partner: a) – c) To what degree ...

UNTERRICHTS-
KONZEPT
In dieser Aufgabe sollen die S sich darüber bewusst werden, dass sie oder andere sich über die Sprache als einer bestimmten Gruppe zugehörig ausweisen und sich damit auch abgrenzen. Je nach Situation und Adressat werden sie sich sprachlich unterschiedlich verhalten. Abwertende Begriffe wie „Alter" zu verwenden deutet nicht auf eine Degradierung des Adressaten zum Beispiel hin, sondern eher auf eine bestimmte Altersgruppe.

LÖSUNGSVORSCHLAG
a) **To what degree is Thao a typical male teenager? Explain your reasons.**
Individual answers expected.

b) **Do men talk differently from women and if so, under what circumstances?**
Individual answers expected.

c) **How do men address each other? Do they talk differently if women are not around?**
Individual answers expected.

COMPREHENSION
2 Skimming: Watch the scenes and compare Walt's assessment of Thao ...

LÖSUNGSVORSCHLAG
• get a job to provide for yourself in construction (= physical work)
• talk like a man

ANALYSIS
3 (1:10:38 – 1:13:32) a) – i) 👥 / 👥👥 Watch the scene at the barber ...   → S23

UNTERRICHTS-
KONZEPT
Walt initiiert Thao nicht nur in die Welt der Männer, sondern auch in die Welt der white working class. Hierfür empfiehlt sich der 1,5-minütige Filmbeitrag von CNN auf der Website: http://edition.cnn.com/2016/09/25/politics/white-working-class-overview-kff-poll/ (siehe Aufgabe g); The Chintz and Shag Game (siehe Aufgabe i) findet man unter: http://www.cnam.com/people-like-us/games_shocked/flash.html. Die SuS verwenden die Useful phrases zu Analysing communicative behaviour. Bei Teilaufgabe f) erfolgt ein Hinweis auf Skill 23 Dialogue (Green Line Oberstufe Baden-Württemberg).

LÖSUNGSVORSCHLAG
a) **What can you conclude about the conventions of a conversation between men?**
Individual answers expected.

b) **Comprehension: Some of the following words are used in this scene. Consult a . . .**

Word	Meaning
Polack	offensive for sb from Poland
Chink	offensive for sb from China
crazy Italian prick	stupid, unpleasant person
Nip	offensive for sb from Japan
pussy (kid)	sweet and effeminate male; male homosexual
goddamn dick-smoking gook	dick: informal, not polite for penis dick smoking: homosexual gook: offensive for sb from East and Southeast Asia

→ **My conclusion about this male conversations:**
   ethnically, sexually and nationalistically charged labels

c) **Analysis: Explain the conditions/circumstances under which they are used as well as . . .**
Generally, the use of racial slurs is based on stereotyping and intended to put oneself above other races, women and/or people with different cultural backgrounds; but neither Walt nor Martin are offended; their ritual is to say the opposite of what they mean, namely to demonstrate and enhance their bonding and familiarity/belonging together (male, white, same socio-economic background, both first-generation Americans). They enjoy their bantering as indicated by their facial reactions (smile, laughter) and tone of voice; it is obvious that the way the labels are interpreted depends on the context and the addressee i.e. the familiarity with a person. Anybody who meets them together and does not know them would be considered an outsider and would first have to earn the respect and follow the rules of the in-group in order to belong and be allowed to follow their conversational rules. The purpose of the visit at the barber shop is to initiate Thao into this kind of male bantering and ultimately to prepare him for the world of construction which is dominated by men. Ironically, Thao, being the victim of racially-charged insults, learns how to use overtly racist language, thus making himself superior to others or at least getting a foot in the door to mainstream America.

d) **Analysis: Now watch Thao again in his first attempt to speak like a man and explain . . .**
Thao copies Walt's very informal style and verbal insults towards Martin. But he is clearly and immediately shown that he has violated the rules when Martin points his gun at him and thus literally and metaphorically holds him at a distance. This reminds the viewer of Walt's behavior in his encounters with the black and Hmong gangs when racial labels were used in a confrontational way to indicate separation, not inclusion.
In this case Thao is not entitled to use this kind of language for two reasons: he has never met Martin before and he is much younger than Martin. He therefore does not belong and has no right to follow the rules of the in-group (white, middle-aged, lower-middle class, male friends sharing the same language). Instead he violates these inofficial rules and comes across as extremely offensive. Walt then teaches Thao how to interact with a person of a "group" that he does not belong to, thus inititating him into their group: only if Thao accepts that he is inferior in age and ethnicity and therefore does not belong is he accepted as a friend of the "group". As a result he is advised or even told to swear about other people but not at the people when you first meet them. This clearly shows the ambiguity of the idea of belonging in this case.
Thao does not feel comfortable and does not really learn the rules either: he still addresses the barber as an "Italian son-of-a-bitch prick barber" and he does use rude language when he talks about his sore behind from the construction work, but a man is not supposed to say that he is too weak to work in construction.

e) **Evaluation: Racial slurs should never be used, not even in a humorous way. Comment.**
Individual answers expected.

f) 👤👤👤 **Pre-viewing: Next Walt takes Thao to his friend Tim Kennedy, supervisor . . .**   → S23
Individual answers expected.

g) **Comprehension (1:13:33 – 1:17:07): Watch the scene and compare your version with the ...**
Thao has learnt the lesson: he is polite when he first meets Mr. Kennedy, he makes up for the embarrassment of not having a car by lying about his car being at the repair shop. He has learnt that cars are a main feature of manliness and help you bond with a person like Mr Kennedy. He uses the "right" language, swearing about the repair shop and the high costs. His body language is also important: he is upright and swings a bit showing his resolve and energy to do the job. He thus shows that he can belong to this kind of milieu. When they leave the office Walt calls him "zipperhead" (offensive for a person from Asia) thus ironically showing his approval of how he has presented himself to Mr. Kennedy. At the hardware store their bonding becomes evident in the handshake that Walt offers Thao.

h) **Analysis: Thao gets initiated not only into a man's world, but also into a sector of ...**
European background, possibly second generation; like to fix things and do manual work; like routine, working class/blue collar, stereotyping, guns, interests: cars, women and how they do the shopping, sports

i) **Play the "Chintz and Shag Game" on the internet. Find out how Walt's house makes ...**
- floor: hardwood, some throw rugs
- shelves: in the kitchen have extra food, a cookbook, a phone and a teapot on them; in the basement are cans of paint
- wall hanging: beer poster in the garage, florals in the kitchen, map and picture of wild animal in the garage
- chair: sofa and comfortable chairs in the living room, nice dining room chairs
- TV: large colour TV
- furnishing: China cabinet with porcelain dishes, other large cabinets with dark wood, sheer curtains, big refrigerator

Note: In this task students could also play with the different categories to see what his house looks like inside to make it "working class" – sort of do it backwards. The film does not show much of the interior so this might be a better way of using this (fun) game. The dog (labrador) certainly does not do much to make him fit into the working class, the beer advertisement is in the garage and the TV, though, can be identified.

Sequence 6: Dealing with the gang (1:17:08 – 1:26:13)

UNTERRICHTS-
KONZEPT *Ein weiteres Mal drangsalieren die Mitglieder der Hmong Gang Thao, doch diesmal brutaler, denn sie rächen sich an Thao dafür, dass er ihnen nicht angehören will. Sie wissen, dass sich Thao längst für Walt entschieden hat, was sich in dieser Sequenz bestätigt. Damit wird aber auch der ultimative Showdown zwischen der Gang und Walt aus der Schlusssequenz anberaumt. Walt wiederum fühlt sich verantwortlich für die Notsituation, in der Thao und seine Familie stecken und der Zuschauer befindet sich auf der Höhe des Spannungsbogens, denn Walt erläutert auch Father Janovich nicht, was er plant. Wie mit einem Boomerang wird Walt stattdessen mit Thaos neuer „Männlichkeit" konfrontiert, wenn dieser gemeinsame Rache an der Gang für Sues Misshandlung fordert. Walt lässt sich aber nicht auf seinen Wunsch ein, sondern schützt ihn, indem er ihn einsperrt, und handelt im Alleingang.*

PRE-VIEWING **1 Imagine Walt sees this scene from his lawn. Speculate how the script ...**

LÖSUNGSVORSCHLAG Individual answers expected.

COMPREHENSION **2 Read the paraphrases of quotes below from the following sequence ...**

LÖSUNGSVORSCHLAG **Watch the sequence, compare and fill in who actually says it. (1:17:08 – 1:26:13)**

Paraphrases of quotes	Character	Significance
"I'm coming home from work – not that you guys would know much about that."	Thao	First time he talks to the gang members in self-defence; has adopted Walt's and thus the American's work ethic in contrast to the gang members.

"Why the fuck do you have to make me look bad?"	Gang members	Initially Thao has been drawn between the expectations of his mostly female family members and the male gang members; ironically Smokie is just as concerned about his image/honor as Walt was in the previous scene; so both "compete" for Thao to make him belong to him.
"Don't worry about the tools. Where does your cousin live?"	Walt	The gang members took away the tools and hurt him on his cheek. Walt is no longer concerned about material things but Thao's well-being. He is protective and wants to deal with Smokie in person. He does not leave it up to Thao to solve the problem. Walt then confronts Smokie with his weapon, beats him and threatens him if he does not leave Thao alone.
"You'd let me take the Gran Torino? Really?"	Thao	Walt helps Thao to go on his first date with Wa Xam and entrusts his cherished car to him. This is the ultimate sign of trust and friendship and a sign that he has won him over.
"I knew this would happen. What the hell am I doing here?"	Walt	After the shooting by the gang members: Sitting motionlessly wondering why he is here amidst the misery is ambiguous. On the one hand, it shows how attached he is to the Hmong family, on the other hand, he seems afraid of experiencing the emotional hardship of death and loss again as he did during the Korean War.

ANALYSIS **3 Explain the significance of what the characters say and fill in the third ...**

UNTERRICHTS-KONZEPT *Die SuS sollten diese Szene auf alle Fälle zweimal sehen und sie sollten nach jedem Durchlauf genügend Zeit erhalten, sich Notizen zu machen, da sie während des Sehens nur begrenzt mitschreiben können.*

LÖSUNGSVORSCHLAG See third column in task 2.

CREATIVE WRITING **4 When Sue comes home all bloodied after her awful encounter ...**

UNTERRICHTS-KONZEPT *In dieser Aufgabe können die SuS vieles von dem, was sie bisher zu Walt und seiner Beziehung zu Sue und ihrer Familie erkannt haben, zusammenführen und Walts Gefühlen und Gedanken Ausdruck verleihen.*

LÖSUNGSVORSCHLAG Possible thoughts: paralysed, haunting memories of the war when he saw wounded Koreans, feeling of guilt about then and now, sense of responsibility, anger, helplessness, urge to leave (logical connection to the film: he has just mentioned the war, the loss of friends; he has triggered the attack and the rape because he beat up Smokie)

COMPREHENSION/ANALYSIS **5 (1:27:13 – 1:29:58): a) – h) 🮲 You will listen to the ...**   → S14.2, S29.2, S29.3

UNTERRICHTS-KONZEPT *Die SuS werden bei den Teilaufgaben c) und d) auf Skill 29.2 Analysing films und Skill 29.3 Making a film (Green Line Oberstufe Baden-Württemberg) hingewiesen. Bei Teilaufgabe h) erfolgt ein Verweis auf Skill 14.2 Comment.*

LÖSUNGSVORSCHLAG **a) You will listen to the conversation between Father Janovich and Walt at his house ...**
- the Hmong: remain silent, not helpful to the police; Sue in the hospital
- the gang members: omnipresent, will harrass and threaten the Hmong family forever
- emotions: the Hmong are scared, Walt is not
- expectations: Thao is waiting for Walt to take revenge with him
- plans: Father Janovich: without a plan; Walt: does not know yet

b) **On a scale of 1 to 4 (with 4 being extremely close), how close have Walt and Father ...?**
Individual answers expected. Indicators:
Walt suggests he stay and have a beer; Father Janovich uses impolite language for the first time → Walt immediately allows the priest to call him by his first name; lets Father Janovich get the beer himself; Walt asks him existential questions and thus accepts him as a partner in an important situation; his respect and closeness is suggested when he continues to call him 'Father' and not by his first name; they agree in their final assessment that nothing is fair.

c) 🗣 **Speaking: Look at the film analysis pages at the back of this book. ...**   → S29.3
Individual answers expected.

d) **Analysis: Analyse the cinematic devices used in this scene and how they ...**   → S29.2
- in the dark, only faces are partially lit → no distraction by the surroundings, focus only on conversation given the seriousness of the issues; very intimate situation yet marked by distance (= respect) as they sit opposite each other
- close-ups of black and white i.e. very old photo album suggesting Walt has been sentimental about his past or seeking comfort in looking back at his forefathers
- he and the priest look at each other at eye-level → underlines that they see each other on equal terms; Walt remains seated and thus static, indicating that he is pensive and not sure yet what to do.

e) **Watch the second scene with Father Janovich (1:32:44 – 1:34:40). Explain why Walt ...**
- Walt goes to confess three things: he kissed a woman, he failed to pay some taxes and he was not able to establish a good relationship with his sons.
- Walt is very matter-of-fact, so is Father Janovich, who actually mistrusts Walt and is rather short with him; he suspects that Walt plans an act of retaliation.

f) 🗣 **Explain Thao's and Walt's states of mind, how and why they want to solve ...**

	Thao	Walt
state of mind	mad with rage, agitated, impatient	very pensive, calm, purposeful and concentrated
plan	ambiguous: wants to take revenge but only with Walt; not clear what he wants to do	ambiguous: wants to think about it first but seems to know what he is doing: plans to do it himself, not telling anyone (Thao, Father Janovich)
obvious reason	wants to prove that he can stand up to them; does not want to be passive = short-term solution	wants to protect Thao and his family from the gang forever = long-term solution
realisation	locked up in the basement by Walt like an animal in a cage; too late to watch Walt confront the gang members	has himself shot by the gang members, with neighbours watching and thus being witnesses → gang members can be arrested and Hmong family will be safe
significance	his determination shows that he has learnt to be a man (according to the old school); he has learnt the lesson from Walt: ready to use a weapon and defend himself	sacrifices himself for the family because he is terminally ill, but Thao has a long life ahead of him; feels responsible for the Hmong; punishes himself for his guilt; redeems himself and the Hmong family = ultimate sense of belonging

g) 🗣 **Speaking: Discuss the following viewer's comment about the ending of the film. ...**
→ **Your personal conclusion:**
Individual answers expected.

h) Writing: Then write a comment in which you state your personal opinion at ...   → S14.2
Individual answers expected.

Sequence 7: Ultimate belonging (1:43:36 – 1:46:00)

In der Abschlusssequenz bedenken die SuS nochmals alles, was die Beziehung zwischen Walt und Thao ausgemacht hat, wobei die von Walt vererbten Dinge für die Werte stehen, die Walt wichtig sind und die er deshalb an Thao weitergibt. Damit ist Thao vollkommen assimiliert, was das letzte Bild, in dem er am See im Gran Torino entlang fährt, versinnbildlilcht. Er entfernt sich von seiner Familie und Umgebung, an Bord ist lediglich Walts – betagter – Hund. Er fährt aber auch in eine unbekannte Welt hinein und insofern kann das Ende auch als ambig interpretiert werden.

PRE-VIEWING   **1** 👥 **Speculate on the similarities and differences between Walt's funeral ...**

**UNTERRICHTS-
KONZEPT**

Die SuS berücksichten die Informationen im Tipp für ihre Argumentation.

LÖSUNGSVORSCHLAG
- Similar: grandchildren equally disrespectful
- Different: Hmong family present, Father Janovich finds more personable words and refers to Walt's life as a veteran and how he sacrificed himself

ANALYSIS   **2** **Compare your ideas with the actual scene in the movie.**

LÖSUNGSVORSCHLAG
- Father Janovich stands close to the coffin which reflects his closeness to Walt; he speaks personally and very honestly about his encounter with the deceased and he is rather informal ("boy did I learn") which underlines his closeness to Walt.
- Walt's family is there, the granddaughter dressed just as informally as in the opening scene; this shows that nothing has changed in the relationship between Walt and his family; at the same time Walt's family suspiciously looks over to the Hmong family, who do not seem to notice; with the Hmong family sitting in first row as well, they come across as significant as Walt's actual family; they are dressed in their traditional costume, thus showing their respect for Walt but also their sense of belonging to their original culture.
- The coffin is open and we see that Walt is cleanly shaven, has had a haircut and is dressed in his newly tailored suit.

CREATIVE WRITING   **3** **Imagine you are Sue. Write a eulogy on behalf of the neighbours. ...**   → S15

**UNTERRICHTS-
KONZEPT**

Die Lehrkraft verweist auf Skill 15 Speech *(Green Line Oberstufe Baden-Württemberg) und den Tipp zu* Eulogy.

LÖSUNGSVORSCHLAG

Imagine you are Sue. Write a eulogy on behalf of the neighbours. Be prepared to deliver ...
Individual answers expected.

OR:
Imagine you are Walt and want to write your will. Fill in the chart and then write the will.
Individual answers expected.

ANALYSIS   **4** **Compare your classmates' imagined wills to Walt's will as presented ...**

LÖSUNGSVORSCHLAG

Even in death and afterwards he holds onto his ideals of the past: loyalty and hard work; he trusts in Thao rather than in his own family to pursue this legacy; he educated Thao in a way that he did not succeed in doing with his sons; the Gran Torino is the torch that he passes on along with the responsibility (you can have it "only if you do not change anything …").

PRE-VIEWING   **5** 👥 **a) After having listened ... b) Watch the final scene (1:46:00 – the end) ...**

LÖSUNGSVORSCHLAG
a) If you were the director, where should Thao take his new car and what kind of music …?
   Individual answers expected.

b) **Compare the ending to your ideas. Then take notes on the following:**

	Description	Significance
characters	Thao and Daisy, the dog	The most precious beings for Walt are together with the cherished war; Thao will take care of Daisy, who is with him in the driver's seat = he is in charge
mood and atmosphere	Thao: smiling, head up; sunshine, clear view	content, proud to have the Gran Torino; weather conveys positive feeling: freedom, no obstacles ahead i.e. in Thao's way = optimistic ending
scenery	inside the Gran Torino driving along Lake Michigan i.e. in nature	He has left his old life and neighbourhood behind, it suggests his full assimilation according to Walt
music	song sung by Walt	Walt will always be with him: sentimental/ melancholic, yet optimistic

C Wrapping up the film

FINAL ASSESSMENT

1 a) – h) There are various groups of people and individuals with whom the . . .

CD-ROM

→ **Kopiervorlage 1 (How comfortable are you (= Walt) with uncertainty?)**

LÖSUNGSVORSCHLAG

a) **Assess to what degree the protagonists' sense of belonging can be called ambiguous, . . .**

Walt

- His own family: He disrespects everyone in his immediate famliy as shown right after the funeral, during the birthday visit of his son and daughter-in-law, or when he simply hangs up when his son calls him about the season ticket; on the other hand, he calls his son after he returns from the doctor, having learned that he is terminally ill, just to find out that his call is not quite welcome or that he is so estranged from his son that he doesn't find a way of tellng him the sad news
- Church: He does not have much respect for Father Janovich at the beginning and rejects his call for a confession; later he reluctantly listens to him and tells him about his Korean War experiences; after Sue has been beaten, he opens up to Father Janovich and offers him a beer; he does go to confession after he has learnt about his illness, in order to confess that he had kissed a woman when he was already married, that he evaded taxes on $900 and was never close to his sons because he did not know how to; he claims he is at peace after he has confessed. It is not clear whether he goes to confession to please his wife or whether he feels the need to do so. He leaves the house to the church because it was his wife's wish, not because he feels he belongs. So it is his former wife who makes him connect with the church, which shows that he does not belong whole-heartedly.
- Thao and his family: After rejecting the Hmong family completely because they do not conform to his idea of a suitable neighbour (run-down house and garden), he does get close to them for reasons that are never openly mentioned but up to the reader's interpretation: They could be loneliness on his part, his loyalty to a tribe that helped the US in the Vietnam War, taking Thao under his wing because of his deteriorated relationship with his sons and in order to protect him from the injustice of the gang. Later in the film he claims that he has more in common with his neighbours than with his own family. His sense of belonging in the current neighbourhood is still called into question though because he feels the need to assimilate Thao into mainstream American society rather than to accept him as a Hmong member.

Thao

- His own family: Even though he is a blood relative and does not give up his family by joining the Hmong gang, he is an outsider within his family after all. He does not meet the female family members' expectations that they have of a man because he does women's work and cannot defend his family from harm. Only when Walt teaches him how to talk and how to fix things does he become a real man, but then he fulfills American mainstream expectations rather than Hmong standards. He expresses his sense of belonging to the Hmong tradition by wearing traditional clothes at the church service for Walt yet he drives Walt's car, the epitome of US culture in this film, at the end of the movie.
- Gang members: He does not want to join them even though they promise him protection from other gangs, yet he allows them to talk him into stealing the Gran Torino. Ironically, this brings him closer to Walt because he then has to make up for his attempted theft by working for him.
- American society (represented by Walt): After his attempted theft he does want to have anything to do with Walt on account of his guilt. When he is pushed by his mother and sister to make up for his wrong-doing, he starts getting close to Walt, who becomes a mentor or father figure for him. Just like his sister he is open-minded toward the American way of life, which is shown when he helps an elderly white neighbour with her groceries. He can easily and comfortably live in both worlds – see above "His own family".

Sue

- Her own family and American society: Unlike her mother and grandmother she has learned to live in both worlds and, as she tells Walt later in the movie, Hmong girls slip in and out of the culture more easily. She also wears Hmong clothes at Walt's funeral service but teases Walt just like an American would. So she can live comfortably with the ambiguity of belonging (to the American and Hmong cultures). The fact that she thanks Walt for being a father figure to Thao shows that she is realistic enough to see that this is the way for Thao to go.

b) **To evaluate how Walt feels about ambiguity – which always involves uncertainty – you …**
See solutions to *KV 1 (CD-ROM)*.

c) **What is your overall assessment of Walt's feeling of uncertainty?**
Walt does not like uncertainty. He wants everything to be as he is used to (neighbourhood, significance of American cars).

d) **Now read the following excerpt from …, and relate its message to Walt's character.**
Issues relating to Walt who tends to become crazy when confronted with uncertainty and ambiguity:
- stress (= death of his wife, new and foreign neighbours, his weak health)
- quick decision when confronted with foreign neighbours and jumping to conclusions ("urgency effect") → stereotyping (racial slurs against Hmong)
- experience abroad (Korea) helps him to connect with the Hmong neighbours
- role of food (party at the Hmong house)
- job (= assembly line rather than innovative work)
- permanence effect as shown in the end: he has carefully planned his death and the salvation of Thao's family; he sticks to his beliefs, symbolically expressed by passing on his Gran Torino to Thao after he has managed to assimilate the Hmong teenager into 'his' America

e) **Analysis: Analyse instances of confusion which Walt experiences.**
- his opponent, the Shaman in the Hmongs' house, tells him what his real problem is, i.e. that he is not liked and not at peace with himself
- former white male doctor no longer there; new Asian female doctor tells him about his terminal illness
- his son does not respond to Walt's worried state of mind on the phone after he has learnt about his terminal illness
- he has not been able to protect the Hmong family from harm (by the gang members)

f) **Analysis: Comment on the role that Father Janovich and Sue play in this respect.**
They both help him "to push through confusion" since they have no problem confronting Walt with his peculiarities – they are both rather direct, insistent, and are not afraid of his grouchiness. Father Janovich keeps urging Walt to confess or at least deal with his past while Sue knows how to take him by using a similar language with Walt that he likes to use when dealing with his peers. She calls him "Wally" and does not hesitate to order him around when it comes to "hiring" Thao. Being female might make the challenge of getting through to Walt a little easier for Sue than for Father Janovich, who battles Walt until the very end. Yet in the final funeral service Father Janovich admits that he has learnt a lot from Walt. If it were not for Father Janovich and Sue, Walt would not open up to his environment and acknowledge that things are more complex (and therefore ambiguous) than he thinks. They both help him clear his mind and come to terms with the ambiguities and conflicts that he faces.

g) **Comment on whether Walt's relationship with the Hmong proves he has a tolerance ...**
He seems to tolerate cultural differences with the Hmong women but not with Thao, whom he is willing to assimilate into mainstream America and thus be acceptable to Walt. Walt learns to appreciate their food, their insistence on their cultural conventions and their spirituality (see the Shahman's explanations). On the other hand, Sue has adapted to American culture by being self-confident and teasing Walt in a way that makes him like her but would not suit Hmong culture. In other words, she makes it easy for him to deal with her because she knows how to adapt.

h) **Explain how Walt's death shows his "need for closure".**
His decision to sacrifice himself to protect Thao and his family from the gang brings his life some closure because he seems to redeem his guilt of having a bad relationship with his sons, having killed a Korean boy of similar age as Thao and having escalated the conflict with the gang and thus indirectly inflicted more violence on Thao's family. His bath in the tub before he confronts the gang symbolises his cleansing his sins, thus having arrived at moral certainty.

D Further activities

EVALUATION   **1 Watch the following scene (1:06:50 – 1:07:49). Starting from this ...**   → S29.2

UNTERRICHTS-
KONZEPT

Die SuS werden auf Skill 29.2 Analysing films (*Green Line Oberstufe Baden-Württemberg*) *und den Tipp aufmerksam gemacht.*

LÖSUNGSVORSCHLAG

Sue has been direct and rather informal with Walt from the very beginning and this shows again in this scene. She is Thao's big sister and appreciates that Walt has taken over the father role for her brother. In view of an absent father Walt has served as a role model, something which he rejects in modesty and which shows that he does not have a lot of self-esteem for himself as a father. Early on she cares for him, does not take no for an answer and gently urges him to connect with her family on his birthday. She is the one who explains her culture to him in the car after the encounter with the gang and at the party in her family's house. She is the bridge between his and her world and subtly teaches him to deal with and accept the ambivalent nature of their neighbourhood.

EVALUATION   **2 Belonging means dependence. Discuss this thesis with reference ...**

LÖSUNGSVORSCHLAG

Walt feels he no longer belongs in his neighbourhood due to the arrival of Asian neighbours who neglect their houses and yards. He isolates himself completely from them, which is underlined by the fact that he scares off any intruders with his weapon. He claims to be independent from his neighbours and his sense of beloning is reduced to his house and lot, and he would deny the thesis.

His idea is ironically called into question, however, when he runs out of beer and depends on Sue to meet his drinking needs. When Walt allows Thao to work for him to make up for his attempted theft of the Gran Torino, he depends on the teenager to fix the houses and trim the trees in the neighbourhood so that he can feel a sense of belonging again.

Another case in point is that he assumes he and his children do not belong together. When he learns of his terminal illness, his phone call to his son proves that he does depend on them and therefore feels or longs for a sense of belonging.

EVALUATION   **3 Read the following passage and explain the various concepts of ...**

LÖSUNGSVORSCHLAG   The Hmong family is an example of 'segmented assimilation'. Those family members who have joined the gang represent downward assimilation: they own a car and define themselves in terms of their vehicle, yet socially they have not moved up but down because they don't have work and don't mind being involved in car thefts and possibly other illegal activities. They also own weapons and in that way have assimilated as well.

Walt, on the other hand, can be called a nativitist initially because he also builds fences and avoids any contact with the Hmong. When he finally gives in to the pressure of the neighbours, his goal is to assimilate Thao, i.e. he turns Thao into an American. To what degree this is 'forced' assimilation is up to the viewer. Thao does not have any other role model to follow except the negative one of his cousin so he is forced to turn to Walt in a way. On the other hand, he does not mind in the end; on the contrary, his mood in the Gran Torino at the very end shows that he seems to be happy with his assimilation.

EVALUATION   **4 "Heimat ist kein Ort. Heimat ist ein Gefühl", says Stefan Kuzmany ...**

LÖSUNGSVORSCHLAG   Initially Walt would not agree with this statement as he defines his sense of belonging clearly in territorial terms. He defends his home against trespassers and feels very protective of his property. He feels disrespected by his Asian neighbours. But even though he has his house, his dog, his Gran Torino and his lawn which he is proud of, he learns during the course of the film that "Heimat" is more than a place. It is where the heart is, where he feels understood and where there are caring relationships which provide a deeper sense of belonging.

EVALUATION   **5 The German philosopher Theodor Adorno once said, "Intolerance of ..."**

LÖSUNGSVORSCHLAG   Walt cannot tolerate ambiguity at the beginning of the movie. He rather isolates himself completely from his neighbours and his family because he cannot accept that two worlds, that of the Hmong family and that of his materialistic and self-interested own family, can coexist and even connect with his own world and values. Instead he is very categorical and therefore authoritarian with his neighbours and family members. He expects everyone around him to follow his set of values and rules (i.e. his sons to work with American cars, the Hmong family to leave him alone, his neighbourhood to look like it used to, etc.). Even later when he becomes more relaxed around and tolerant of Thao's family, he still asserts his authority when he initiates Thao into the American world and even more so when he locks him up in the basement to prevent his intervention during the final scene with the gang.

EVALUATION   **6 Imagine Thao has become a father himself later in life and tells his ...**   → S12.2

UNTERRICHTS-
KONZEPT   *Bevor die S diese Aufgabe bearbeiten, wäre es sinvoll, dass sie sich Fragen des Sohnes/der Tochter zu dem Auto überlegen, damit es aus dem Text tatsächlich ein Dialog wird. Zudem erfolgt ein Hinweis auf Skill 12.2 Material-based writing (Green Line Oberstufe Baden-Württemberg).*

LÖSUNGSVORSCHLAG   Thao looks back in appreciation of Walt and what he has done for him: he has become a real man, has learnt to connect with mainstream America and to get himself a job. He takes great care of the Gran Torino and probably wants his son or daughter to cherish the car and what it stands for just as much as he does.

CREATIVE WRITING	**7** a)–d) Bringing the novel and film together: a) Walt and Thao drive ... → S12
UNTERRICHTS-KONZEPT	*Die SuS berücksichtigen Skill 12 Creative writing (**Green Line Oberstufe Baden-Württemberg**).*
LÖSUNGSVORSCHLAG	**a)–d)** Individual answers expected.
ZUSATZMATERIAL	*Zu diesem Kapitel gibt es im Anhang zwei Klausurvorschläge mit Erwartungshorizonten. Klausurvorschlag 1 enthält einen Mediationstext, Klausurvorschlag 2 eine Hörverstehensaufgabe. Die Klausurvorschläge und das Transkript stehen zusätzlich editierbar auf der CD-ROM zur Verfügung.*
CD-ROM	→ Klausurvorschlag 1 mit Erwartungshorizont (Mediation: Große Mehrheit der Zuwanderer liebt Deutschland) • Klausurvorschlag 2 mit Erwartungshorizont (Listening: My 'Oriental' father: On the words we use to describe ourselves)

3 Crooked Letter, Crooked Letter

Didaktisches Inhaltsverzeichnis

Titel	Textsorte	Thema	Unterrichtsmethoden	Kompetenzen Textproduktion
A Introduction				
Ideas about belonging	Visuals, Word bank	General aspects of belonging	*Unterrichtsgespräch* *Einzelarbeit* *Gruppenarbeit* Think–Pair–Share	Dealing with vocabulary Creating a wall display Using a dictionary Doing internet research Giving a presentation
Was ist Heimat?	German newspaper article Statements *Kopiervorlage 1 (CD-ROM)*	Individual aspects of belonging	*Unterrichtsgespräch* *Einzelarbeit* *Mediation*	Mediating Taking notes Writing a comment
B Content				
Crooked Letter, Crooked Letter	Novel (Chapters 1–19) Visuals *Kopiervorlagen 2, 3 (CD-ROM)*	The plot The main characters The crimes Crimes and police work The setting The role of families	*Unterrichtsgespräch* *Einzelarbeit* *Partnerarbeit* *Gruppenarbeit* Touch–Turn–Talk Think–Pair–Share	Extensive reading Taking notes Comparing aspects Analysing characters and themes Summing up information
Racism	Dictionary entry	Definition of racism	*Unterrichtsgespräch* *Einzelarbeit*	Working with a dictionary Marking words
Amerika beschimpft und verachtet seine Armen	German newspaper article	Poor people in the US	*Unterrichtsgespräch* *Einzelarbeit* *Mediation*	Speculating about expressions Mediating Summing up findings
Study by American psychologists	Online article	Child health and human development	*Unterrichtsgespräch* *Einzelarbeit* *Partnerarbeit* *Gruppenarbeit* Think–Pair–Share	Reading for detail Paraphrasing findings Comparing results
C Analysis				
Crooked Letter, Crooked Letter	Novel (Chapters 1–19) *Kopiervorlage 4 (CD-ROM)*	The use of foreshadowing The role of time shifts Narrative perspective and genre Creation of suspense	*Unterrichtsgespräch* *Einzelarbeit*	Close reading Literary analysis: Analysing narrative structure and narrative perspective Analysing language and style
Bildungsroman	Dictionary entry	Definition of coming-of-age novel	*Unterrichtsgespräch* *Einzelarbeit*	Close reading Marking up a text Making a grid

D Further activities				
Crooked Letter, Crooked Letter	Book review	The plot	*Unterrichtsgespräch Einzelarbeit*	Writing a response for the comment section
Interview with Tom Franklin	⊚ Interview, Transcript *(CD-ROM)*	Radio show	*Unterrichtsgespräch Einzelarbeit Hörverstehen*	Listening for detail
Crooked Letter, Crooked Letter	Further tasks *Zusatzmaterial: Klausurvorschläge 1, 2 mit Erwartungs- horizonten (CD-ROM)*	The plot	*Unterrichtsgespräch Einzelarbeit*	Writing a diary entry Creating a freeze frame Writing a newspaper article Analysing a quote Writing a composition Creating a book cover

Anmerkungen zur didaktischen Konzeption

UNTERRICHTS-KONZEPT

Das Kapitel Crooked Letter, Crooked Letter *umfasst die komplette inhaltliche Erschließung des Romans von Tom Franklin, eine Analyse ausgewählter erzähltechnischer Aspekte, die Behandlung generischer Fragen sowie einen kursorischen Überblick über die Rezeption des Textes. Da der Roman nicht als eigenständige Lektüre zu behandeln, sondern in das Schwerpunktthema* The Ambiguity of Belonging *einzubinden ist, liegt der Schwerpunkt dieses Kapitels sowohl auf der inhaltlichen als auch auf der thematischen Erschließung des Textes. Dort, wo eine Unter- suchung erzähltechnischer Aspekte das Verständnis des Romans im Kontext des Schwerpunkt- themas unterstützen kann, wird diese begleitend herangezogen.*

Die Kapitel sind je nach Umfang zusammengefasst. Eine Reading portion *umfasst in der Regel zwischen 21 und 65 Seiten. Es wird das sukzessive Vorgehen im Unterricht empfohlen – die einzelnen* Portions *können so bearbeiten werden, dass damit in der Regel eine Doppelstunde gefüllt wird (Ausnahme:* Chapters 3, 5, 7*). Hausaufgabe ist dann der Leseauftrag für die nächste Doppelstunde. Um die Arbeitsbelastung der SuS zu reduzieren, sollte auf weitere Hausaufgaben – vor allem bei den längeren Leseaufträgen – verzichtet werden. Dazu kann es nötig werden, Pufferstunden einzubauen, um den Zeitraum, den die SuS zur Verfügung haben, zu verlängern. Als Pufferstunden eignen sich die beiden Kopiervorlagen (KV 2: vertiefter Umgang mit* Setting *und* Atmosphere*; KV 3:* “Crooked Letter, Crooked Letter” in the tradition of Southern literature*). Auch kann bei der Unterrichtsplanung ein Abschnitt aus dem Eingangskapitel zu* Identity and belonging *zurückgestellt und erst im Rahmen der Romanlektüre behandelt werden.*

Für jede Reading portion *gibt es eine Aufgabe zur Überprüfung des Leseverstehens. Bei der Zusammenstellung der Aufgaben wurde darauf geachtet, die SuS vor allem mit Formaten zu konfrontieren, die auch in der schriflichen Abiturprüfung zum Einsatz kommen. Abgefragt wer- den jeweils die zentralen Handlungsschritte. Im Einzelnen werden darüberhinaus noch weitere Informationen abgefragt, die später im Bereich* Analysis *wieder aufgegriffen werden können (z.B. bei der Charakterisierung der Personen). Die ausgefüllten und verbesserten* Reading comprehension tasks *dienen den SuS deshalb als* Word bank *bzw.* Language support *zur Bewältigung weiterer Aufgaben. Die Lehrkraft sollte den Kurs bei Bedarf darauf hinweisen.*

Um eine einigermaßen gleichmäßige Aufteilung der Reading portions *zu erreichen, wird folgen- de Aufteilung des Romans vorgeschlagen (die Seitenzahlen beziehen sich auf die Klett-Ausgabe, ISBN 978-3-12-579900-4):*
- Chapter 1: *9 S.*
- Chapter 2: *30 S. (39 S.)*
- *Einführung in die lektürebegleitenden Aufgaben:* Case files, Qs and As
- Chapter 3: *26 S.*
- Spot on vocabulary: Crime and policing

Im Sinne des integrativen Unterrichts erfolgt im Anschluss an die Überprüfung des Leseverstehens eine Vertiefung im Rahmen der Textanalyse oder im Sinne der Wortschatzerweiterung (Language work). Zusätzlich gibt es Aufgaben, die gezielt die Schreibkompetenz der SuS trainieren. Die Lehrkraft kann an geeigneter Stelle Aufgaben aus dem Bereich C Analysis in die fortlaufende Bearbeitung der Lektüre integrieren. Es finden sich dazu bei den Hinweisen zum Unterrichtsablauf in Kapitel C Angaben, ab welchem Kapitel diese zusätzlichen Analyse-Aufgaben sinnvoll eingesetzt werden können. Folgende Aspekte des Romans spielen im Zusammenhang mit dem Schwerpunktthema eine Rolle:

Class and race: *Oberflächlich betrachtet, erfüllt der weiße Protagonist Larry Ott alle Voraussetzungen, um ein erfolgreiches Leben zu führen. Er entstammt einer Familie aus der weißen Mittelschicht, die es zu bescheidenem Wohlstand gebracht hat. Der Vater, Carl, ist Eigentümer einer Autowerkstatt, Landbesitzer und angesehener Bürger der Kleinstadt Chabot, während seine Frau Ina sich als Hausfrau vor allem um das Wohlergehen ihres einzigen Kindes kümmert. Und doch erweist sich diese vermeintliche Sicherheit als trügerisch. Durch den Verdacht, der nach Cindy Walkers Verschwinden auf Larry fällt, zerbricht nicht nur die Familie, sondern wird auch deren wirtschaftliche Grundlage zerstört. Die Kunden meiden Carls Werkstatt, sein bereits latent vorhandener Alkoholismus wird offensichtlich und er stirbt angetrunken bei einem Autounfall. Ina flieht wenig später in die Demenz. Larry muss nach Cindys Verschwinden Chabot verlassen und kehrt dennoch als Erwachsener zurück. Um sich finanziell über Wasser zu halten, muss er Stück für Stück seinen Landbesitz verkaufen. Er fristet ein einsames Dasein im abgelegenen Elternhaus, geächtet von den Bürgern der Ortschaft. Genau gegenläufig verläuft dagegen der Werdegang von Silas Jones, der zunächst eine denkbar schlechtere Ausgangsposition innehat. Er wächst ohne Vater auf und muss nach der Inhaftierung des Lebensgefährten seiner Mutter überstürzt ein recht behütetes Leben im aufgeklärten Chicago gegen eine heruntergekommene Jagdhütte ohne Heizung und fließendes Wasser in einer Kleinstadt in Mississippi tauschen, dem Bundesstaat, der neben Alabama wohl als Inbegriff des alten, rassistischen Südens gilt. Trotz dieser widrigen Umstände wird Silas zum angesehenen Sportler an der örtlichen High school und später zum einzigen Polizisten der Gemeinde. Rassismus spielt im Leben der beiden Hauptfiguren vor allem während ihrer Kindheit und Jugend eine entscheidende Rolle, wenn auch nur unterschwellig – Silas' Mutter Alice wird ungewollt von Carl schwanger und muss Chabot verlassen. Gleichzeitig müssen Cindy und Silas ihre Beziehung geheim halten, was zum folgenschweren Date mit Larry führt.*

Family: *Bei der Frage nach Zugehörigkeit und den damit verbundenen Gefühlen von Sicherheit, Geborgenheit und Vertrauen, spielt die Familie eine zentrale Rolle. Für Larry Ott bedeutet Familie die (teils überbordende) Fürsorge seiner Mutter auf der einen Seite und die Verachtung seines Vaters, dessen Ansprüchen er nie genügen kann, auf der anderen Seite. Statt gegen den autoritären Vater zu rebellieren, versucht Larry alles, um sich die Gunst des Vaters zu sichern – letztlich opfert er sogar seine Freundschaft mit Silas dafür. Silas' Kindheit dagegen ist geprägt von der Abwesenheit eines Vaters und dem Bemühen seiner Mutter, Silas ein besseres Leben zu ermöglichen. Auch Silas' Mutter ist von ihrem Sohn enttäuscht, da ihm in ihren Augen etwas fehlt. Während sich Carl Ott allerdings einen athletischen, handwerklich geschickten Sohn wünscht, ist es die mangelnde Empathiefähigkeit von Silas, die Alice Jones bemängelt. Cindy Walker schließlich leidet unter ihrem gewalttätigen, alkoholkranken Stiefvater, dem ihre meist abwesende Mutter nichts entgegensetzen kann oder will. Obwohl dies letztendlich nicht eindeutig geklärt wird, wird Cecil offensichtlich auch zu ihrem Mörder.*

The American South – the land and its people: Crooked Letter, Crooked Letter *ist auch ein Roman über den wirtschaftlich abgehängten, ländlichen amerikanischen Süden. Die Ortschaft Chabot wirkt vergessen, einigen ihrer Einwohner fehlt eine Perspektive. Dennoch haben sich diese Menschen entschieden, diesen Ort nicht zu verlassen. In diesem Zusammenhang gilt es herauszuarbeiten, inwiefern die Verbundenheit (Belonging) zu einem Landstrich neben einem Gefühl von Vertrautheit und Sicherheit auch Enge und Perspektivlosigkeit bedeuten kann. Während Larry sich dagegen entscheidet, Chabot zu verlassen, kommt Silas zurück.*

High school as a microcosm: *Wenngleich der Roman auf die erwachsenen Protagonisten Larry und Silas fokussiert, so spielen doch ihre Erfahrungen als Kinder und Jugendliche eine prägende Rolle. Dabei geht es vor allem um die Rolle, die beide in ihrer* Peer group *einnehmen. Sowohl Larry als auch Silas werden maßgeblich in ihren Entscheidungen von den Erwartungen ihrer* Peer group *beeinflusst: Larry in seinem Bestreben, bei den anderen Jugendlichen Anerkennung zu finden; Silas in seinem Bestreben, seine Position durch eine mögliche Freundschaft zu Larry nicht zu gefährden. Auch Silas' Beziehung zu Cindy kann in diesem Kontext als ein Versuch des jungen Mannes gesehen werden, seine Position innerhalb dieses sozialen Gefüges zu stärken, auch wenn die beiden diese Beziehung – allerdings aus Angst vor Cindys Stiefvater – geheim halten.*

Clothing and identity: *Der Erzähler beschreibt die Kleidung der Charaktere mit viel Detail. Tatsächlich lassen sich daran identitätsstiftende Merkmale festmachen. Vor allem die Einstellung, die die Figuren gegenüber ihrer Kleidung zeigen, lässt Rückschlüsse darauf zu, inwiefern sie sich in der ihnen zugewiesenen oder selbstgewählten Rolle wohlfühlen, ob sich also in diesem Zusammenhang ein Gefühl des* Belonging *einstellt, bzw. inwiefern die Zugehörigkeit auch durchaus negative Begleiterscheinungen mit sich bringt, was dem Gefühl der Zugehörigkeit einen schalen Beigeschmack verleiht.*

Genre: Crooked Letter, Crooked Letter *ist ein vielschichtiger Roman, der sowohl ein anschauliches Bild des ländlichen Südens zeichnet als auch Aspekte der Kriminalliteratur und des Bildungsromans in sich vereint. Um den SuS die inhaltliche Erschließung des Romans zu erleichtern, spielen Aspekte der Kriminalliteratur bereits während der Lektüre eine große Rolle (durch das Erstellen von sog.* Case files *und der regelmäßigen Überprüfung offener Fragen). Eine Untersuchung von Aspekten des Bildungsromans findet innerhalb der* Analysis *statt. Optional ist die vertiefte Behandlung des Romans als Beispiel für* Southern Literature *(Kopiervorlage 3) und als* Crime novel *(Kopiervorlage 4).*

ZUSATZMATERIAL   *Zu dem Kapitel liegen zwei Klausurvorschläge mit Erwartungshorizonten im Anhang vor. Sie stehen zusätzlich in editierbarer Form auf der CD-ROM zur Verfügung.*

CD-ROM   **→ Klausurvorschlag 1 mit Erwartungshorizont (How has the Confederate flag lasted so long in Mississippi?) • Klausurvorschlag 2 mit Erwartungshorizont (The new president will inherit a profoundly divided United States)**

Unterrichtsverlauf

A Introduction

SPEAKING

1 Look at the pictures. Jot down your first impressions. Share . . .   → S28.1

UNTERRICHTS-
KONZEPT

Die SuS machen sich zunächst in Stillarbeit Notizen zu den Bildern. Dabei geht es nicht darum, die Bilder inhaltlich zu beschreiben, sondern um eine affektive Reaktion. Die SuS sollen den Gefühlen, die sie mit dem Dargestellten verbinden, Ausdruck verleihen. Der Austausch in der Klasse kann mit der Methode „Blitzlicht" erfolgen. Die Lehrkraft kann dazu die Bilder auf Folie kopieren und einzeln auflegen. Die SuS nennen reihum dazu Begriffe, die von der Lehrkraft auf der Folie festgehalten werden. Alternativ kann die Rolle des Protokollanten auch einzelnen SuS übertragen werden. Es erfolgt ein Hinweis auf Skill 28.1 Working with visuals: Pictures (**Green Line Oberstufe Baden-Württemberg**).*

METHODISCHE
TIPPS

In dieser Übung entwickeln die SuS eine eigene Word file, *die in der Folgeaufgabe als Differenzierungsmaßnahme* (Language support) *verwendet werden kann. Die Bilder wurden so ausgewählt, dass sie ohne besondere Wortschatzkenntnisse beschrieben werden können.*

LÖSUNGSVORSCHLAG

Individual answers expected, e.g. trust, love, happiness, understanding, comfort, peace, togetherness, belonging, home, success, partnership, reliability, etc.

THINK-PAIR-SHARE

2 a) – c) 👥 / 👥👥 Write down the first three words or ideas that you . . .

UNTERRICHTS-
KONZEPT

Ausgehend von ihren Notizen zu Aufgabe 1 wählen die SuS in Stillarbeit diejenigen Begriffe aus, die zum Oberbegriff Belonging *gehören. Sie berücksichtigen dabei die* Useful phrases: Working with a partner and in a group. *Als zusätzliche Unterstützung dient die* Word bank, *mit der die SuS ihre Liste ergänzen können. In einer zweiten Phase vergleichen die SuS ihre Wortlisten mit einem Partner und wählen gemeinsam vier Begriffe aus, die sie in die folgende Gruppendiskussion einbringen möchten. Jeweils zwei Paare vergleichen ihre vier Begriffe und einigen sich erneut auf vier Begriffe, die sie auf DIN A4-Zetteln mit Markern notieren. Falls es zu viele identische oder ähnliche Begriffe gibt, kann die Lehrkraft weitere Ideen hinzufügen (siehe* Word bank), *bzw. bei der Benennung von Oberbegriffen stützend eingreifen. Folgende Bereiche sollten genannt werden, so dass im Rahmen der Romananalyse darauf zurückgegriffen werden kann:* geography (e.g. home town / country, land, place of birth, etc.), groups (e.g. family, friends, team, school, etc.), emotions (e.g. safety, support, courage, satisfaction, etc.), exclusion (e.g. bullying, (peer) pressure, etc.).*

METHODISCHE
TIPPS

Diese Methode nennt sich Pyramid discussion *oder Schneeballdiskussion. Sie fördert die sprachliche Interaktion zwischen den SuS und hilft beim Sammeln von Ideen in einer Einstiegsphase, die Anzahl an Dopplungen zu verringern. Beispielsweise gibt es bei einer üblichen Kursgröße von 20 SuS fünf Gruppen, die insgesamt 20 Begriffe präsentieren. In Klassen, die mit dieser Methode noch nicht vertraut sind, kann es hilfreich sein, einen Musterzettel an die Tafel zu heften (Aufschrift:* Use the entire space!) *um kleingeschriebene, unleserliche Zettel zu verhindern. Lehrkräfte halten Papier, Marker und Magnete bereit. Die Lehrkraft legt für jede der Phasen ein Zeitlimit fest, das den SuS zu Beginn der Arbeitsphase bekanntgegeben wird. Für die Einzelarbeit genügen drei bis fünf Minuten, für die Partnerarbeit muss die Arbeitszeit verdoppelt werden, in der Gruppenarbeit schließlich benötigen die SuS die dreifache Menge an Zeit.*

LÖSUNGSVORSCHLAG

a) – c) Individual answers expected.

PRESENTATION

3 Present your ideas to the class by clustering them on the . . .   → S22

UNTERRICHTS-
KONZEPT

Der in dieser Aufgabe erarbeitete Wortschatz sollte den SuS während der gesamten Unterrichtseinheit zur Verfügung stehen. Es empfiehlt sich daher, das Cluster, sobald es seinen endgültigen Zustand erreicht hat, auf Packpapier zu kleben und an einer Wand des Klassenzimmers anzubringen. Die Postergröße ist so zu wählen, dass im Laufe der Einheit bei Bedarf weiterer Wortschatz hinzugefügt werden kann. Als zusätzliche Sicherung können die SuS dazu angehalten werden, das Cluster auf ein A3-Blatt abzuschreiben und im weiteren Verlauf der Unterrichts-

einheit zu ergänzen. Alternativ könnte die Lehrkraft das Poster abfotografieren und für die SuS kopieren. Auch hier empfiehlt sich eine Kopie im A3-Format, da die SuS im Laufe der Einheit Ergänzungen vornehmen werden. Es erfolgt ein Verweis auf Skill 22 Presentation (**Green Line Oberstufe Baden-Württemberg**).

LÖSUNGSVORSCHLAG   Individual answers expected.

RESEARCH   **4** 👥👥👥 **Each group chooses a cluster to explore further. With the help …**

UNTERRICHTS-
KONZEPT   *Diese Aufgabe kann in die Hausaufgabe gegeben werden. Die SuS berücksichtigen dabei den Tipp zu* Digital version. *Alternativ dazu findet diese Phase des Unterrichts im Computerraum statt. Es gibt zahlreiche Mind-Mapping-Programme, die im kostenlosen Download erhältlich sind oder browserbasiert arbeiten, z. B.:*
FreeMind (open source), FreePlane (open source), *http://www.xmind.net/de/ (kostenlose Version erhältlich), https://www.mindmeister.com/de (Anmeldung nötig, kostenlos). Aufgrund des ständig wechselnden Angebots sollte die Lehrkraft die Gültigkeit der Links überprüfen.*
- Dictionaries: *www.dictionary.cambridge.org/, www.oxfordlearnersdictionaries.com/, https://www.merriam-webster.com /*
- Word family finders: *https://www.learnenglish.org.uk/wff/index.html, http://www. oxfordlearnersdictionaries.com/topic/* (choose from a "topic" and go from there).
- Finding synonyms / antonyms: *www.thesaurus.com*
- Finding collocations: *http://www.ozdic.com/*

Die Suche nach lizenzfreien Bildern kann über folgende Metasuchmaschine gestartet werden: https: / / search.creativecommons.org /.

LÖSUNGSVORSCHLAG   Individual answers expected.

PRESENTATION   **5** **Present your illustration to the class. In your presentation, use as many …**

UNTERRICHTS-
KONZEPT   *Die Ergebnisse der SuS ergänzen das in Aufgabe 3 entworfene Plakat (bzw. ihre eigenen Aufschriebe davon).*

LÖSUNGSVORSCHLAG   Individual answers expected.

MEDIATION   **6** **The novel you are going to read deals with the connection people …**   → S26

CD-ROM   → Kopiervorlage 1 (Mediation: Was ist Heimat?)

UNTERRICHTS-
KONZEPT   *Vor Bearbeitung der Aufgabe kann die Lehrkraft zunächst die SuS nach ihren spontanen Assoziationen mit dem Begriff „Heimat" fragen. Je nach Leistungsstärke der Klasse kann diese Aufgabe im Plenum oder in Einzelarbeit (auch als Hausaufgabe) bearbeitet werden. Dazu sind folgende Arbeitsschritte durchzuführen:*
1. *Die SuS identifizieren die Aufgabenanforderungen in der Arbeitsanweisung und kreisen diese ein.*
2. *Die SuS lesen den deutschen Text und suchen gezielt nach Informationen, die sie markieren.*
3. *Die SuS übertragen die markierten Passagen ins Englische.*
4. *Die SuS schreiben einen zusammenhängenden englischen Text auf der Grundlage ihrer englischen Notizen.*
Die SuS berücksichtigen Skill 26 Mediation (***Green Line Oberstufe Baden-Württemberg***).

LÖSUNGSVORSCHLAG   See solutions to *KV 1 (CD-ROM).*

DISCUSSION   **7** **Drawing from your cluster on the previous page, find links between …**

UNTERRICHTS-
KONZEPT   *Diese Aufgabe dient sowohl der Umwälzung des bereits erarbeiteten Wortfelds zum Thema* Belonging *als auch der Vorentlastung der nachfolgenden Schreibaufgabe. Die SuS setzen sich unter Einbeziehung des zuvor entwickelten Wortschatzes (Plakat mit Clustern) mit der Definition Kuzmanys auseinander und äußern sich in diesem Zusammenhang mündlich zu ihrer per-*

sönlichen Definition von Heimat. SuS mit Migrationshintergrund können sich äußern, inwiefern auch unterschiedliche Länder und Kulturräume als persönliche „Heimat" empfunden werden. Vor allem die Aussage Kuzmanys, dass ein Ort, der keine persönliche Entfaltung ermöglicht, keine Heimat sein kann, kann im Zusammenhang mit der Romananalyse im weiteren Verlauf der Unterrichtseinheit wieder aufgegriffen werden (siehe Chapter 9, Task 2: Analysing the location und Task 5: Analysing the people, Schülerheft, S. 57/58). Des Weiteren können Begriffe, die sich noch nicht auf dem Plakat befinden in die entsprechenden Cluster (bzw. dem eigenen Aufschrieb) ergänzt werden. Denkbar wäre es auch, ein neues Cluster zum Thema „Heimat" zu entwickeln und zu ergänzen.

LÖSUNGSVORSCHLAG Individual answers expected.

WRITING/ PRESENTING **8** 👥 **Drawing from the discussion, the cluster and the word files, …**

UNTERRICHTS- KONZEPT *Die SuS machen sich Notizen (keine vollständigen Sätze) zu ihrer persönlichen Definition von Heimat. Sie verwenden dabei den Wortschatz, der auf dem Plakat gemeinsam erarbeitet wurde. Die Sicherung der Ergebnisse erfolgt zunächst in Partnerarbeit. Bei der Methode Conversation competition geht es darum, möglichst viele Begriffe aus einem zuvor definierten Wortfeld zu verwenden. Der Partner kontrolliert die Verwendung (z.B. durch Abhaken der Begriffe mit Bleistift im eigenen Aufschrieb oder im Aufschrieb des Partners). Im Anschluss werden einzelne Definitionen im Plenum vorgetragen. Die Klasse einigt sich auf eine Definition und ergänzt diese im Cluster. Diese Definition kann bei der Besprechung des Romans im Zusammenhang mit der Heimatverbundenheit der Hauptfiguren Larry und Silas wieder in Erinnerung gerufen und diskutiert werden.*

LÖSUNGSVORSCHLAG Individual answers expected.

B Content

READING LOG **1 Tracking your reading progress:** *Crooked Letter, Crooked Letter …*

UNTERRICHTS- KONZEPT *Bedingt durch die zahlreichen Zeitsprünge sollte den SuS die Notwendigkeit verdeutlicht werden, ein – wenn auch knapp gefasstes – Reading journal zu führen. Diese Aufgabe erfüllt mehrere Zwecke. Zum einen wird das grobe Leseverständnis der SuS gesichert. Zudem erarbeiten sich die SuS eine individuelle Kurzübersicht über den Roman, der im Rahmen der Vorbereitung der Abiturprüfung eingesetzt werden kann. Zuletzt dient diese Aufgabe auch der Schreibschulung. Mit der Textsorte der sog. one sentence summary, die oft im Zusammenhang von Writing courses für angehende Schriftsteller eingesetzt wird, werden die SuS veranlasst, sich noch einmal mit den wesentlichen Ereignissen eines Kapitels auseinanderzusetzen und diese so knapp wie möglich wiederzugeben.*

METHODISCHE TIPPS *Eine one sentence summary zu schreiben, stellt die SuS erfahrungsgemäß vor eine große Herausforderung. In leistungsschwachen Klassen kann die Lehrkraft die SuS bei der Besprechung der Beispiel-Summaries im Schülerheft auf die Verwendung von Haupt- und Nebensätzen sowie den Einsatz von participle constructions hinweisen. Die Bearbeitung jedes Kapitels im Schülerheft beginnt mit einer Leseverstehensaufgabe. Die Sätze aus diesen Aufgaben können von den SuS als Word bank für ihre one sentence summaries verwendet werden (vgl. Tipp auf S. 45). Die SuS berücksichtigen die beiden Tipps zu Summary und Flashbacks. Die vierspaltige Tabelle aus dem Schülerheft (chapter – character in focus – time span – one sentence summary) wurde in dem folgenden Lösungsvorschlag aufgelöst.*

LÖSUNGSVORSCHLAG
- Chapter 3: Larry; the past (late 1970s); this chapter introduces us to a teenage Larry, who, while desperately trying to live up to his father's standards, starts a tentative friendship with a black boy, Silas.
- Chapter 4: Silas; the present; after Silas and Chief French have begun a preliminary investigation of Larry's assault, Silas comes home to find Larry's message about having important information he wants to share.

- Chapter 5: Larry; the past (late 1970s); Silas intervenes when an intoxicated Cecil bullies Cindy, but both Larry and Silas let an equally drunk Carl coerce them into fighting, after which their friendship dissolves.
- Chapter 6: Silas; the present (+ flashback); as Silas goes through Larry's possessions, he reminisces about coming to Chabot with his mother, who, he now discovers, had previously worked for the Ott family.
- Chapter 7: Larry; the past (early 1980s); this chapter describes the events of Larry's date with Cindy, her subsequent disappearance and the consequences for Larry and the entire Ott family.
- Chapter 8: Silas; the present; after revealing to Angie details of his former friendship with Larry, Silas visits both Larry, who is still in a coma, and Ina, who does not recognise him, before returning to the cabin he once shared with this mother.
- Chapter 9: Larry, the (more recent) past; this chapter describes the growing friendship between Wallace and Larry, which ends abruptly in Wallace revealing his violent nature by both threatening Larry and demolishing his truck.
- Chapter 10: Silas; the past and present; shifting repeatedly between present and past, this chapter reveals the location of Tina Rutherford's corpse, the role Silas played in Cindy's disappearance and the reason behind Alice's dismissal from the Ott's household: her pregnancy.
- Chapter 11: Larry; the present; this chapter describes a confused Larry slowly regaining consciousness and being interviewed by the police in regard to the Rutherford case.
- Chapter 12: Silas; the present; after Silas admits his involvement in Cindy's disappearance to his superiors while at the same trying to reconnect with Larry, he meets with Irina, who points him to Wallace Stringfellow as a possible suspect for the rattlesnake attack.
- Chapter 13: Larry, the present; having fully recovered from his painkiller-induced haze, Larry decides to divulge his knowledge about Wallace Stringfellow to Chief French and to initiate change in his life by at least repairing and fortifying his mailbox.
- Chapter 14: Silas; the present; Silas visits Wallace Stringfellow at his home and attempts to question him, whereupon Stringfellow opens fire and hurts Silas before – having been shot himself – he flees into the woods.
- Chapter 15: Larry; the present; Chief French informs Larry that Wallace Stringfellow – now the major suspect in the murder of Tina Rutherford – has been killed on the run and that Larry subsequently has been cleared of both Tina's and Cindy's abductions.
- Chapter 16: Silas; the present; sharing a hospital room, Silas and Larry first learn that the police found evidence which implicates Stringfellow in the Rutherford case before exploring the idea that they are brothers and thus both have Carl as a father.
- Chapter 17: Larry; the present; Larry and Silas receive numerous visitors at the hospital, all of whom are keen to let bygones be bygones and move forward, with Angie inviting Larry to her church and the mayor expressing his eagerness for Silas to return to his job.
- Chapter 18: Silas; the present; Silas struggles to make amends for his past mistakes, visiting both Ina and Larry and setting about to clean Larry's house together with Angie.
- Chapter 19: Larry and Silas; the present; moving back and forth between the two main characters, this final chapter describes how Larry discharges himself from the hospital and is picked up by Silas, whereupon Silas attempts to rekindle their friendship, ending the story on a note of optimism and the promise of a future that would allow both characters to find peace at last.

NOTE-TAKING ## 2 Keeping track of the aspects of belonging: While reading the ... → S11.2

UNTERRICHTS-
KONZEPT

Den zentralen Begriff der übergreifenden Unterrichtseinheit aufnehmend, sammeln die SuS in dieser Tabelle stichpunktartig Ideen zur Frage, inwiefern Belonging für die beiden Hauptfiguren Larry und Silas eine Rolle spielt. Ggf. kann die Lehrkraft unterstützend auf die bereits eingetragenen Begriffe im Cluster hinweisen, die z.T. für eine oder beide Figuren übernommen werden können. In diesem Zusammenhang dient diese Aufgabe auch der Umwälzung des Wortfelds aus der Introduction. Diese Tabelle sollte während der Bearbeitung der Lektüre immer wieder zu Stundenende aufgegriffen werden. Ggf. durch Impulsfragen der Lehrkraft angeleitet, ergänzen die SuS darin auch Überlegungen, inwiefern das Gefühl von Belonging *bei beiden Charakteren als ungewiss, doppelsinnig oder gar mehrdeutig (ambiguous) betrachtet werden kann. Besonders nach den Abschnitten zum* Rural South *und* Teenage popularity and high school *(S. 55/56) kann jeweils ein Zwischenfazit gezogen werden. Die SuS berücksichtigen den Tipp zu* Chart *sowie* Skill 11.2 Taking notes *(Green Line Oberstufe Baden-Württemberg).*

LÖSUNGSVORSCHLAG

Aspects of belonging or exclusion

Larry Ott	Silas Jones
• class identity (ambiguity: even though Larry belongs to the middle class, he is excluded from society due to his dubious past) • racial identity (ambiguity: even though Larry is white, he is excluded by the other kids at school and tries to win their admiration by bullying a black girl) • community member as a land and business owner (ambiguity: Larry has to sell his land and his business is shunned by the local populace yet he feels comfortable in his work clothes and his garage) • Southern identity (ambiguity: is unsure how to deal with his father's latent racism; yet feels at home / comfortable in his natural surroundings) • peer group (ambiguity: Larry is isolated among the others because he doesn't fulfill (their) stereotypical expectations – he isn't physically attractive or athletic and pursues unpopular hobbies – reading and collecting snakes yet he is desperate to belong)	• class identity (ambiguity: Silas succeeds in escaping the lower class and becoming a respected citizen yet his secrets from the past make his position seem volatile; he is also troubled by financial problems and a lack of funding) • racial identity (ambiguity: by becoming a successful athlete and respected constable Silas is able to overcome racial bias; it is mostly his childhood and early teenage years that are marked by the social exclusion accompanying racism – his living situation in the cabin, the need to keep his friendship with Cindy a secret) • community member as a constable (ambiguity: as long as Silas chooses not reveal his role in Cindy's disappearance his position is volatile, see above) • Southern identity (ambiguity: although he has chosen to return to Chabot, he feels much more uncomfortable with the area; evidence: his descent into the ravine, his discomfort with the humid heat) • peer group (ambiguity: Silas has managed to be well-respected for his athletic success yet is unwilling to reveal neither his romantic involvement with Cindy nor his acquaintance with Larry for fear of losing the others' respect)

NOTE-TAKING

3 Tracking the protagonists: While reading the novel, take notes on . . . → S11.2

UNTERRICHTS-KONZEPT

Als Grundlage für die spätere Analyse dient das Character profile, *in dem die SuS zentrale Informationen über Larry und Silas sammeln (direkte Charakterisierung). Diese sollen im Analysis-Teil bei der indirekten Charakterisierung wieder aufgegriffen werden. Diese Aufgabe kann auch in arbeitsteiliger Partnerarbeit erledigt werden. Die Aktualisierung der* Personal profiles *sollte dann regelmäßig zum Stundenbeginn (z.B. einmal wöchentlich) erfolgen. Um eine gründlichere Sicherung der Ergebnisse sicherzustellen, kann dazu jeweils ein* Partner puzzle *durchgeführt werden. Arbeitsgleiche SuS vergleichen dabei zunächst ihre Notizen zu ihrer Figur, bevor sie ihre Ergebnisse einem Partner präsentieren, der die andere Hauptfigur bearbeitet. Es erfolgt ein Hinweis auf den Tipp zu* Personal profile *und auf* Skill 11.2 Taking notes *(Green Line Oberstufe Baden-Württemberg).*

LÖSUNGSVORSCHLAG	Larry	Silas
	• white, lower middle-class background	• black, lower class background, becomes middle class
	• 41 years old	• in his forties
	• a mechanic and garage owner ("Ottomotive")	• successful athlete as a teenager
	• practical and tidy (evidence: the portable pen for his hens, his spotless house, the way he keeps his clothes)	• police constable as an adult
		• reserved, aloof (both as a child and as an adult)
	• lives by routines (evidence: how he prepares for work in the mornings)	• tenacious investigator
	• polite / obliging (evidence: how he treats Wallace)	• ambivalent sense of justice (evidence: helps Cindy when Cecil is harassing her but leaves Larry behind to face the consequences of Cindy's disappearance)
	• cautious (evidence: hesitant to allow Wallace into his home, unsure of how to deal with Silas' confession)	• as a child / teenager: yearns to be accepted (evidence: Cindy possibly as a "trophy", doesn't openly admit to his former friendship with Larry)
	• loves to read horror stories	
	• as a child / teenager: desperate to please others (his father, the kids at school)	
	• as an adult: resigned, exhausted	

Chapters 1 and 2

TRUE OR FALSE

1 Read the statements carefully. While reading the chapters, … → S5.1

UNTERRICHTS-
KONZEPT

Um eine Vergleichbarkeit mit dem Abiturformat zu erhalten, werden die SuS hier aufgefordert, ihre Antwort mit einem Textzitat zu belegen. Anders als in einem begrenzten Abiturtext ist es bei einem längeren Lesetext allerdings nicht möglich, sämtliche Zitate in den Lösungsvorschlägen aufzulisten. Auch handelt es sich bei den Belegen oft um längere narrative Passagen (siehe Aufgabe 2 unten), so dass es nicht immer möglich ist, einen Beleg zu nennen, der sich auf einen Satz oder ein Satzfragment beschränkt. Es wird daher exemplarisch auf jeweils eine Stelle verwiesen, die als Beleg angeführt werden kann. Die Bewertung weiterer Lösungsvorschläge der SuS liegt im Ermessen der Lehrkraft. Die SuS werden auf die beiden Tipps zu Key words *und* Literary genre *sowie auf* Skill 5.1 Understanding narrative text types and typical features *(**Green Line Oberstufe Baden-Württemberg**) aufmerksam gemacht.*

LÖSUNGSVORSCHLAG

Chapter 1

1. false; He takes great care of the house, the garden and the barn. quote: p. 17, ll. 9 – 10 ("He acted more … and paying bills.")
2. true; quote: p. 19, ll. 1 – 21 ("The new pen … twice as good.")
3. true; quote: p. 21, ll. 1 – 3 ("a toolbox on … a road call"), also possible: "his mobile pen for the hens"
4. true; quote: p. 21, ll. 5 – 6 ("But even before … own a gun.")
5. false; There are no customers. quote: p. 20, l. 25 ("A mechanic, but only in theory.") or: p. 21, l. 29 to p. 22, l. 1 ("For a moment … job or something.")
6. false; Larry accepts Chief French's explanation without objecting. quote: p. 23, ll. 5 – 6 ("And Larry did … come here, too.")
7. false; Larry tries to talk to the intruder to calm him down. quote: p. 23, ll. 28 – 29 ("'Larry opened his … 'Wait,' he said.")
8. false; Larry believes he has seen the man's eyes before. quote: p. 24, ll. 1 – 2 ("Larry for a … familiar in there.")
9. true; quote: p. 25, ll. 5 – 6 ("'Die,' he said again. Okay with Larry.")

Chapter 2

1. false; Silas is alarmed by circling buzzards. quote: p. 26, ll. 9 – 11 ("He glanced out … dozens of them.")
2. true; quote: p. 27, ll. 9 – 16 ("Least of all … had gone out.")
3. true; quote: p. 32, ll. 3 – 13 ("M&M had sold … for that matter.")

4. false; After the Rutherford girl disappears, the police devote less attention to M&M's case. quote: p. 32, ll. 24 – 26 ("But since the … but forgotten M&M.")
5. true; quote: p. 33, ll. 1 – 6 ("Silas was sitting … in the water.")
6. true; quote: p. 36, ll. 20 – 22 ("He and M&M … could've done something.")
7. false; The narrator describes the town's center and the evidence of its economic decline.; quote: p. 38, ll. 1 – 20 ("Mayor Mo's real … fleet as spirits.")
8. false; Silas is alarmed by the garage being closed and wants to investigate.; quote: p. 46, ll. 7 – 13 ("Where the hell … sudden you care?")
9. true; quote: p. 45, l. 31 to p. 46, l. 2 ("But you wouldn't … Larry never confessed.")
10. true; quote: p. 46, ll. 16 – 17 ("'You need to … in somebody's mailbox.'")
11. false; Silas had expected sth better after reading the advertisement for the job. quote: p. 54, ll. 17-20 ("He'd thought this … hours, a vehicle.")
12. true; quote: p. 55, ll. 9 – 12 ("'We at Larry …God,' she said.")

NOTE-TAKING

2 Keeping track of the criminal cases: Chapters 1 and 2 introduce …   → S11.2

UNTERRICHTS-
KONZEPT

Um die Entschlüsselung der Kriminalfälle auch in Phasen des extensiven Lesens sicherzustellen, werden die SuS dazu angehalten, während der Lektüre sogenannte Case files *zu führen. Dies erhöht zudem die Motivation, selbst die dargestellten Kriminalfälle zu lösen bzw. Querverbindungen zu erkennen. Der regelmäßige Austausch über diese* Case files, *der routinemäßig in den Unterrichtsablauf eingebaut werden kann (z.B. einmal pro Woche), dient auch der sprachlichen Aktivierung der SuS. Methodisch eignet sich dazu die sog. A-R-M-Methode (Accept – Reject – Modify). Nach der kurzen Ergänzung der Fakten in die jeweiligen* Case files *präsentieren einzelne SuS dazu ihre Schlussfolgerungen. Diese können von der Lehrkraft (oder Protokollanten aus dem Kurs) an der Tafel notiert werden. Die Klasse bespricht dann jedes einzelne Statement zunächst in Partnerarbeit. Die Partner äußern sich dabei nach einem vorgegebenen Schema:*
I accept this conclusion because … / I reject this conclusion because … / I'd like to modify this conclusion because …
In leistungsschwachen Gruppen kann die Lehrkraft den entsprechenden Funktionswortschatz an die Tafel schreiben. In der Klasse kann im Anschluss eine kurze Abstimmung erfolgen (die SuS äußern sich per Handzeichen zu den einzelnen Thesen). Umstrittene Statements werden dann noch einmal im Plenum thematisiert. Fragen, die aus dieser Diskussion entstehen, können in den Wall display *integriert werden, der in der Folgeaufgabe beschrieben wird. Die* Case files *können ebenfalls auf einem* Wall display *im Klassenzimmer ausgestellt werden. Die SuS berücksichtigen* Skill 11.2 Taking notes *(**Green Line Oberstufe Baden-Württemberg**).*

METHODISCHE
TIPPS

In schwächeren Klassen ist es möglich, als binnendifferenzierende Maßnahme hier Kategorien vorzugeben: time of death, manner of death, personal background (age, sex, occupation, socioeconomic situation, etc.), possible motives / suspects.

LÖSUNGSVORSCHLAG

Cindy Walker	Tina Rutherford
• white female teenager • during the evening: after Larry had dropped her off and before they were set to meet at 11 pm • reliability of Larry as a witness doubtful • identity of the boyfriend unclear • claims to have been impregnated by her boyfriend • body was never discovered • violent stepfather and negligent mother	• 19-year-old white female from wealthy family • college student who disappeared on her way back to university • no witnesses • kidnapping not probable: no ransom note • dead body found in state of decay buried under a bed in an abandoned cabin on the Ott property

Morton Morrissette (M & M)	Larry Ott
• black man in his forties • a local drug dealer • disappeared • found murdered in a ravine on Rutherford property and had been dead for a while	• 41-year-old white male • mechanic, business and landowner • shot in the chest in his own home by a person (man?) wearing a zombie mask • suspect must have been known to Larry: no signs of a struggle • time of attack: noon / early afternoon (after phone call from the nursing home) • identity of the assailant is unknown (scruffy jeans, Larry seems to recognizes his eyes) • evidence found at his house: tracks (from a four-wheeler), numerous footprints, marijuana stubs, beer in his refrigerator (although Larry did not drink alcohol) • possible suicide attempt?

Connections:
- Tina – Cindy (both young women, possibly a sexually motivated crime?, crimes seem to resemble each other)
- Tina – Cindy – Morton (all three disappeared without a trace)
- Morton – Tina (Morton was found on the Rutherford's land, Tina is a Rutherford)
- Morton – Larry (possibly both associated with Wallace, who was a drug user)

CREATIVE TASK

3 Chapters 1 and 2 raise several questions about Larry's and Silas' past …

UNTERRICHTS-
KONZEPT

Bedingt durch die zeitliche Verflechtung von Gegenwart und Vergangenheit sowie die allmähli-che Enthüllung von Hinweisen, die zur Aufklärung der Verbrechen dienen, ist zu erwarten, dass im Laufe der Lektüre bei den SuS Fragen auftauchen, die nicht sofort geklärt werden können. Es bietet sich daher an, diese regelmäßig im Unterricht zu thematisieren (beispielsweise in der Einstiegsphase). In der Anfangsphase der Lektüre werden die SuS dabei vor allem neue Fragen notieren. Die Fragen werden gesammelt und auf von der Lehrkraft vorbereitete Vorlagen (Sprechblasen im A4-Format, z.B. aus Microsoft Word oder als Clipart im Download erhältlich) notiert. Neben dem Wortschatzspeicher und den Case files *entsteht somit auch ein interaktiver Fragenspeicher, der sukzessive im Laufe der Lektüre abgearbeitet werden kann. Es ist vorteil-haft, die Fragen für alle sichtbar zu dokumentieren, so dass bei deren Besprechung die Lehr-kraft in den Hintergrund treten und die SuS die Moderation des Unterrichtsgesprächs überneh-men können. Auch wird dadurch sichergestellt, dass die Behandlung der Lektüre auf die tat-sächlichen Bedürfnisse der Klasse zugeschnitten ist, da sich die SuS mit Fragen beschäftigen, die sie selbst formuliert haben. Sobald sich bei der weiteren Lektüre Antworten ergeben, werden diese ebenfalls durch Sprechblasen (ggf. mit einer anderen Farbe) ergänzt. Diese* Qs and As *können den SuS auch bei der Vervollständigung der* Case files *helfen.*

METHODISCHE
TIPPS

Sehr zurückhaltende Klassen bzw. SuS, die noch wenig Erfahrung mit der Behandlung englisch-sprachiger Ganzschriften haben, benötigen hier möglicherweise Impulse der Lehrkraft. Die Lehr-kraft sollte daher zu jeder Reading portion *auch eigene Fragen notieren, die ggf. den Anstoß für ein Unterrichtsgespräch bieten können.*

LÖSUNGSVORSCHLAG

Individual answers expected. Possible aspects:
- How did Alice and Silas come to live in the cabin? / What is the link between the two families?
- What happened to Cindy after Larry dropped her off?
- How did the friendship between Larry and Silas come to an end?
- Who do the tracks / evidence (beer, marijuana) belong to that were found at Larry's house?
- Why did Wallace Stringfellow want to become Larry's friend?

Chapter 3

SHORT ANSWERS **1** **Read through chapter 3 carefully. While reading, answer the following . . .**

LÖSUNGSVORSCHLAG
1. Carl Ott gives Silas and Alice a lift to school.
2. Larry is one of the only white kids in the school after integration / redistricting.
3. She gives Larry a ride and hands Silas and Alice old coats, telling Alice not to expect a ride in the future.
4. He tries to make himself useful at the shop (and willingly takes over chores at home).
5. He calls a black girl names – she beats him up – he is humiliated in front of the other white kids.
6. a rifle his father has lent him

SPOT ON VOCAB **2** **Crimes and police work: Go through the following word file on crimes . . .**

UNTERRICHTS-
KONZEPT
Die SuS berücksichtigen den Tipp zu Individual learning processes. *Als Differenzierungsmöglichkeit bietet es sich an, leistungsstärkere SuS nach weiteren Begriffen aus dem Text suchen zu lassen.*

LÖSUNGSVORSCHLAG
Individual answers expected. Possible categories:
perpetrators, criminal actions, investigators, investigative actions, characteristics describing criminals, etc.

WRITING **3** ⚇ **Get together in groups of four. Each of you chooses one of the . . .**

UNTERRICHTS-
KONZEPT
Die SuS bilden Gruppen mit mindestens vier Personen und arbeiten zunächst still an ihrem Text. Sie berücksichtigen den Hinweis im Tipp zu Present tense. *Danach werden die Texte in der Gruppe präsentiert – entweder mündlich oder in einer stummen Schreibkonferenz. In einer Auswertungsphase sprechen die SuS innerhalb der Gruppe über mögliche Verbindungen und nehmen auch entsprechende Ergänzungen in ihren* Case files *vor. Um eine Doppelung bei der Ergebnissicherung zu vermeiden, werden nur diese Spekulationen im Plenum vorgetragen. Falls gewünscht und diese Form des Kursgesprächs ritualisiert werden soll, bietet sich für die Reaktion der Mitschüler/innen wiederum die A-R-M-Methode an (vgl. S. 68).*

LÖSUNGSVORSCHLAG
Individual answers expected.

Chapter 4

MULTIPLE CHOICE **1** **While going through chapter 4, tick the one correct answer for each task.**

UNTERRICHTS-
KONZEPT
Die SuS müssen zu dieser Aufgabe keine Belegstellen angeben. Sie wurden hier für die Hand der Lehrkraft ergänzt.

LÖSUNGSVORSCHLAG
1. c) calls Chief French with the news. quote: p. 82, l. 24 ("Next he called … office in Fulsom.")
2. d) begins a preliminary investigation of the crime scene. quote: p. 85, l. 19 ("He checked out the truck first." and the following pages until p. 88, l. 33
3. b) is startled by the chickens. quote: p. 88, ll. 29–31 ("He poked his … other birds aflight.")
4. c) abstinent. quote: p. 92, l. 33 ("Larry has been … all his life.")
5. b) indifference. quote: p. 96, l. 29 ("Well it was … it. Too late.")

SPEAKING **2** **Speaking about clothing: For each of the pictures, think about . . .** → S28.1

UNTERRICHTS-
KONZEPT
Diese Aufgabe dient der sprachlichen und gedanklichen Vorentlastung von Aufgabe 3. Die SuS erarbeiten sich eine eigene Word bank, *die in Aufgabe 3 als Grundlage für die Beschreibung der Romanfiguren herangezogen werden kann. Es erfolgt ein Hinweis auf* Skill 28.1 Working with visuals: Pictures (**Green Line Oberstufe Baden-Württemberg**).

LÖSUNGSVORSCHLAG
Individual answers expected.

CLOSE READING   **3**   Gathering information: a) 🎭 Get together ... b) Present your results ...

UNTERRICHTS-
KONZEPT   *Die SuS sollen bewusst dazu angehalten werden, den in Aufgabe 2 erarbeiteten Wortschatz nun umzuwälzen. Grundsätzlich kann diese Aufgabe auch in Einzelarbeit bearbeitet werden. Wenn sie als Hausaufgabe aufgegeben wird, können die SuS den Arbeitsauftrag erhalten, im Internet nach einer Person zu suchen, die ihrer Ansicht nach die Romanfigur am besten verkörpert. Die Angaben zu Larry stammen aus* Chapter 1, *zu Silas und Chief French aus* Chapter 2 *und* Chapter 4. *Durch diesen Hinweis kann die Lehrkraft den SuS die Suche nach geeigneten Textstellen erleichtern. Die SuS berücksichtigen den Tipp zu* Indirect characterisation. *Die Sicherung in Aufgabe b) kann dann zunächst in Gruppenarbeit erfolgen. Alternativ können einzelne SuS ihre Ergebnisse auf Folie festhalten und der Klasse präsentieren.*

LÖSUNGSVORSCHLAG   a) **Collect clothes your character wears:**

Larry Ott	Silas Jones
• shirt with his name printed on the front • sensible pants and shoes • Saturdays: jeans instead of work pants • clothes make him feel safe, they signify the responsibility he has accepted to keep the family business running; the way he keeps his clothes also shows that he is neat and takes care of his appearance • this characteristic of neatness may lead the reader to believe he is an upstanding figure	• police uniform • vest while directing traffic • clothes make him feel uncomfortable, they are less suited to the warm and humid weather; the way he wears his clothes shows that he doesn't feel entirely comfortable with his role and might already indicate that the job wasn't his real reason for coming back to Chabot

Chief French

• motto T-shirt with explicit content
• sensible shoes and clothes for examining a crime scene
• clothes show that he feels self-confident and is an experienced investigator who doesn't need to fulfil people's expectations of what a respectable person should look like; the fact that he can wear his personal clothes to work also shows his superior position compared to Silas.

b) **Discuss how the three characters differ in regard to their clothing.**
   Individual answers expected.

BUZZ GROUP   **4**   🎭 **Think about how clothes signify belonging (to a group, a profession, ...**

UNTERRICHTS-
KONZEPT   *Gerade zurückhaltende SuS profitieren von einer Vorentlastung eines Unterrichtsgesprächs in der Partnerarbeit oder der Kleingruppe. Je nach Gruppengröße kann dieser Austausch entweder mit dem Nebensitzer oder mit weiteren SuS stattfinden. Die Lehrkraft kann die Zeit nutzen, um durch das Klassenzimmer zu gehen und bei einzelnen SuS-Gesprächen mitzuhören. Beim anschließenden Unterrichtsgespräch können dann gezielt SuS aufgerufen werden, die interessante Beiträge geleistet hatten, sich generell aber nur selten aus Eigeninitiative melden.*

WRITING   **5**   **Assess whether this statement by American humourist Mark Twain ...**   → S14.2

UNTERRICHTS-
KONZEPT   *Diese Aufgabe eignet sich als Hausaufgabe. Sie kann auch erst am Ende der Lektürebehandlung zur Bearbeitung aufgegeben werden. Die SuS sollten vor der Bearbeitung darauf hingewiesen werden, dass diese Schreibaufgabe eine Analyseleistung sowie eine eigene Stellungnahme beinhaltet. Der Aufbau des Textes sollte sich an folgende Struktur halten (siehe Tipp zu* Three steps *und* Skill 14.2 Comment, **Green Line Oberstufe Baden-Württemberg**):*
   1. Auseinandersetzung mit der Bedeutung des Zitats.
   2. Darstellung von Belegen aus dem Text, die das Zitat entweder unterstützen oder widerlegen.
   3. Abschließende, eigene Stellungnahme.

LÖSUNGSVORSCHLAG   Individual answers expected.

Chapter 5

SEQUENCING   **1 Read the statements carefully. While reading chapter 5, put the . . .**

LÖSUNGSVORSCHLAG

No.	Event
7	Carl asks Larry to give back the rifle he has lent him.
5	Silas intervenes, but runs away before he is caught.
1	Larry is busy with chores around the house.
3	Silas and Larry hope to see Cindy Walker in her bathing suit.
11	Silas physically dominates Larry, provoking Larry to call him a "nigger".
8	Larry's confession about the rifle leads to his parents quarreling about Alice and Silas' living arrangements.
6	Larry is able to slip away without being seen.
9	Carl follows Larry to Silas.
4	The boys witness Carl and Cecil Walker harassing Cindy.
10	Carl bullies the two boys into fighting for the gun.
12	Silas deserts Larry.
2	Larry remembers spending time with Silas during springtime.

SPOT ON VOCAB   **2 Verbs of motion and speaking: To improve your writing style, it is . . .**   → S3

UNTERRICHTS-
KONZEPT

Die SuS berücksichtigen den Tipp zu Thesaurus *und* Skill 3 Working with a dictionary *(**Green Line Oberstufe Baden-Württemberg**). Da einsprachige Wörterbücher in der Regel keine ausreichende Anzahl an Synonymen bereitstellen, empfiehlt es sich, für diese Stunde den Computerraum zu reservieren. Die SuS bearbeiten Aufgabe 2 dann mithilfe von www.thesaurus.com. Es sollten jeweils ca. 15 – 20 Verben aufgeschrieben werden sollten.*

LÖSUNGSVORSCHLAG   Individual answers expected. Possible answers:
- Verbs of motion ordered from slowest to fastest: limp, amble, shuffle, lumber, trudge, roam, wander, stroll, jog, march, stride, strut, scamper, scoot, hustle, sprint, rush, race, bolt, dart, dash, etc.
- Verbs of speaking ordered from weakest to strongest: whimper, mumble, murmur, stammer, stutter, mutter, drawl, drone, grumble, talk, say, chatter, prattle, call (out), shout, wail, holler, cry, shriek, scream, etc.

COMPREHENSION   **3 ⚇ Putting everything together: a) – b) Work with a partner. Each of . . .**   → S10

UNTERRICHTS-
KONZEPT

Falls die Stunde in den Computerraum verlegt wurde, kann die Schreibaufgabe ebenfalls am Computer erledigt werden. Die SuS können in ihrem Dokument die ersetzten bzw. ergänzten Verben dann entsprechend farblich hervorheben bzw. unterschiedliche Verben ausprobieren, bevor sie sich für eine endgültige Variante entscheiden. Nach dem gegenseitigen Vortrag der Texte besprechen die SuS die Änderungen zunächst in PA. Im Plenum werden ihre Versionen dann mit dem Original verglichen (ggf. durch erneutes lautes Vorlesen) und die unterschiedliche Wirkung diskutiert. Die S berücksichtigen die beiden Tipps zu Verbs of speaking *und* Style/Tone *sowie* Skill 10 Style and stylistic devices *(**Green Line Oberstufe Baden-Württemberg**).*

LÖSUNGSVORSCHLAG   **a) Rewrite the passage and replace the verbs of motion or speaking with . . .**
A: p. 109, l. 29 – p. 110, l. 17 (Verbs of motion)
Folgende Verben könnten ersetzt werden: striding away, walk up, turned, went, was walking, heading for, came down, sprinted away, to inch down, trudge, stepped, etc.

B: p. 113, ll. 1–27 (Verbs of speaking)
SuS, die diese Textpassage bearbeiten, sollten nicht nur die wenigen im Text vorhandenen speaking verbs *ersetzen, sondern weitere hinzufügen:* told, said (3x), whispered, said through his teeth, called, said, etc.

b) **Comment on the effect that results when the author does not always use ...**
Individual answers expected.

Chapter 6

SENTENCE
COMPLETION

1 **Read the sentence beginnings carefully. While reading chapter 6, ...**

LÖSUNGSVORSCHLAG

1. The new pieces of evidence Silas collects at Larry's house are a <u>butt end of a marijuana cigarette, broken glass, four-wheel tracks</u>.
2. Larry's phone bills reveal that he <u>only received calls from a single phone number</u>.
3. When Silas goes through Larry's things in the attic, he is shocked to find <u>a photo of his mother Alice holding Larry on her lap when he was a baby</u>.
4. In a flashback, Silas remembers living in <u>Chicago with his mum and her boyfriend</u>.
5. On their trip South, Silas and Alice lose <u>all of their possessions, including their clothes</u>.
6. Upon arriving in Chabot, they walk <u>to the cabin on the Ott property</u>.
7. Back in the present, Silas decides to break the law by <u>taking evidence from the crime scene (the photo showing Alice and Larry)</u>.

BUZZ GROUP

2 👥 **Referring to the images above, talk to a partner about the ...**

UNTERRICHTS-
KONZEPT

Da das Thema American South *nicht mehr fester Bestandteil des Bildungsplans ist, ist damit zu rechnen, dass die SuS unterschiedliche Vorkenntnisse mitbringen. Um auch SuS mit weniger Vorkenntnissen die Teilnahme an einem Gespräch zu ermöglichen, erfolgt diese Phase der Vorentlastung bewusst im geschützen Raum – in SuS-Gruppen ohne eine verbindliche Sicherung im Plenum. Sollten nur wenig Vorkenntnisse vorhanden sein, können die SuS-Gruppen aufgefordert werden, den Inhalt der Bilder zu verbalisieren und über deren Bedeutung zu spekulieren. Zur Differenzierung kann die Lehrkraft dazu passende Satzanfänge an die Tafel schreiben:* This picture shows ..., The man in the picture is ..., This image reminds me of ... *Es erfolgt ein Hinweis auf den Tipp zur Gestaltung des* Fact file.

LÖSUNGSVORSCHLAG

Individual answers expected.

VOCABULARY

3 **The dictionary gives the following definition of racism: ...**

UNTERRICHTS-
KONZEPT

Diese Aufgabe kann dazu verwendet werden, mit den SuS den Umgang mit dem einsprachigen Wörterbuch zu üben.

LÖSUNGSVORSCHLAG

Individual answers expected. Possible word field:
(subtle/open) racism – racist – race – racial (discrimination), superiority – (feeling of) inferiority, supremacy – (white) supremacist, dominance – dominant - to dominate, prejudice – prejudiced, animosity, injustice – unjust – to justify, intolerance – intolerant – to tolerate, stereotype – stereotypical (behaviour), discrimination – to discriminate against – to be discriminated against, bias – biased, partiality, bigotry, ethnicity – ethnic (group), to oppress – oppression, subjugation – to subjugate, etc.

TOUCH-TURN-TALK

4 👥👥 **a) Get together in groups of ... b) Then turn the cards around. ...**

UNTERRICHTS-
KONZEPT

Diese Aufgabe führt die Ergebnisse aus den Aufgaben 2 und 3 zusammen. Die SuS sollen den neu erarbeiteten Wortschatz nun einsetzen, um über ihre Vorkenntnisse zu sprechen. Sie erhalten dazu weitere Stichworte, die ihnen helfen sollen, sich über das Thema Rassendiskriminierung zu äußern, was dem Gespräch nun ein höheres Maß an Verbindlichkeit verleiht. Bewusst erfolgt weiterhin keine Sicherung im Plenum, da alle in dieser Aufgabe vorgesehen Begriffe in Aufgabe 5 wieder aufgegriffen werden und dann bei Bedarf von der Lehrkraft mit zusätzlichen Informationen unterfüttert werden können. Es ist zu erwarten, dass zu den Begriffen poll tax *und* Little Rock Nine *wenig Vorkenntnisse vorhanden sind, andere Begriffe (*desegregation*) können auch erschlossen werden.* Poll tax *kann ggf. von leistungsstärkeren SuS über das Wörterbuch erschlossen werden.*

LÖSUNGSVORSCHLAG   See task 5.

TIMELINE   **5   In class, match the events / terms / names above with the years to create ...**

LÖSUNGSVORSCHLAG
- 1865: The Ku Klux Klan is founded with the intention of oppressing the black population.
- 1896: In the Plessy vs. Ferguson decision, the Supreme Court sanctions a "separate but equal" segregation of the races, laying the groundwork for separate educational facilities.
- 1954: The Supreme Court rules in the landmark case Brown vs. Board of Education of Topeka, Kansas, agreeing that segregation in public schools is unconstitutional.
- 1955 (Montgomery, Alabama): Rosa Parks refuses to give up her seat at the front of the "colored section" of a bus to a white passenger, openly defying a Southern custom of the time. Upon her arrest the Montgomery black community begins a bus boycott, which lasts for more than a year, until the buses are desegregated Dec. 21, 1956. Reverend Martin Luther King, Jr., is instrumental in leading the boycott.
- 1957 (Little Rock, Arkansas): Nine black students are blocked from entering the formerly all-white Central High School on the orders of Governor Orval Faubus. President Eisenhower sends federal troops and the National Guard to intervene on behalf of the students, who become known as the "Little Rock Nine".
- 1963 (Washington, D.C.): About 200,000 people take part in the March on Washington. Coming together at the Lincoln Memorial, participants listen as Martin Luther King delivers his famous "I Have a Dream" speech.
- 1964: The 24th Amendment abolishes the poll tax, which originally had been instituted in eleven Southern states to make it difficult for poor blacks to vote.
- 1964: President Johnson signs the Civil Rights Act of 1964. The most sweeping civil rights legislation since Reconstruction, the Civil Rights Act prohibits discrimination of all kinds based on race, color, religion, or national origin. The law also provides the federal government with the powers to enforce desegregation.
- 1992 (Los Angeles, California): The first race riots in decades erupt in south-central Los Angeles after a jury acquits four white police officers for the videotaped beating of African American Rodney King.

CLOSE READING   **6   👥 a) *Crooked Letter, Crooked Letter* ... b) Discuss: To what extent ...**

UNTERRICHTS-
KONZEPT   *Aufgrund der unterschiedlichen Menge an Fundstellen sollte die Klasse in drei große Gruppen aufgeteilt werden. Gruppe 1: Larry, Gruppe 2: Carl, Gruppe 3: white kids at school und Cecil. Diese Aufgabe kann auch als Gruppenpuzzle durchgeführt werden. Die SuS berücksichtigen den Tipp zu* Conflict *und* Theme.

LÖSUNGSVORSCHLAG   **a)   Collect evidence for racism in the novel by exploring the characters. Divide the class up ...**

Carl Ott	Larry Ott
Examples for racist thinking: • p. 64, l. 25ff.: Carl making fun of Devoid Chapman and his hair style (p. 65, l. 3: "nest of hair") • p. 64, l. 22: black man called "crazy nigger" by Cecil p. 111: Carl calling Silas a "nigger boy" • p. 112: Carl provoking Ina by asking her to invite Alice and Silas over "after church" • p. 117, l. 23: Carl calls the fight over the gun a "dispute between the races" and asks them to "fight it out. Man to man. White to colored." (l. 118)	Examples for racist thinking: • p. 58: Larry "terrified" of black kids (l. 2) • p. 58: "unusual and inappropriate" for black people to be seen in a white man's car (ll. 23 – 25) when Silas and Alice get out of Carl's car Examples for racist actions: • p. 72: Larry trying to impress Ken and David by jumping off the swing and calling Jackie "Monkey Lips" • pp. 73 – 75: Larry being assaulted in the classroom by Carolyn, a black girl • p. 119, l. 30: Larry calling Silas a "nigger" in order to get back at him

Cecil Walker	white kids at school
Examples for racist thinking: • p. 110, l. 25 / 26: Cecil calling Silas a "native"	Examples for racist thinking: • p. 69, ll. 13 – 15: white boy calls the desegregated school a "jungle" • p. 70, l. 10 "Them nigger girls sound like a bunch of monkeys" • p. 70, ll. 20 – 27: The boys making fun of Jackie Simmons because of her dark skin color and her lips (Larry, Ken and David)

b) **To what extent can the black kids at Larry's school be accused of racism as well?**
Larry is afraid of the black kids, if they catch him looking they are sure to "beat him up later" (p. 59, ll. 4 – 5). They physically abuse Larry after the incident with Jackie Simmons, cleverly eluding the teachers.

EVALUATION/ SPECULATION

7 a) What would have been different …? b) Talk about whether racism …

UNTERRICHTS- KONZEPT

Diese Aufgabe dient der sprachlichen Aktivierung der SuS. Sie erstellen zunächst in Stillarbeit eine Liste möglicher Fragen, die sie dann einem Partner oder dem Plenum stellen. Abschließend wird im Plenum zunächst geklärt, ob diese unterschiedlichen Abläufe tatsächlich etwas für Larry geändert hätten. Im Anschluss daran tauschen sich die SuS über die Frage 7 b) aus.

LÖSUNGSVORSCHLAG

a) **Fight in the schoolyard:**
- What if Larry had apologized to Jackie?
- What if the black kids had ignored Larry and simply walked away?
- What if the white kids in the classroom had stood up for Larry?
- What if the teachers had intervened in the school yard and reprimanded Larry?
- etc.

Fight in the forest:
- What if Larry had refused to fight Silas?
- What if Silas had simply walked away?
- What if Larry had not called Silas a nigger and silently accepted his defeat?
- What if Carl had accepted the boys' initial refusal to fight each other?
- etc.

Résumé: In either case, Larry can only lose.
- School yard fight: The black kids bullied him before the incident and will continue to do so; the white kids will continue to ignore him.
- Fight in the woods: Carl's intrusion has ended the boys' fragile friendship and the only change now is that Larry feels guilty about it.

b) **Talk about whether racism is a major theme in the novel so far.**
Racism is less a part of the mystery plotline and more part of the friendship plotline. It is the reason why Silas and Larry have to hide their friendship, which eventually falls apart under the pressure of their parents' animosity towards each other. In addition to that, the underlying racism shown by Cecil and Carl serves as a backdrop to illustrate the mindset of the rural population in Mississippi at this time.

SPECULATION

8 In chapter 6, Silas makes a shocking discovery about his past. …

LÖSUNGSVORSCHLAG

It is implied that Silas is the illegitimate child of Alice and Carl. Ironically, while Carl is the missing father Silas never had, Carl despises Silas. Perhaps this animosity is not only due to Carl's inherent racism, but also to his knowledge of Silas' true parentage. For an adult Silas, this robs him of any sense of belonging.

Chapter 7

SEQUENCING   **1 Put the following statements into the correct chronological order.**

LÖSUNGSVORSCHLAG

No.	Event
14	Carl dies in a drunk-driving accident.
13	Larry joins the army.
7	On the street leading to their houses, Larry waits for Cindy in vain.
16	Needing money, Larry gradually sells off his land to the Rutherfords.
8	Eventually, Larry informs Cindy's parents of her disappearance.
1	Larry tells his parents about his date with Cindy Walker.
9	When interrogated by the sheriff, Larry doesn't give him all the facts.
11	Larry doesn't return to school after the date.
3	Cindy insists on driving herself.
15	Larry comes back home and takes over the garage.
5	Cindy presses Larry to keep her pregnancy a secret.
10	Larry is forced to tell the whole truth.
4	Having reached a secluded spot, Cindy reveals that their date is a sham.
6	At the drive-in, Larry pretends to be in the car with Cindy.
12	The garage loses customers and Carl becomes an alcoholic.
2	After telling the others about his upcoming date, Larry gets some attention from his peers at school.

SPOT ON WRITING   **2 After Larry has given his second statement to the police, a report …**   → S13

UNTERRICHTS-
KONZEPT   *Die SuS berücksichtigen den Tipp zu* Report. *Da die SuS die Faktengrundlage für ihren Bericht aus der* comprehension task *beziehen, sollte das Augenmerk bei der Schreibaufgabe auf der Verwendung eines neutralen und objektiven Stils und dem Einsatz geeigneter* linking words *liegen. Bei dieser Szene handelt es sich um eine entscheidende Szene für den Roman, weshalb sichergestellt werden muss, dass die SuS verstanden haben, was auf der Verabredung passiert ist und warum Larry folglich des Mordes verdächtigt wird.*

LÖSUNGSVORSCHLAG   Individual answers expected. The report should contain the facts as presented in chapter 7. Most of these can be extracted from the comprehension task.

Chapter 8

MULTIPLE CHOICE   **1 Read the tasks. While going through chapter 8, tick the one correct …**

LÖSUNGSVORSCHLAG   1. c) compassion.
2. c) ingratiate himself with the other kids.
3. a) Silas' need of a father.
4. c) being a racist.
5. d) discovers that someone has disturbed the ground.

SPOT ON ANALYSIS   **2 Popularity in high school: a) 🧍🧍🧍 Pass on a … b) Dealing with …**

UNTERRICHTS-
KONZEPT   *Die Methode* Pass a problem *stammt aus dem kooperativen Lernen und fördert die sprachliche Interaktion der SuS. Die Klasse wird zunächst in sechs Gruppen geteilt. Ausgehend von den Bildimpulsen notieren sich die SuS zunächst Fragen zu der auf ihrem Bild abgebildeten Person. Es sollen Informationen erfragt werden, die die SuS an dieser Person interessieren. Beispiele:* How did this person feel when the picture was taken? Does he / she have many friends? Does he / she like school? What is his / her favorite hobby? etc. *Diese Fragen werden auf einem separaten Blatt notiert und nach einem vorgegebenen Zeitlimit (3 – 5 Minuten je nach Leistungs-*

stärke der Klasse) an die nächste Gruppe weitergegeben. Diese versucht nun, Antworten auf die Fragen zu geben. Selbstverständlich darf dabei spekuliert werden. Nach weiteren 5 Minuten wird das Blatt mit den Fragen und Antworten an eine weitere Gruppe gegeben. Diese notiert nun Adjektive, die sich zur Charakterisierung / Beschreibung der auf dem Bild gezeigten Person eignen. Nach 5 Minuten wird das Blatt ein letztes Mal weitergegeben. Die letzte Gruppe wertet die Ergebnisse nun aus und markiert neutrale Beobachtungen und stereotype Feststellungen mit unterschiedlichen Farben. Die SuS fassen ihre Ergebnisse mündlich zusammen und präsentieren sie der Klasse. Im Unterrichtsgespräch wird geklärt, bei welchen Bildern stereotype Äußerungen besonders häufig aufgetreten sind und woran dies liegen könnte. Es erfolgt Hinweis auf den Tipp zu Stereotype.

LÖSUNGSVORSCHLAG

a) **Pass on a problem: Get into groups of four. Each group deals with one of these images.**
Individual answers expected.

b) **Dealing with stereotypes: Using your worksheets as a starting point, discuss the …**
Individual answers expected. Possible answers:
beauty, athleticism, eloquence, success (with the opposite sex, in student offices), wealth, intelligence, commitment, etc.

CLOSE READING **3** **Which roles do Larry, Silas and Cindy fulfil at school and among their peers?**

UNTERRICHTS-KONZEPT

Die Ergebnissicherung kann zunächst in Gruppenarbeit und im Anschluss im Plenum erfolgen. Einzelne SuS können aufgefordert werden, ihre Ergebnisse auf Folie festzuhalten und der Klasse zu präsentieren. Die SuS wissen zu diesem Zeitpunkt noch nichts über das Verhältnis zwischen Silas und Cindy. Dieses Wissen spielt bei der Beurteilung ihrer jeweiligen Rollen an der Schule allerdings keine Rolle. Die Lehrkraft kann die SuS erneut eine Bewertung der drei Figuren nach Chapter 10 vornehmen lassen – als Silas Angie gesteht, der heimliche Freund gewesen zu sein.

LÖSUNGSVORSCHLAG

Larry	Cindy	Silas
the role he plays: • the outsider / "loser" / "geek" / "weirdo" / "nerd" • bookish type (doesn't excel at sports) • not successful or popular with girls	**the role she plays:** • the pretty girl, yet rebellious • goes out with a lot of different boys – easy to get? • popular	**the role he plays:** • good baseball player • popular, well-liked for his athletic qualities
corresponding passages from the novel: • loves horror stories (carries Steven King novels around) (ch. 3, 8) • bullied by both black and white kids at school: Jackie Simmons episode (ch. 3) • date with Cindy (ch. 7) • "the hick nobody liked" (ch. 8, p. 178) • brings snakes to school (ch. 8) • doesn't take part in any school activities (prom, games, etc.; ch. 8) • used, then ignored by the popular kids: haunted house episode (ch. 8)	**corresponding passages from the novel:** • the date (ch. 7) • Cindy talking about her mother's and Cecil's parenting methods (ch. 7) • haunted house episode: part of the group / laughs about Larry	**corresponding passages from the novel:** • has his "name in the paper all the time" (ch. 8) • haunted house episode: part of the group / laughs about Larry (ch. 8)

EVALUATION

4 **By examining the socioeconomic background of all three characters, ...**

UNTERRICHTS-
KONZEPT

Diese Aufgabe kann bei knapper Zeit auch arbeitsteilig bearbeitet werden. Bei der Auswertung kann mit den SuS besprochen werden, inwiefern die vermeintlich besseren Ausgangsbedingungen von Larry und Cindy aufgrund ihrer Familiensituation (beide haben zwei Eltern) und ihrer Hautfarbe nicht zwingend in einen Vorteil münden müssen, sondern sogar eher zur Belastung werden (Ambiguity of belonging).

LÖSUNGSVORSCHLAG

Larry	Silas	Cindy
• white, middle-class background; father owns a business, family owns their own house and lots of land; doting mother; problematic relationship with his father • chances: superficially, chances at succeeding are good: stable family life, no financial worries	• black, lower-class background, illegitimate child, problematic relationship with his mother, spends his first months in Chabot illegally in a cabin with no water and heat, then moves to a trailer home • chances: disadvantaged – needs to rely on his athletic qualities (and physical appearance) to become accepted (then again: in a place where many blacks were poor, his financial situation does not necessarily set him apart)	• white, lower-class background; disabled, alcoholic and abusive step-father; problematic relationship with both parents; live in a run-down place • chances: disadvantaged – needs to rely on her physical appearance (in an economically depressed area, many whites were poor, so that her financial situation is not necessarily a problem at school)

Résumé: Even though Larry has the best starting point, his "qualities" prove useless in his peer group, whereas Cindy and Silas, being far less privileged, succeed at becoming accepted at school (= the ambiguity of belonging).

WRAP UP

5 **All three teenagers are on their personal quest for belonging. For each ...**

UNTERRICHTS-
KONZEPT

Diese Aufgabe kann abschließend im Unterrichtsgespräch bearbeitet werden. Alternativ kann sie zur Differenzierung eingesetzt werden, um schnelle SuS nach der Bearbeitung von Aufgabe 4 mit einer anspruchsvolleren Aufgabe zu betrauen.

LÖSUNGSVORSCHLAG

Larry	Silas	Cindy
• quest: wants to be part of the group – to be accepted (to this end, he bullies Jackie Simmons, he brings snakes and his zombie mask to school) • success: Larry fails – even before the date with Cindy, everything he does seems to alienate him more and more from the others	• quest: wants to be accepted by the other kids • success: Silas succeeds – he has friends, is part of the baseball team, has a girlfriend	• quest: is looking for love or approval (her actual motives remain shady and she remains more opaque than Larry and Silas) – later we learn her goal is to get away from Cecil and her mother • success: superficially, Cindy seems to be accepted by her peers

Résumé: Larry's desperate attempt to belong makes him a murder suspect – he goes along with Cindy's deception at the date instead of driving her back home. Out of loyalty, he is reluctant to reveal her supposed pregnancy to the police.

Chapter 9

TRUE OR FALSE **1 Read the statements carefully and tick the correct answer. Provide ...**

LÖSUNGSVORSCHLAG

1. true; quote: p. 196, ll. 9 – 23 ("He had his ... went to work.")
2. false; Wallace comes to Larry's house on purpose under false pretences. quote: p. 208, ll. 24 – 29 ("'How come you ... the water.' 'Yeah.'")
3. false; Wallace actively seeks out Larry's friendship. (No single quote possible – this item refers to the entire chapter.)
4. true; quote: p. 219, ll. 5 – 6 ("So if you ... you raped her.")
5. false; Wallace is disappointed in Larry's rejection. quote: p. 220, ll. 8 – 29 ("For a moment ... you, Scary Larry!"). There is no actual quote for this passage as the students are required to read between the lines.
6. true; quote: p. 221, ll. 23 – 26 ("When he visited ... last, this friend.")

ANALYSIS **2 Analysing the location: You have read a lot about the town of ... → S28.1**

UNTERRICHTS-KONZEPT

Hier soll den SuS die Gelegenheit gegeben werden, ohne direkte Bezugnahme auf den Text ihren Eindruck von Chabot wiederzugeben. Denkbar wäre auch, die SuS als Hausaufgabe im Internet nach einem geeigneten Bild suchen zu lassen. SuS, die kein geeignetes Bild gefunden haben bzw. die Hausaufgabe nicht erledigt haben, können sich dann aus dem Fundus des Schülerhefts bedienen. Sollte diese Art der Durchführung gewählt werden, kann die Lehrkraft die SuS auffordern, sich zu Unterschieden zwischen den mitgebrachten Bildern und denen des Schülerhefts zu äußern. Es erfolgt ein Hinweis auf Skill 28.1 Working with visuals: Pictures *(Green Line Oberstufe Baden-Württemberg).*

Als differenzierende Maßnahme kann die Lehrkraft deskriptiven Wortschatz auf Folie zur Verfügung stellen, der über den alltäglichen Wortschatz der SuS hinausgeht. Die SuS verwenden diesen Wortschatz, um ihre Wahl zu begründen. Es geht an dieser Stelle noch nicht um eine detaillierte Beschreibung des ausgewählten Bildes (vgl. Aufgabe 3). Denkbar wäre ein Wortspeicher mit folgenden Einträgen:

- *negative Attribute:* dilapidated, run down, closed off, shut down, neglected, derelict, grubby, gloomy, forgotten, depressing, etc.
- *positive Attribute:* lively, vibrant, booming, prosperous, budding, flourishing, dynamic, romantic, nostalgic, traditional, etc.

Alternativ kann dieser Wortschatz auch mit den SuS gemeinsam entwickelt werden: In der Einstiegsphase werden die SuS in zwei Gruppen aufgeteilt und erhalten den Arbeitsauftrag, möglichst viele positive bzw. negative Begriffe zur Beschreibung von Gebäuden und Ortschaften zu sammeln. Die Lehrkraft ergänzt diese Sammlung durch weitere Begriffe, die nicht dem gängigen Wortschatz der SuS entstammen (siehe Word bank*).*

METHODISCHE TIPPS

Um allen SuS die Gelegenheit zu geben sich zu äußern, kann eine Präsentation zunächst in Partnerarbeit erfolgen. Im Plenum können die SuS dann – um eine Redundanz bei der Ergebnissicherung zu vermeiden – aufgefordert werden zu beschreiben, welcher Eindruck von der Stadt Chabot durch die Wahl ihres Bildes entsteht (idyllic, romantic, downtrodden, etc.).

LÖSUNGSVORSCHLAG Individual answers expected.

CLOSE READING **3 Go back to the novel to collect more detailed information about ...**

UNTERRICHTS-KONZEPT

Diese Aufgabe eignet sich als Stillarbeitsphase nach dem vorangegangenen Unterrichtsgespräch.

LÖSUNGSVORSCHLAG

- only two full-time employees; can only afford an old, run-down jeep for their constable
- town economically dependent on the Rutherford Mill
- mayor only works part-time and is a real estate agent with an office across from town hall
- the only buildings in town: Mayor Mo's real estate office, the post office, a bank that mostly services the mill, a diner/convenience store called The Hub, an IGA grocery store and a

drugstore (both going out of business because of the Wal-Mart in Fulsom), a clothing store, a cheap motel and Ottomotive Repair (Larry Ott's garage)
- the Chabot Bus, an old yellow school bus on blocks that has been converted into a bar
- last two buildings are empty offices with boarded up windows; vacant lot where the barber's builder have been dismantled
- town built on the edge of a gully which is full of weeds and trash
- buildings all face the Rutherford Mill, which is a "city" in itself (dirty, loud, obstructing the view of nature and "burning" the sky with its smoke)

VOCABULARY IN USE   **4** **Go through your notes from task 2 and circle descriptive adjectives …**

UNTERRICHTS-KONZEPT   *Diese Aufgabe kann auch als Hausaufgabe gestellt werden. Die Besprechung erfolgt dann als* Peer correction. *Dazu sollten mit den SuS gemeinsam Kriterien zur Bewertung erarbeitet werden. Es hat sich bewährt, die SuS nur anhand von wenigen, klar formulierten Kriterien arbeiten zu lassen, um möglichst aussagekräftige Feedback-Ergebnisse zu erhalten.*
Dies könnten hier z. B. sein: usage of the present tense, usage of descriptive adjectives, usage of correct descriptive phrases (in the foreground, on the left, etc.). *Die SuS verwenden zur Korrektur unterschiedliche Farben für die jeweiligen Kategorien. Bei der Erarbeitung kann auf den Tipp zu* Descriptive phrases *hingewiesen werden. Wenn in Aufgabe 1 der Schwerpunkt auf die Wortschatzerweiterung gelegt wurde, dann sollte die Lehrkraft darauf achten, dass der neu erworbene Wortschatz von den SuS bei den Beschreibungen eingesetzt wird. Dazu können die SuS auch aufgefordert werden, alle verwendeten Adjektive in ihrem Text farblich zu kennzeichnen bzw. zu unterstreichen.*

LÖSUNGSVORSCHLAG   Individual answers expected.

ANALYSIS   **5** **Analysing the people: a) – b)** 👥 **The minor characters in …**   → S7

UNTERRICHTS-KONZEPT   *Zur gemeinsamen Erarbeitung von Aufgabe a) im Plenum bietet es sich an, DIN A4-Zettel für die einzelnen Personen(gruppen)/Familien zu erstellen und diese von den SuS mit Magneten auf einer aufgezeichneter Pyramide an der Tafel anbringen zu lassen. Alternativ wäre es auch denkbar, ein Poster (z. B. aus Packpapier) herzustellen, so dass die Gesellschaftspyramide den SuS für die weitere Unterrichtseinheit zur Verfügung steht und ggf. bei der Besprechung späterer Aufgaben oder der Wiederholung für das Abitur wieder herangezogen werden kann, auch wenn das Schülerheft einmal nicht zur Hand ist. Die Lehrkraft verweist auf den Tipp zu* Direct / Indirect characterisation *und auf* Skill 7 Characterisation *(**Green Line Oberstufe Baden-Württemberg**).*
In Aufgabe b) verengt sich der Fokus auf die unterste Schicht der Gesellschaft und erfordert ein genaues Lesen des Textes. Aus Zeitgründen kann ein arbeitsteiliges Verfahren im Partnerpuzzle gewählt werden. Die Arbeitsschritte sind dann wie folgt abzuarbeiten:
1. *Bearbeitung der Teilaufgabe (Irina oder Wallace) in Einzelarbeit.*
2. *Vergleich der Ergebnisse mit einem arbeitsgleichen Partner und ggf. Ergänzung der eigenen Ergebnisse.*
3. *Präsentation der Ergebnisse in arbeitsungleichen Teams.*

Eine anschließende Sicherung aller erarbeiteten Ergebnisse im Plenum ist redundant und für die SuS wenig motivierend. Daher könnte nach Abschluss der Ergebnissicherung im Plenum mit folgender Frage weitergearbeitet werden: How is the notion of belonging reflected in these characters? Are Irina and Wallace similar characters? Why or why not? *Über den Unterschied, der zwischen den Figuren deutlich wird, kann sich das Unterrichtsgespräch dem Aspekt der Ambiguität annähern: Während Irina und Wallace einen ähnlich sozioökonomischen Hintergrund haben, wirken Irina und ihre Nachbarinnen – anders als Wallace - mit sich selbst im Reinen* (they are less uncertain, less ambiguous about their identities than Wallace, who is still adrift). *In diesem Zusammenhang könnte mit den SuS besprochen werden, ob die Frauen deshalb selbstbewusster und zufriedener auftreten, weil sie in einer Gemeinschaft leben und sich gegenseitig unterstützen.*

LÖSUNGSVORSCHLAG   **a)** Arrange the characters of present-day Chabot in a pyramid. Using a different colour, . . .

the Rutherford family

the mayor

the Ott family

Miss Voncille, Silas Jones (constable)

Irina Mott

Wallace Stringfellow

the Walker family

Larry Ott

the Jones family

Reasons:

- The Rutherford Mill provides the town and its inhabitants with their livelihood. None of the family members personally appear in the novel.
- The mayor remains equally aloof. (Chief French is from Fulsom and thus not included.)
- Miss Voncille and Silas Jones are figures of authority in town. Together with the mayor, they are the only respected members of the middle class in the novel.
- Irina Mott and her neighbours cannot be considered middle class due to their living conditions. Still, their lives seem more structured and stable than Wallace Stringfellow's.
- As a small business and land owner, Larry Ott should be on a level with Miss Voncille and Silas Jones. However, he is an outcast of society – essentially positioned on a lower level than Wallace.
- Before Cindy's death, the Otts as business and landowners would have been situated just below the Rutherfords. The Walkers would have been comparable to Irina Mott, the Joneses would have been on the lowest tier due to their socioeconomic background and possibly their ethnicity as well.

b) 🧍🧍 While the Rutherfords remain mysteriously invisible behind the curtain of . . .

Irina Mott and her neighbours	Wallace Stringfellow
<ul><li>live on "White Trash Avenue"</li><li>described as "rednecks"</li><li>appearance: thin tattooed bleach-blond women with babies on their laps, strained-looking grandmothers in housedresses smoking cigarettes</li><li>kids on four-wheelers with BB guns, shirtless, dirty</li><li>properties seem neglected: garbage in the yards; clotheslines with sheets, sheer panties, nylons; old car in the yard with bitterweed growing through the engine block, windows broken, the trunk open and cast-off car parts speared by grass</li><li>animals: an old camper shell used for a chicken coop and chickens and guinea hens in the weeds, half a dozen dogs on each property running wild</li><li>language: colloquial ("It's done pissed on my phone bill.", "'Hell, Officer,' Irina said. 'It's three of us divorced girls live here.'")</li></ul>	<ul><li>skinny, drives a four-wheeler</li><li>an alcoholic ("Once I start dranking, I don't like to stop.")</li><li>smokes marijuana</li><li>gets into brawls</li><li>as a kid: dirty, cut-off blue jeans, no shoes</li><li>as an adult: goatee, scruffy beard on his cheeks, bony, still dirty</li><li>a loner, quit school, paints houses</li><li>loves guns</li><li>owns a dog named for a serial killer who raped and killed boys / young men; ruthless: obviously had no scruples drowning puppies, brags about his former dogs' brutal deaths; maltreated armadillos as a child</li><li>has fantasies about brutal abductions, rapes</li><li>language: colloquial, faulty grammar, deep southern accent</li></ul>

c) **Discuss your results: Comment on the effect the chosen methods of characterisation . . .**
Indirect characterisation is prevalent.

- For the women, there is some direct characterisation (white trash, rednecks) and numerous instances of indirect characterisation (through Silas' eyes). While the direct characterisation is openly critical, the indirect characterisation is more descriptive and neutral. Silas has a fairly unbiased view of these women and remains courteous at all times. Still, the descriptions also focus on the negative (the looks of the children, the derelict state of the properties).
- Wallace is mostly characterised indirectly (partially through Silas, mostly through Larry). At first, he comes across as harmless, even positive, tentatively offering his friendship to Larry in an unbiased and naïve way. Layer by layer, his true character is then revealed, mostly by what he says about his behaviour towards animals. By refraining from direct characterisation, the narrator allows the reader to piece together Wallace's personality on his own. If the students have not read the novel any further than chapter nine at this point, they might not suspect Wallace's involvement in Tina Rutherford's disappearance.

MEDIATION
6 Dealing with stereotypes: a) – b) Pejorative terms used to label . . .   → S26

UNTERRICHTS-KONZEPT
Durch die Kürze des Textes eignet sich diese Mediationsaufgabe besonders für die gemeinsame Bearbeitung im Plenum. Die Lehrkraft kopiert dazu den Text in entsprechender Größe auf eine Folie. Es erfolgt ein Hinweis auf Skill 26 Mediating and translating skills *(**Green Line Oberstufe Baden-Württemberg**).*

LÖSUNGSVORSCHLAG
a) **Pejorative terms used to label poor people in the South include "white trash", . . .**
Individual answers expected.

b) **The historian Nancy Isenberg has done extensive work on the perception of the . . .**
The summary should contain the following points:
- first settlers were seen as human "waste" by the British
- this is because the mother country mostly sent poor people across the Atlantic – those who had been a burden on society at home (among them many teenagers sold as slaves)
- owing to its strong agrarian economy, US society long valued those owning fertile land as productive members of society – those without land or living on barren soil were relegated to society's lowest tier
- barren land was said to yield both inferior livestock and inferior men
- thus, the poor were seen as expendable

DISCUSSION
7 Discussing stereotypes: Evaluate whether the novel meets these . . .

UNTERRICHTS-KONZEPT
Diese Aufgabe kann auch als schriftliche Hausaufgabe und damit als Composition task *gestellt werden. Dazu kann – vor allem in leistungsschwachen Klassen – die Textarbeit im Unterricht erfolgen (ggf. auch in arbeitsteiliger Gruppenarbeit), die schriftliche Ausarbeitung dann zuhause.*

LÖSUNGSVORSCHLAG
- Irina: Superficially, Irina fulfils the stereotype: she lives on run-down land in a bad neighbourhood and has obviously made some bad choices regarding men; her tattoos and choice of clothes also fit the cliché, labelling her as promiscuous.
- Wallace: Wallace's personality and behaviour exceed the negative connotations of the stereotype: while coming across as a harmless rapscallion at first, he comes from a broken home and has no steady job; when turning on Larry towards the end of chapter nine, he reveals himself as a truly vicious character who has nothing to lose.
- Cecil: Cecil fulfils the stereotype as well: he is portrayed as a steady drinker who is unwilling to work and a violent man who has no scruples making sexual advances towards his step daughter. Carl and Ina Ott remember him as a poor kid who ran barefoot all summer. As an adult, he lives on run-down property.

ANALYSIS   **8 The place and the people: Going back to your work on tasks 2 and 3 on . . .**

Diese Aufgabe führt die Erkenntnisse, die die SuS zum Ort Chabot gesammelt haben, mit ihren Ergebnissen zur Analyse des Figurenpersonals zusammen. In diesem Zusammenhang kann auch erörtert werden, inwiefern sich diese Menschen dem Ort Chabot zugehörig fühlen bzw. inwiefern sie diese Zugehörigkeit auch als zwiespältig (z. B. einengend, beschränkend, erdrückend) empfinden.

LÖSUNGSVORSCHLAG   The sense of hopelessness pervading Chabot's town centre and its economic prospects correspond to many characters in the novel, foremost to Wallace and Cecil and secondly to the inhabitants of "White Trash Ave". While some of them haven't got the economic means to leave Chabot behind (Wallace, Cindy, Cecil, at first: Alice), others feel a sense of belonging that keeps them there – Silas and Larry. For Larry, the garage, their house and their land are the only things left from the family's well-ordered life before everything broke down with Cindy Walker's disappearance. For Silas, the situation is not as obvious: most likely, he has subconsciously decided to come back to discover what his mother had said was "missing in him", his ability for empathy and thus his loyalty to Larry. For these reasons, the sense of belonging these characters feel towards their hometown can be described as ambiguous.

ANALYSIS   **9 Going beyond the novel: In light of the 2016 presidential election, many . . .**

Diese Aufgabe kann auch als Vertiefung des im Unterricht behandelten Themas als Hausaufgabe aufgegeben werden.

LÖSUNGSVORSCHLAG

	How his anger manifests itself	Towards whom it is directed	Reason for his anger
Wallace Stringfellow (chapter 9)	• abuses animals • fantasises about beating/raping women • vandalises Larry's truck • threatens to tell the police Larry has confessed to Cindy's murder	• those who are (physically) weaker than he is (animals, women, Larry as a social outcast)	• remains obscure (broken home? no future? economic distress?)
Cecil Walker (chapters 5 and 7)	• bullies his daughter and strikes Larry	• those who are (physically) weaker than he is (women, children/teenagers)	• economic failure, physical weakness (especially when compared to Carl Ott, a businessman and land owner)

Both characters are white men and thus feel privileged (in that they belong to this group).
• Cecil is described as being one of the "boys" listening to Carl's anecdotes after work at the garage or drinking with Carl on several occasions. Still, even as a teenager, he didn't actually belong (cf. the episode Ina and Carl talk about before Larry's date). Thus, his sense of belonging can certainly be seen as ambiguous, his position among his peers volatile.
• Wallace impresses his peers by cursing in church and claiming knowledge of Larry Ott. He achieves belonging not through his own capabilities but by apparently profitting from Larry's reputation, thus making his own position highly precarious (= ambiguous).
• Both Wallace and Cecil are emasculated by their socioeconomic failure – Cecil relies on his wife to provide financial support for the family. His stepdaughter openly defies his attempts at asserting his authority over her. Wallace is a high school dropout who has neither a steady job nor a steady girlfriend. Essentially, he is alone.

Chapter 10

SHORT ANSWERS

1 Answer these questions with short answers.

LÖSUNGSVORSCHLAG

1. Tina Rutherford's
2. a stringy looking man trying to contact Larry
3. Silas was the secret boyfriend Cindy had – she went to see him the night she disappeared
4. she wanted Cindy's relationship with Silas to end
5. on the road leading to her home
6. his mother sent him to a different high school – he left Chabot for 25 years
7. he feels guilty, can't understand what he did back then – believes that what he has been "missing" is courage
8. Larry has woken up

SPECULATING

2 👥 Get together with a partner and make a list of the choices ...

UNTERRICHTS-KONZEPT

Diese Aufgabe kann auch mit dem kooperativen Verfahren Trade a problem *unterrichtet werden. Dazu notieren sich alle SuS-Paare zunächst nur die* Choices, *die Silas nun hat. Sie geben ihre Liste daraufhin einem weiteren SuS-Paar, das sich nun über die daraus entstehenden Konsequenzen berät. Im anschließenden Plenum könnten sich die SuS darüber äußern, was sich aus ihrer Sicht als realistischen Fortgang der Geschichte darstellt und welchen weiteren Plot-Verlauf sie für eher unwahrscheinlich halten.*

LÖSUNGSVORSCHLAG

Individual answers expected. Possible answers:
- he quits his job and leaves Larry to his own devices → he is unable to conquer the demons of his past and will not become a happy and content person
- he comes clean and risks losing his own job → he becomes an outsider in the town as well and has to leave, which resolves nothing for him and leaves him with the same consequences as his first choice
- he patches things up with Larry → he could be shunned by the town and lose his job or he could be able to convince the others of Larry's innocence

Chapter 11 and 12

WEED READING

1 Read the following summary of chapters 11 and 12. There are ten ...

LÖSUNGSVORSCHLAG

1. ll. 1/2: At the beginning of this chapter, Larry's memories of being shot, taken to the hospital and having <u>his mother</u> there attending to him slowly return. Correction: Silas
2. ll. 3/4: The police go on to inform Larry that the dead body of <u>Cindy Walker</u> has been discovered on his land. Correction: Tina Rutherford
3. ll. 6-8: While both the Sheriff and Chief French try to persuade Larry to admit to these killings, Larry is increasingly less able to distinguish between <u>both cases</u>. Correction: reality and his imagination
4. ll. 10/11: Silas discloses his knowledge about what happened on the night <u>Tina Rutherford died</u>. Correction: Cindy Walker disappeared
5. ll. 11/12: He tells Larry that he does not think Cindy was actually pregnant and suggests that it was <u>Carl Ott</u> who killed her. Correction: her stepfather Cecil/Cecil Walker
6. ll. 13/14: Having withheld information pertaining to a murder investigation, Silas is <u>fired</u> by Chief French. Correction: interviewed
7. ll. 17/18: Back at the hospital, Silas maneuvers his way into Larry's room where he wants to persuade him to talk about his <u>father</u>. Correction: assault
8. ll. 18-20: But Larry is more interested in discussing the past, specifically the night Cindy died and the <u>day Silas provoked Cecil when he helped Cindy</u>. Correction: fight Carl incited that broke up the two boys' friendship
9. ll. 20-22: Later, at the bar, Silas meets <u>Angie</u>, who informs him about Wallace Stringfellow and his store of firearms and snakes. Correction: Irina
10. ll. 22/23: At her home, Silas is tempted to have sex with <u>Angie</u>, but eventually leaves, disgusted with himself. Correction: Irina

THINK-PAIR-SHARE   **2**   👥👤 **How important is the family for the well-being of a child …?**

UNTERRICHTS-KONZEPT   *Zur visuellen Unterstützung dieser Aufgabe kann die Lehrkraft Bilder präsentieren, die Familien in typischen Alltagssituationen zeigen: beim Essen, beim gemeinsamen Spielen, auf einem Ausflug, bei einer Umarmung, etc. Die Ergebnisse der SuS sollen an der Tafel festgehalten werden, um sie für eine der folgenden Aufgaben nutzbar zu machen.*

LÖSUNGSVORSCHLAG   Individual answers expected.

BACKGROUND   **3**   **a) – b) The following text summarises a recent study by American …**

UNTERRICHTS-KONZEPT   *Die Textquelle lautet:*
https://www.nichd.nih.gov/news/releases/Pages/042715-time-with-parents.aspx.

LÖSUNGSVORSCHLAG   **a) Read the text and mark its key passages. Then paraphrase the findings below.**
- the amount of time mothers spend together with their children has a positive effect on their behavior (the teens less are likely get in trouble)
- in addition to that teenagers engaging in activities with both parents also do better in school and are less likely to use drugs
- these results are only true for teenagers, not for younger children

b) Compare the findings of this study with the results of your initial discussion. …
Individual answers expected. Possible discrepancy:
The amount of time that parents spend with their older children seems more important for these children's well-being than the time spent with younger kids.

CLOSE READING   **4**   **Re-read the following passages in the text. Summarise the information …**

UNTERRICHTS-KONZEPT   *Diese Aufgabe kann aus Zeitgründen arbeitsteilig durchgeführt, die Besprechung dann im Plenum erfolgen. Alternativ dazu eignet sich für die Bearbeitung von Aufgaben 4, 5 und 6 die Durchführung eines Gruppenpuzzles: In den Stammgruppen werden vier Experten bestimmt, wobei sich von drei Experten je einer um eine Familie kümmert (Ott, Jones, Walker). Ein vierter Experte erhält die Aufgabe, sich ausschließlich um die Rolle von Silas zu kümmern (Aufgabe 6). Diese Aufgabe ist deutlich anspruchsvoller als Aufgaben 4 und 5 und kann daher als binnendifferenzierende Maßnahme zur Förderung besonders leistungsstarker SuS genutzt werden. Die Experten arbeiten zunächst eng am Text und schreiben Belegstellen heraus. Nach der Präsentation dieser Belegstellen in der Stammgruppe bearbeiten die Stammgruppen dann gemeinsam Aufgabe 5. Die Lehrkraft kann diese Phase nutzen, um einzelnen SuS-Gruppen individuelle Hilfen zukommen zu lassen. In einer abschließenden Plenumsphase sollten nicht die Ergebnisse der Stammgruppenarbeit erneut vorgetragen werden, um Redundanzen zu vermeiden. Vielmehr sollten weitergehende Fragen gemeinsam erörtert werden, deren Beantwortung sich aus den Arbeitsergebnissen der vorangegangenen Aufgaben speist (vgl. dazu auch Aufgabe 7). Beispiele dazu sind:*
- Which parent is more influential for the teenager's development?
- Have the parents failed their children? Why or why not?
- Have the children failed their parents? Why or why not?
- How important is it for the teenagers to belong to their families? etc.

LÖSUNGSVORSCHLAG   1. Carl and Larry – p. 61, l. 20 to p. 63, l. 27: Larry fails to meets Carl's expectations. Larry doesn't resemble his father physically and prefers books to athletic pursuits. Carl also criticises Larry's manual skills at the garage.
2. Ina and Larry – p. 113, l. 28 to p. 115, l. 18: Ina is very protective of Larry, praying for him to find a true friend and to become healthy and strong. Larry doesn't seem to resent his mother's devotion.
3. Alice and Silas – p. 134, l. 28 to p. 143, l. 25: there is almost a total lack of communication between the two, leading to a fateful chain of events: Alice hitting Silas, Silas running off, Silas and Alice losing almost all of their possessions when they are robbed during his flight
4. Alice and Silas – p. 246, l. 13 to p. 248, l.14: Alice wants to protect her son from the repercussions of having a white girlfriend (possibly because she herself has suffered the consequences of her relationship with Carl Ott)

5. Cecil and Cindy – p. 109, l. 3 to p. 110, l. 7 and p. 245, l. 14 to p. 246, l. 9: Cecil makes sexual advances towards Cindy (perhaps in order to control her?)
6. Cecil and Cindy – p. 158, l. 17 to p. 161, l. 10: while Cindy is both openly and covertly defiant, Cecil tries to control her actions (obviously without success which is why he uses Larry as an outlet for his aggression)

EVALUATION

5 👥 **In groups, use your results from above as a starting point . . .**

UNTERRICHTS-KONZEPT

Siehe die methodisch-didaktischen Hinweise zu Aufgabe 4.

Larry	Cindy	Silas
mother: • Ina accepts Larry for who he is • defends him in front of Carl • prays for him (= provides reassurance) father: • wants his son to be athletic and manually skilled • teaches him how to shoot a gun, lends him a gun • bullies him into a physical confrontation and doesn't help him reaction of the teenager: • wanting to please his father at all costs (at the garage, in the fight with Silas) • takes care of his mother's chickens • continues his father's business even after his death and looks after his truck/his tractor (as an adult)	mother: • is practically non-existent • seems to prefer her husband over her child • wants her to stop messing around with boys father: • (stepfather) • wants to control Cindy in every possible way reaction of the teenager: • open and covert defiance (is this why she subconsciously chooses Silas as a boyfriend?)	mother: • tries to offer him a stable and secure home (works several jobs, supports him through college, protects him from Cecil's wrath by sending him away) • wants him to be "a different boy" and be successful father: • as a child and teenager, he doesn't really know who his father is reaction of the teenager: • at first he defies his mother, in the end he submits to her (because it makes his life simpler → he chooses the easy way out)

ANALYSIS

6 Two sons – one father: The presence of Silas strongly affects the . . .

UNTERRICHTS-KONZEPT

Siehe die methodisch-didaktischen Hinweise zu Aufgabe 4. Sollte diese Aufgabe losgelöst von den Aufgaben 4 und 5 behandelt werden, kann sie aufgrund ihres Anspruchs auch teilweise im Plenum behandelt werden. Die Lehrkraft könnte dazu die Ereignisse bereits vorgeben (What happened?), und diese von den SuS zunächst in die richtige Reihenfolge bringen lassen. In einer Lesephase konsultieren die SuS dann zunächst ihren Reading log und die gelösten Comprehension tasks zu den betreffenden Kapiteln und notieren sich – ggf. auch nach einer weiteren Stilllesephase – ihre Ergebnisse zur Rolle von Silas und der Reaktion von Carl. Die Ergebnisse werden im Plenum verglichen und ergänzt.

	Chapter 1: meeting Alice and Silas	Chapter 3: with Ina's brother and at the garage	Chapter 5: fighting for the rifle	Chapter 7: the aftermath of the date	Chapter 7: Carl's death
What happens	Larry asks Carl to give Alice and Silas a lift; Larry tells his mother	Larry doesn't meet his father's physical expectations	Larry gives Silas his father's rifle; Carl forces Silas to play out his physical dominance and subsequently destroys their friendship	Larry is accused of murder – the public condemnation breaks his parents; Larry is sent off and has to leave the family	Carl becomes an alcoholic and dies in a car accident
Silas's role	he is the reason Alice needs a lift (Silas needs to get to school) and thus indirectly causes a conflict between father and son	Silas is athletic (something Carl expects in a son)	serves to illustrate Larry's supposed faults in Carl's eyes	as the secret boyfriend, Silas is the reason for Cindy's sham date	Silas has already left Chabot behind, not caring about the conse- quences Cindy's death had for Larry
Carl's reaction	initial betrayal of trust (Carl silently shows his disdain)	disappoint- ment (Carl walks away from the table)	Is Carl angry that his "secret son" is all he wanted a son to be? Carl openly shows his disdain	final estrange- ment between father and son	Carl seeks solace through alcohol which leads to his death and to Larry's ultimate loss of his father

EVALUATION **7 Relate the familial situation of the story's adolescents with the results …**

UNTERRICHTS-
KONZEPT
Diese Aufgabe eignet sich zur vertieften Auseinandersetzung mit den Ergebnissen aus der arbeitsteiligen Gruppenarbeit in den Aufgaben 4 und 5.

LÖSUNGSVORSCHLAG
- Alice could have supported Silas in telling the truth and thus vindicating Larry (only to make himself a suspect).
- Cindy's mother could have stood up for her daughter and defied Cecil.
- Carl could have accepted his son's personality. Carl and Ina could have supported Larry's friendship with Silas, thus improving Larry's position at school.
- Both Alice and Cindy's mother spend little time with their children due to financial concerns – obviously this is a luxury they cannot afford. In this respect, Larry turns out the "best" – his only "flaws" are being in the wrong place at the wrong time and defending Cindy's honour.

Chapter 13 – 15

SENTENCE
COMPLETION

1 Read the sentence beginnings carefully. While reading chapters . . .

CD-ROM   → Kopiervorlage 3 (Southern literature) • Kopiervorlage 4 (Crime novel)

UNTERRICHTS-
KONZEPT

Aufgrund der geringen Kapitellänge und der einheitlichen Zeitstruktur erhalten die SuS in dieser Lesephase jeweils mehrere Kapitel zur Lektüre. Die Lehrkraft kann parallel zur Überprüfung des Leseverständnisses bereits mit Aufgaben aus Teil C Analysis *beginnen. Alternativ dazu können an dieser Stelle Kopiervorlagen zum Einsatz kommen (KV 3:* Southern literature, *KV4:* Crime novel). *Weiter kann die Unterrichtszeit nach der Besprechung der* Comprehension task *nun dafür reserviert werden, den Abschluss der Kriminalfälle zu besprechen. Da der* mystery plot *nun aufgelöst wird bzw. kurz vor seiner Auflösung steht, sollten die SuS in der Lage sein, letzte offene Fragen von ihrem* Wall display *(vgl. S. 46 im Schülerheft) zu beantworten und die* Case files *(vgl. S. 46/47) abzuschließen. Die gelösten* Comprehension tasks *helfen vor allem leistungsschwächeren SuS dabei. Dazu kann ein* Role play *simuliert werden:*

Task: Imagine you are a deputy working for Chief French. The chief has called a meeting to compare all the evidence in the "cold" Walker case and the open Ott, Rutherford and Morrissette cases. Each of you is asked to take over one case and present all of your findings and provide your theory as to who you believe to be the culprit. As a team, work out possible connections between the cases and sum up your findings.

Im Plenum können die Schlussfolgerungen der SuS und ihre Mutmaßungen über mögliche Motive in die gemeinsam geführten Case files *eingetragen werden.*

LÖSUNGSVORSCHLAG

1. Watching television triggers Larry's memory of Wallace Stringfellow <u>being the man behind the mask</u>.
2. Larry realises that only four people know <u>about the hunting cabin on his land</u>.
3. Larry's decision to fix his mailbox symbolises his wish to <u>repair his life, become stronger and to not let himself be bullied anymore</u>.
4. Meanwhile, Silas decides to <u>look in on Wallace Stringfellow because of the rattlesnake in Irina's mailbox</u>.
5. At Wallace Stringfellow's house, Silas finds <u>an aggressive dog and lots of snakes</u>.
6. In a confrontation with Stringfellow, Silas is <u>wounded by the dog</u>.
7. Stringfellow is able to <u>get away (even though he is shot by Silas)</u>.
8. The chapter ends with Silas <u>lying on the floor in Wallace's house with a rattlesnake closing in on him</u>.
9. Back at the hospital, Larry informs <u>Detective French about his suspicions concerning Wallace Stringfellow</u>.
10. Larry feels guilty about <u>not having listened to Wallace and not having told Silas about his suspicions</u>.
11. At the end of chapter 15, a recovering Silas is <u>moved into Larry's room</u>.

Chapter 16 – 19

MATCHING

1 Match the sentence beginnings and endings to create a summary . . .

UNTERRICHTS-
KONZEPT

Vor der Besprechung der Comprehension task *kann die Lehrkraft die SuS zu einer ersten, spontanen Reaktion* (one-sentence-reaction) *über den Roman auffordern. Dabei sind folgende Alternativen denkbar:*

1. Four corners-*Methode: Die Lehrkraft bereitet vier DINA4-Schilder für den Unterricht vor. Sie tragen folgende Aufschrift (1+2: Auszüge aus Rezensionen, die auf www.amazon.de zitiert sind; 3+4: Zitate aus dem Forum von goodreads.com, Quelle: http://www.goodreads.com/ book/show/7948230-crooked-letter-crooked-letter):*

• "Franklin's characters are captivating, and the sadness of the story stains your soul." (Metro-Books of the Year)
• "[W]hat sticks at the end is Franklin's heart-breaking depiction of loneliness." (Observer)

- "The plot itself was too neatly constructed in many places, and tied way too conveniently for my taste." (Maciek)
- "Larry is harmless, incapable of having a mean streak that would have otherwise given him a more rounded out character (and made his involvement in the crime more ambiguous)." (Jason)

Die SuS erhalten zunächst Zeit, sich alle vier Zitate durchzulesen, ggf. werden Wortschatzfragen geklärt. Im Anschluss stellen sie sich zu dem Zitat, das sie am meisten anspricht. Sie tauschen mit den anderen SuS in ihrer Ecke Meinungen aus und werden dann aufgefordert, diese auch im Plenum zu äußern. SuS, die sich von keinem der Zitate angesprochen fühlen, bleiben in der Mitte und werden am Ende des Gesprächs aufgefordert, ihre eigene one-sentence-reaction *vorzutragen und zu begründen.*

2. *Alternativ werden die SuS aufgefordert, sich in einer Reihe aufzustellen und damit (zunächst) nonverbal ihre Meinung zum Buch zum Ausdruck zu bringen. Das eine Ende der Reihe wird mit dem von der Lehrkraft vorbereiteten DINA4-Schild* "I would recommend this book to a friend". *beschildert, das andere Ende mit dem Hinweis* "I wouldn't recommend this book to a friend". *Die SuS positionieren sich zunächst stumm. In einem nächsten Schritt tauschen sie sich mit den anderen in ihrer Nähe aus. Zuletzt fordert die Lehrkraft einzelne SuS auf, ihre Einschätzung gegenüber der Gruppe zu begründen. Die Lehrkraft kann aus dem Unterrichtsgespräch heraus auf die Besprechung der* Comprehension task *überleiten. Neben der inhaltlichen Besprechung der* Task *kann die Lehrkraft auch auf Lösungsstrategien hinweisen, indem im Unterrichtsgespräch die Satzanschlüsse auf Hinweise untersucht werden, die bei der Vervollständigung helfen.*

LÖSUNGSVORSCHLAG

The news reveals Wallace	to be tied to Tina Rutherford's death.
Larry admits to Silas that	he had guessed at Carl being Silas' father.
Unable to endure Silas' proximity, Larry asks	to be moved to another room.
Meanwhile, Silas receives	a flurry of visitors.
Among them is Chief French, who	reports that Wallace Stringfellow might also be responsible for M&M's death.
French asks Silas and Larry	to keep their mutual animosity to themselves when interviewed by the press.
After being released from the hospital,	Silas is surprised to find he is offered a promotion.
The next day	Silas and Angie tidy Larry's house.
Silas returns Larry's gun, which	he has cleaned for him.
In order to elude the waiting press,	Larry leaves the hospital in the middle of the night.
Alerted by the security guard,	Silas picks Larry up and drives him home.
Back home, Larry discovers what	Silas and Angie have done for him.
The two men part amicably,	with Larry deciding to repair Silas' jeep.

C Analysis

FORESHADOWING

1 a) – d) **Write down the first sentence of the novel below and read it again . . .**

UNTERRICHTS-KONZEPT

Die Bearbeitung des ersten Satzes erfolgt kleinschrittig und kann damit exemplarisch für das Close reading *von Textpassagen stehen. Als Einstieg in diese Aufgabe eignet sich die Impuls-frage:* What should a perfect first sentence in a novel be like? *Am Ende stellt die Lehrkraft dann als* Wrap-up *die Frage:* Did this first sentence fulfil your expectations? Why or why not? *Die SuS berücksichtigen den Tipp zu* Check your notes.

LÖSUNGSVORSCHLAG

a) **Write down the first sentence of the novel below and read it again carefully.**
"The <u>Rutherford girl</u> had been missing for eight days when <u>Larry</u> Ott returned <u>home</u> and found a <u>monster</u> waiting in his house."

b) **Write down the key words on the lines below. Examine what questions they spark . . .**

the Rutherford girl	Larry's home/house	a monster
• significance of the name? • what happened to the girl (mystery – criminal case)? • girl or young woman?	• why was Larry's private space invaded?	• connection to the Rutherford girl? • what kind of monster? • what will the monster do to Larry (second criminal case)?

c) **Go through the chapters 1 and 2 again and find more elements of foreshadowing.**

Elements of foreshadowing in chapters 1 and 2		Their significance later in the novel
the zombie mask		• illustrates Larry's attempt to ingratiate himself with the others • used to scare Wallace off • Wallace wears it during Larry's assault and can thus be identified
the eyes behind the zombie mask	→	Larry knows the attacker
the snake in the mailbox		provides Silas with the link to Wallace
the character of Irina		• gives Silas vital information on Wallace • involvement with Irina give Silas pause to think about his life
the allusion to a conflict between Larry and Silas in the past		the estrangement between the two boys is a key factor in Larry's alienation

d) **Use of foreshadowing in a novel:**
   • to build up dramatic tension
   • heightens the readers' anticipation
   • can include false clues to mislead the reader
   • can help reader understand later plot development (and thus "prepare" him/her)

Use of foreshadowing in a mystery or crime story:
   • elements of foreshadowing serve as clues
   • resolution of the conflict/the mystery seems more believable to the reader
   • use of misleading "red herrings" (false clues)

ANALYSIS   **2   Narrative structure (time): a) – c) Review your reading log in regard to the …**

UNTERRICHTS-
KONZEPT   *Aufgaben 2 bis 6 beschäftigen sich hauptsächlich mit der Erzähltechnik und können in einer
Doppelstunde in Gruppenarbeit erarbeitet werden. Dadurch, dass die Aufgaben kleinschrittig
aufgebaut sind, können diese von den SuS auch ohne Anleitung der Lehrkraft bearbeitet werden. Die Präsentation der Ergebnisse kann auf verschiedene Arten erfolgen, u.a.:*

- One stays, the rest stray: *Jeweils ein Gruppenmitglied bleibt am Gruppentisch zurück. Die
  restlichen Gruppenmitglieder gehen von einem Gruppentisch zum nächsten und notieren
  sich bei den Präsentationen ihrer Mitschüler/innen deren Ergebnisse. Nach 2–3 Stationen
  übernimmt ein anderer Schüler die Präsentationsrolle am eigenen Gruppentisch. Die
  Präsentationsphase wird abgeschlossen, indem die Gruppenmitglieder ihren Präsentatoren
  die fehlenden Informationen vorstellen.*
- Gallery walk: *Die Gruppen füllen großkopierte Plakate ihrer Aufgaben aus. Danach gehen
  alle durch den Raum und informieren sich an den Plakaten über die Ergebnisse der anderen.
  Offene Fragen werden auf den Plakaten mit einem farbigen Textmarker notiert und am Ende
  von Lehrkraft im Plenum aufgegriffen.*
- *Schülerpräsentation: Die SuS erhalten eine Folie ihrer Aufgabe und verwenden diese zur
  Präsentation der Arbeitsergebnisse.*

*Alternativ dazu können Aufgaben 2 bis 6 auch arbeitsteilig als Hausaufgabe aufgegeben wer-
den. Die SuS erhalten in der darauffolgenden Stunde dann zunächst den Arbeitsauftrag, ihre
Ergebnisse grafisch für die anderen aufzuarbeiten (auf einem Plakat oder als Folie). Diese Plakate werden dann als Grundlage für die nachfolgenden Präsentationen herangezogen. Die SuS
werden auf den Tipp zu* Fractured tandem *hingewiesen.*

LÖSUNGSVORSCHLAG   **a)   Time: Review your reading log in regard to the time periods covered by each chapter. …**
The narration keeps shifting from the present to the past. Usually one chapter covers a time
period. When the momentum of the story picks up, flashbacks are added to the chapters
written in the present.

b)   Examine how the narrator uses flashbacks to relate the present to the past …
Answers posed in the present are partially answered by the flashbacks. In the case of
Cindy's disappearance, questions from the past are answered in the present. This shows the
truth as multi-layered and the intrinsic connection between the present and the past.

c)   Examine why chapter 10 can be considered pivotal.
As soon as Silas reveals his part in the Walker case (this happens in chapter 10), there are
no more time shifts to the past. In a sense, this 'chapter' of the past is closed, allowing the
characters to move forward.

ANALYSIS   **3   Narrative perspective and the crime novel: a) – e) Re-read the …**   → S8

UNTERRICHTS-
KONZEPT   *Die SuS berücksichtigen* Skill 8 Narrative perspectives *(**Green Line Oberstufe Baden-Württemberg**) und den Tipp zu* Types of narrative perspective*.*

LÖSUNGSVORSCHLAG   **a)   Examine the point of view the novel is written from.**
third-person narrative with a limited perspective

b)   To which effect does the narrator employ this technique?
The reader is given only partial truths and has to rely on the perspective of the character
the narration focuses on – as a third-person narrator gives the impression of being
objective and neutral as well as omniscient, the reader is tricked into taking his narration at
face value.

c)   Would the same effect have been possible with a first-person narrator or …?
A first-person narrator would have created problems for Larry – it is unclear whether he
survives the attack in the beginning. Also, Silas holding back information about his past
would be less credible. An omniscient narrator would be impossible in combination with
the fractured tandem.

d) **Why did the narrator choose to give this chapter a different narrative style?**
This chapter is told in a more immediate fashion, giving the reader almost unmitigated access to Larry's thoughts and feelings. For Larry, this is a time of great turmoil – he is putting the pieces together regarding Wallace Stringfellow.

e) **What is different about chapter 19? Why did the narrator choose to end the story in …?**
Chapter 19 uses both Larry's and Silas' perspectives. This could signify that their two lives are converging once again and that a renewal of their friendship is possible.

ANALYSIS   **4   One event – two chapters and viewpoints: a) – b) Retrace the events …**

LÖSUNGSVORSCHLAG   a) **How are these events narrated?**

Chapter	14	15
Events	Silas checks out Stringfellow, is attacked by his dog, shoots Stringfellow and lies incapacitated in Stringfellow's house.	Stringfellow was involved in a confrontation with the police and killed.
Narrated by	Silas	Larry who recollects what Chief French said

b) **What effect does this form of narration have on the development of suspense …?**
Suspense is drawn out which makes the reading experience more pleasurable – at the same time, events that have less of an immediate impact on the main characters (Stringfellow's confrontation with the police) are only briefly summarised.

ANALYSIS   **5   Tension and chapter 14: a) – b) Sum up the events of chapter 14 by writing …**

UNTERRICHTS-
KONZEPT   *Um bei der Bearbeitung dieser Aufgabe Zeit zu sparen, kann die Lehrkraft alle Ereignisse auf Folie kopieren und diese in Streifen schneiden. Die SuS erhalten dann zunächst die Aufgabe, die Ereignisse (ggf. unter Zuhilfenahme der* Comprehension task *als binnendifferenzierende Maß-nahme) in die richtige Reihenfolge zu bringen. In einem zweiten Schritt wird dann die Span-nungskurve im Unterrichtsgespräch entwickelt und visualisiert. Bei Aufgabe b) werden die SuS auf den Tipp zu* Turning point *hingewiesen.*

LÖSUNGSVORSCHLAG   a) **Draw the curve in the space below, labelling the decisive events.**

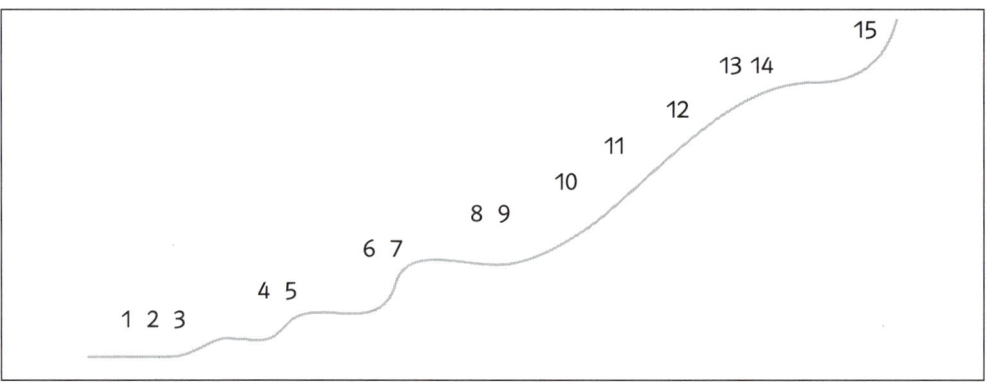

1. Silas checks in at work
2. stops by the hospital
3. feeds the chickens
4. finds out Stringfellow's address
5. goes out to interview him
6. sees the dog and finds Stringfellow on the porch
7. sees aquariums full of snakes and the zombie mask in the house
8. Stringfellow denies knowledge of where the mask came from
9. Stringfellow calms dog
10. Silas unable to call for help

11. Stringfellow lets dog off its chain
12. dog attacks and wounds Silas, who kills it
13. Silas shoots Stringfellow in the leg
14. Stringfellow hobbles into woods, Silas stumbles into house to find a phone
15. Silas breaks one of the aquariums, freeing a rattlesnake

The chapter ends without resolving the situation and leaves the readers in suspense, especially since the next chapter swerves back to the hospital and focuses on Larry again.

b) **Critics have argued that there are several turning points in the novel. ...**
Turning points in the novel:
- Silas reveals the truth about Cindy's date
- Silas confronts Stringfellow
- at the very end of the book, Larry reveals he might renew his friendship with Silas
- revelation that Silas and Larry are brothers
- discovery of Tina's body

ANALYSIS

6 Language and style: a) – b) Re-read chapter 1, p. 21, ll. 15–28 and ... → S10

UNTERRICHTS-KONZEPT

Aufgabe 6 a) kann auch unmittelbar nach der Bearbeitung von Chapter 1 bearbeitet werden. Das Internet hält zahlreiche Videos mit Stimmproben amerikanischer Südstaatler bereit. So gibt es beispielsweise den sogenannten „Accent Tag", bei dem Menschen aufgefordert werden, eine Liste bestimmter Begriffe vorzulesen, sowie Fragen zu beantworten. Entsprechende Videos zu Mississippi findet man über den Suchbegriff „Mississippi Accent Tag".

LÖSUNGSVORSCHLAG

a) **Analyse the style the author uses.**
- monotonous style (simple sentence structures: "A package.", "Several catalogs. The phone bill."; many sentences beginning with "he")
- action-driven (laden with verbs: "detached", "slipped", "picked up", etc.), seems as if the actions of a character are reported with as little embellishment as possible (exception: description of nature)

This makes the narration seem very reliable and straightforward, which might trick the reader into taking everything at face value. It also serves to show what Larry's life is like – monotonous, dull and repetitive.

b) **Illustrate how dialect can signify belonging.**
Passage (page and line numbers):
productive passages include Carl's story-telling at the garage; Silas' conversation with Irina and her neighbours, Silas at "The Hub", Silas and Voncille talking in their shared office, Wallace talking to Larry, ...

Examples from the text	How the use of dialect signifies belonging
Individual answers expected.	- use of dialect creates familiarity and bridges gaps between different classes and races - use of dialect similar to a secret code by which its members reveal themselves to each other as being part of the same group (and at the same distancing themselves from others)

ANALYSIS

7 Symbols: The novel contains a large number of recurring symbols, ...

UNTERRICHTS-KONZEPT

Erfahrungsgemäß fällt es SuS schwer, literarische Symbole und Leitmotive zu entschlüsseln. Die Lehrkraft weist auf den Tipp zu Symbol / Motiv hin. Die im folgenden vorgestellte Drei-Schritt-Methode soll ihnen den Zugang erleichtern, indem der Ausgangspunkt der literarischen Analyse das Weltwissen der SuS ist (Step one). Es ist denkbar, die Drei-Schritt-Methode zunächst für ein bis zwei Symbole im Plenum durchzuführen und die SuS dann in Partnerarbeit an den restlichen

Symbolen arbeiten zu lassen. Eine weitere Vereinfachung kann die Lehrkraft erzielen, indem in einer vorentlastenden Phase zunächst Bilder von allen Symbolen gezeigt werden und die SuS aufgefordert werden, dazu – beispielsweise mittels der Blitzlicht-Methode – Eindrücke zu sammeln. Der stumme Impuls dazu lautet: When I see this image, I think about …

LÖSUNGSVORSCHLAG

Symbol	Step one	Step two	Step three
snakes	• danger • poison/death • deception (Bible)	• Larry likes to collect them, is knowledgeable about them • Wallace imitates Larry; Cindy kills a snake on purpose • link between Wallace, Irina and Silas	• illustrates Larry's alienation (abnormal interests?) • in the end, snakes provide the missing link between the cases
books	• knowledge • learning • fantasy/ • creativity	• Larry loved books as a child/teen • as an adult, they are his only "friends" • Silas uses a book to prop open a window	• Larry uses books to escape from his dreary life; • the different meaning of books for Silas and Larry show their difference in character
guns	• danger • death • power • skill • freedom	• Carl gives Larry a gun, who in turn gives it to Silas • Carl teaches Larry how to shoot • Wallace gives Larry a gun for Christmas and later shoots him with it	• twice, Larry is given guns which trigger fatal developments: the first gun causes the fight, the second gun is used to shoot him
the zombie mask	• fear • non-human behaviour • Halloween	• Larry is proud of the mask and tries to ingratiate himself with the others at the party • he later uses the mask to scare off Wallace, who uses it as a disguise when assaulting Larry	• The mask hides Larry's true identity – that of a kind and responsible person. • However, he is confronted with two real-life monsters (Cecil and Wallace) without suspecting it. • The mask thus distracts from the true monsters in the story.
chickens	• supply eggs – fertility • cycle of life, represent nature • need care/ • protection	• First the chickens are Ina's, then Larry takes care of them. • During Larry's time at the hospital, Silas feeds the animals.	• Illustrate Larry's responsible character (his feeding scheme). • Illustrate Silas' gradual coming of age (taking over responsibility as well).

ANALYSIS   **8** Genre: a) Read the following definition … b) Assess whether *Crooked* …

UNTERRICHTS-KONZEPT   *Die abschließende Frage, ob Larry und Silas tatsächlich als Jugendliche ihre „Bildung" abschließen* (Do they actually come of age as young men?) *kann entweder mündlich besprochen oder als schriftliche Ausarbeitung aufgegeben werden.*

LÖSUNGSVORSCHLAG

a) **Read the definition of a Bildungsroman or coming-of-age novel and circle key words.**

A *Bildungsroman* is a type of novel that traces <u>the psychological and moral growth of its protagonist from birth or early childhood to adulthood and maturity.</u> In most cases, the novel of development <u>starts with a loss or tragedy that disturbs the character emotionally.</u> The hero embarks on a <u>journey of education and growth.</u> During the journey, the protagonist <u>matures gradually and with difficulty.</u> The plot usually depicts a <u>conflict between the protagonist and the values of society.</u> In the end, the hero is <u>able to accept those values and is thus accepted by society, putting an end to the dissatisfaction.</u>

b) **Assess whether *Crooked Letter, Crooked Letter* can be considered a coming-of-age ...**

Component	Larry	Silas
focuses on the growth of a protagonist from youth to adulthood	narration begins when Larry is in middle school, his further development is briefly summarised after his junior year; he re-enters the story as an adult	narration begins when Silas is in middle school and is interrupted after his junior year; he re-enters the story as an adult
starts with a loss or tragedy	because parts of the story are told in retrospect, the multiple tragedies in Larry's life (the break-up of his friendship with Silas and the disappearance of Cindy) lie at the root of his problems but are not immediately revealed at the beginning of the novel; his assault is more or less a culmination of all his personal tragedies	again, due to the retrospective passages, Silas's tragedies (the absence of his father and having to start from scratch in Chabot) are only revealed in the course of the plot's unravelling
journey of education and growth	for both characters, this journey more or less takes place in the present – being sparked by Wallace's assaulting Larry	
conflict between protagonist and society	as a child Larry is shunned because he is different; later, he is shunned by the townspeople and wrongly suspected – in both cases, the conflict is initiated more by society (difference)	the conflict Silas faces with society is due to his socioeconomic and racial background – he succeeds in mastering this conflict by becoming a successful athlete; however, this is only a superficial resolution (see below)
adherence to values ends dissatisfaction	for both characters, the dissatisfaction ends once they have come to accept themselves for what they are, thus being able to (possibly) renew their friendship on equal footing	

Argumentation:

Neither character never came of age as a teenager on account of different factors. Larry was demonised and alienated by the community. Silas turned his back on the truth by leaving Chabot.

The actual coming of age for both Larry and Silas thus takes place as adults. Upon his return to Chabot, Silas finally finds the courage to face the past and reveal his involvement with Cindy. At the same time, he takes over responsibility not only as the town's constable but also by caring for Larry's chickens and visiting his mother, and by pushing the investigation forward.

For Larry, his coming of age is triggered by his "friendship" with Wallace and his subsequent assault. Recuperating in the hospital, he comes across as a more self-confident, resolute man who is actively planning to shape his own future (e.g. be reinforcing his mailbox and repairing Silas' old jeep).

D Further activities

EVALUATION

1 Dealing with a review: a) – c) Read this book review. Which three . . .?

LÖSUNGSVORSCHLAG

a) Which three elements of praise does the review name?
1. startlingly beautiful prose
2. its evocation of Mississippi
3. its shattering, heart-breaking depiction of loneliness

b) For each element of praise, give more evidence from the novel.
Individual answers expected. Examples could be taken from the 1st and 2nd chapters – the description of the fields around the farm or the forest surrounding Silas as he makes his way towards M&M's corpse (examples of "startlingly beautiful prose"), the portrayal of Chabot as a vivid example for rural Mississippi's sad economic state ("its evocation of Mississippi") or of the 1st chapter describing Larry's routine at home and at the garage or his desperate attempt to make Wallace feel at home at the beginning of their friendship (e.g. by buying beer for him; "heart-breaking depiction of loneliness").

c) Write a response to the reviewer for the comment section using no more than . . .
Individual answers expected.

LISTENING

2 ◉ Read the tasks and then listen to the interview twice.

CD-ROM → Interview (NPR Interview with Tom Franklin) • Transcript

UNTERRICHTS-KONZEPT *Diese Aufgabe kann bereits zu einem früheren Zeitpunkt im Unterricht eingesetzt werden (ab Chapter 7). Eine weitere Möglichkeit ist, sie im Rahmen einer Stunde zur Southern literature (KV 3) oder zur Crime novel (KV 4) zu verorten.*

LÖSUNGSVORSCHLAG
1. d) as a novel with many facets.
2. b) already started the book when he came up with its title.
3. Rebecca Roberts describes the title as a so-called "shibboleth", suggesting that only people who grew up in the South will know what it means.
4. She characterises Larry Ott by summing up his troubled past/his bleak childhood and teenage years/his link with a possible crime.
5. false
6. d) getting away with tricking the people in the other cars.
7. a) describing his former relationship with Larry.
8. false
9. Regarding his black and white characters, Tom Franklin wanted his writing to reflect the difference between the races/what goes on in black and white people's heads.
10. c) restriction.
11. d) this is a genre he himself enjoys reading.

CREATIVE WRITING

3 Larry's date with Cindy (chapter 7) completely changes Larry's, his . . .

UNTERRICHTS-KONZEPT *Vor der Durchführung dieser Aufgabe sollte die Lehrkraft gemeinsam mit den SuS Kriterien für einen Tagebucheintrag entwickeln. Dabei sollte auch deutlich werden, dass es sich bei dieser Form des Creative writing um eine alternative Form der Textanalyse handelt. Somit entsteht hinsichtlich der Wiedergabe von Ereignissen und der Darstellung der Figuren eine hohe Verbindlichkeit gegenüber der Textvorlage. Die gemeinsam entwickelten Kriterien können bei der Ergebnissicherung – z.B. im Rahmen einer Schreibkonferenz – zum Einsatz kommen.*
Mögliche Kriterien:
- first-person narrator with a limited perspective
- highly subjective narration of events
- writing reflects the narrator's emotional state: distress, guilt, worry, doubt, fear, etc.

In Kursen, die wenig Erfahrung mit der Erstellung von Tagebucheinträgen haben, bietet es sich an, den nachfolgenden Schreibprozess zunächst gemeinsam zu beschreiben.

1. Re-read the events surrounding Larry's and Cindy's date.
2. Depending on the character you have chosen, pay special attention to his/her role and his/her thoughts (e.g. Silas's feelings when he argues with Cindy and she runs off; Ina's hopes for her son; Larry's sense of loyalty towards Cindy and his fear of being embarrassed).
3. Take notes. For a diary entry, it is not necessary to create a structure. A better way to organize your ideas in this case is by creating a mind map.

LÖSUNGSVORSCHLAG Individual answers expected.

NEWSPAPER ARTICLE **4 After Silas has been discharged from the hospital, he is interviewed …**

UNTERRICHTS-KONZEPT *Der Erzähler lässt offen, wie viel Silas tatsächlich der Reporterin offenbart. Allerdings ist davon auszugehen, dass er sowohl auf seine Freundschaft mit Larry als auch auf seine Beziehung zu Cindy Walker eingehen wird. Fraglich bleibt, ob er offenlegt, dass er zudem Larrys Bruder ist, zumal ihm Chief French im Kapitel zuvor davon abgeraten hat. Diese Aufgabe kann beliebig erweitert werden: Im engsten Sinne verfassen die SuS einen Text mit Reportagecharakter, der auf die vielfältigen Verflechtungen zwischen Larrys und Silas' Leben eingeht – ihre kurze Freundschaft als Kinder, ihre spätere Verwicklung in das Verschwinden Cindy Walkers und schließlich ihre Rolle bei den Verbrechen von Wallace Stringfellow. Die Aufgabe kann durch das Einfügen geeigneter Bilder aus dem Internet, weiterer „Interviews" mit den Rutherfords, Chief French oder dem Bürgermeister und der Gestaltung des Textes am Computer ergänzt werden (Anordnung von Bildern und Texten, Entwurf von Überschriften, etc.). Sollten die SuS damit betraut werden, eine echte Reportage zu simulieren, eignet sich diese Aufgabe auch als kreative Wiederholung des Plots und damit als Vorbereitung in der Phase unmittelbar vor der schriftlichen Abiturprüfung.*

LÖSUNGSVORSCHLAG Individual answers expected.

FORMAL LETTER **5 Before Larry leaves the hospital, Chief French tells him that the …**

UNTERRICHTS-KONZEPT *Diese Aufgabe gibt den SuS einen großen Spielraum bei der inhaltlichen Ausgestaltung, da die Familie Rutherford zwar vielfältig im Roman präsent ist (durch ihren Landbesitz, das Sägewerk, ihre finanzielle Rolle für die Ortschaft und letztlich auch dem Verbrechen, das an ihrer Tochter begangen wurde), aber nie persönlich auftritt. Dennoch wird deutlich, dass die Familie Larry gegenüber ihr Bedauern zum Ausdruck bringen möchte. Entscheidend ist bei der Ausführung und Bewertung der Aufgabe, dass die SuS einen entsprechend formalen, jedoch mindestens neutralen Stil und den für formale Briefe üblichen Funktionswortschatz verwenden.*

LÖSUNGSVORSCHLAG Individual answers expected.

FREEZE FRAME **6 At the end of the novel, Larry and Silas return to Larry's house. Re-read …**

UNTERRICHTS-KONZEPT *Diese Aufgabe kann auch als Vertiefung des Textverständnisses von Chapters 16 to 19 eingesetzt werden. Der Erzähler lässt offen, ob es den beiden gelingen wird, ihre Freundschaft wiederzubeleben. Während Silas offenbar daran gelegen ist, gibt sich Larry vorsichtiger und abwartender. Bei den Darstellungen der SuS sollte diese unterschiedliche Haltung der beiden Figuren zum Ausdruck kommen. Die SuS können darauf hingewiesen werden, dass sie die Haltung der Figuren nicht nur durch einen entsprechenden Gesichtsausdruck, sondern vielmehr auch durch ihre Körperhaltung, die Position beider Figuren zueinander und ihre Gestik zum Ausdruck bringen können. Ausgehend von den Darstellungen der SuS kann dann im Unterrichtsgespräch darüber spekuliert werden, wie sich die Beziehung zwischen Larry und Silas wohl weiterentwickeln wird.*

LÖSUNGSVORSCHLAG Individual answers expected.

ANALYSIS **7 "The land had a way of covering the wrongs of people." (p. 320, ll. 29 – 30). …**

UNTERRICHTS-KONZEPT *Diese Aufgabe eignet sich als schriftliche Hausaufgabe.*

LÖSUNGSVORSCHLAG

- Introduction: Repeatedly, the narrator describes how nature (the forest, weeds, grass) covers what humans have built and left behind; the statement implies that – as nature reclaims the man-made and silent witnesses to human struggle – the past cannot only be overcome but something can grow out of it and new life can begin; a different interpretation could be that the tangled mass of vines and weeds need to be cleared in order to uncover the past wrongs of people to finally set things right.
- Cindy Walker: The Walker place has been overgrown by privet, vines and kudzu (p. 320) thus losing its menacing appearance, invoking pity or even nostalgia and not fear.
- Alice and Silas Jones: The cabin they shared rests forgotten in the woods, at "the heart of some struggle, as if the vegetation were trying to claim the structure back into itself, pull it down, the earth suddenly an organic breathing mass underneath" (p. 193); Silas needs to expend energy to conquer nature's almost menacing seizure of his old dwelling to uncover the crime committed against Tina Rutherford.
- Conclusion: One the one hand, the people and their actions are depicted as part of the cycle of nature (birth, growth, death), also giving them the chance to start afresh. On the other hand, the characters can only move forward once they have freed themselves from their entanglement with the past.

COMPOSITION

8 Choose <u>one</u> of these quotes and relate it to the novel.

UNTERRICHTS-KONZEPT

Vor der Bearbeitung dieser Aufgabe klärt die Lehrkraft den Operator relate *mit den SuS. Die Bearbeitung erfolgt danach in zwei Schritten: Zunächst äußern sich die SuS zu ihrem Verständnis des Zitates, in einem zweiten Schritt belegen sie anschließend anhand von Textbeispielen, inwiefern diese Aussage auf den Roman zutrifft.*

LÖSUNGSVORSCHLAG

"The truth is: belonging starts with self-acceptance."
One interpretation of the quote: before you can feel like you belong to a certain group of people or a place, you have to define who you are and come to terms with that definition

"When I discover who I am, I shall be free."
One interpretation of the quote: only those who truly know themselves can be free of being ruled by what others tell them or expect from them

Text passages suitable for illustrating both quotes:
- Larry stops trying to ingratiate himself to others at all costs (he refuses Silas's first attempts at renewing their friendship), finally deciding to stand up for his own needs (e. g. he decides to repair his mailbox and not tear it down); he takes his life in his own hands by discharging himself from the hospital, ready to move on (now being the one acting and not reacting to what others say or do)
- Silas admits to his former friendship with Larry and his involvement in Cindy Walker's disappearance (he stops trying to hide who he is – from himself and from those around him by first confessing to Angie, then to Chief French and finally to the entire town via newspaper)
- Silas finally realises what he has been missing (compassion, loyalty towards other human beings → something he felt neither towards Larry (whose need for friendship felt alien), towards his mother (whose self-sacrifice repelled him) nor towards Cindy (whose disappearance seems to have hardly bothered him).

CREATIVE TASK

9 After having read the entire novel, create your own cover using a . . .

UNTERRICHTS-KONZEPT

Bei der Bearbeitung dieser Aufgabe können die SuS auch auf die Bilder zurückgreifen, die sie entweder in der Eingangsphase (bei der Erarbeitung des Themenfelds Belonging*) oder aber im Rahmen der Besprechung von Chabot im Internet gesammelt haben. In der Auswertung kann die Lehrkraft unterschiedliche Cover-Entwürfe der SuS mit den tatsächlichen Covern der verschiedenen Romanausgaben vergleichen lassen.*

LÖSUNGSVORSCHLAG

Individual answers expected.

ERWEITERUNG

Compare various aspects of the novel to those in the film.

UNTERRICHTS-
KONZEPT

Nach der Behandlung des Films Gran Torino *und der Lektüre des Romans kann die Lehrkraft folgende Aufgabenvorschläge mit den SuS bearbeiten, die ggf. auch für eine Klausur herangezogen werden können. Daher sind diese Aufgaben nur im Lehrerheft, nicht aber im Schülerheft abgedruckt.*

a) Compare the degree to which the personalities of Walt *(Gran Torino)* and Larry *(Crooked Letter, Crooked Letter)* are formed by loneliness.

b) Compare the ways in which Chabot *(Crooked Letter, Crooked Letter)* and Detroit *(Gran Torino)* are depicted as two cities shaped by an economic depression.

c) Both Thao *(Gran Torino)* and the teenage Larry *(Crooked Letter, Crooked Letter)* are outsiders. Compare the extent to which their families try to compensate for this.

d) Compare the means the film *(Gran Torino)* and the novel *(Crooked Letter, Crooked Letter)* use to facilitate the viewer's/reader's identification with the protagonists. Select one protagonist from each work.

ZUSATZMATERIAL

Zu diesem Kapitel gibt es im Anhang zwei Klausurvorschläge mit Erwartungshorizonten. Die Klausurvorschläge stehen zusätzlich editierbar auf der CD-ROM zur Verfügung.

CD-ROM

→ **Klausurvorschlag 1 mit Erwartungshorizont (How has the Confederate flag lasted so long in Mississippi?)**

• **Klausurvorschlag 2 mit Erwartungshorizont (The new president will inherit a profoundly divided United States)**

White, working-class and angry: Ohio's left-behind help Trump to stunning win

A ferocious roar rang out as each battleground state fell. [...] Inside a strip-mall office in Youngstown, north-eastern Ohio, dozens of white working-class voters were celebrating an extraordinary revenge after eight
5 years of bruising defeat by Barack Obama's rainbow coalition. A rebuke of an economic system that had left them feeling humiliated and hopeless.

"All the media and all the pollsters just didn't understand that the little people like us all over the
10 country were quietly supporting Donald Trump," said John Vass, a 66-year-old engineer and former Democrat. "And today we made our voices heard." [...]

Youngstown is one of many traditionally blue-collar Democratic bastions that voted for Trump on Tuesday,
15 buoyed by the Republican nominee's consistent appeals to those communities that believed they had been left behind. Early polling data shows that around the country the turnout for Trump of white non-college-educated voters was crucial in securing Trump's
20 victory. In 2010, the city was 47% white.

What appears to have made the biggest difference on the right was the turnout for Trump of white voters across the board – of both sexes and almost all ages and education levels.

25 Just a few hours after traipsing into their local Republican party headquarters fearing the worst, amid claims from some pollsters that Hillary Clinton had a 99% chance of victory, Trump's loyalists were suddenly drawing up their wishlists for his first term in
30 office.

"I don't want abortion," said Kerri Smith, a 48-year-old carer for disabled children and another former Democrat. Trump, who has a supreme court vacancy to fill, has pledged to appoint judges who would
35 overturn Roe v Wade, the 1973 ruling protecting a woman's right to termination.

Robin Speece, a 61-year-old retired teacher and yet another former Democrat, said she was eager for Trump to repeal Obama's signature healthcare reform.
40 Her husband, who already pays $700 a month for insurance and has a $7,000 deductible, is facing a 25% increase in his premium next year, she said.

"I am just so ecstatic," Speece said soon after Trump clinched Ohio. "It would have meant socialism in this country if Clinton had won. The end of the 45 American dream." [...]

Headline statistics show Ohio's economy recovering steadily under Obama since the 2008 financial crisis and recession. Unemployment has fallen. But according to US census bureau data, 50 median household income in the county is actually almost 15% lower now than in 2000 once inflation is taken into account. The proportion of [...] residents in poverty has risen by half since then.

Workers have been repeatedly squeezed by 55 bosses who blame aggressive overseas competition. Trump, in turn, was emphatic in blaming America's free trade agreements for exposing working-class people to the ravages of globalization.

Signs of decay are all over Youngstown. Factories 60 and office blocks sit vacant, fronted by overgrown yards and lined by broken windows that are thick with grime. Tufts of grass sprout through cracks in concrete paving that is in dire need of replacement. Signs and shopfronts are dirty and faded. 65

The Republican nominee managed to tie Clinton both to the North American Free Trade Agreement (NAFTA), which was implemented under her husband Bill after being signed by George HW Bush, and to the proposed Trans-Pacific Partnership (TPP), which she 70 once appeared to support but now opposes. At least among his supporters in north-eastern Ohio, whose former glories in steelmaking and heavy industry are legend, Trump in 2016 appeared to succeed in casting the Democrats as the party willing to sell out American 75 labor.

"The Democrats used to be for the working man," said Jasinski, the retired firefighter. "Now they cater to the very poor, who they can keep in bondage with free stuff, and to the very rich in Hollywood, to keep the 80 donations coming in. We in the middle have been forgotten." [...]

"I want him to bring America back," said Smith, the carer for disabled children. "Bring back the jobs, bring our country back." 85

(657 words)

Jon Swaine, *The Guardian*, 9 November 2016

Annotations
line 1   ferocious – aggressive, wild, very strong
line 6   rebuke – strong criticism
line 7   to humiliate – to make sb feel ashamed, to dishonour
line 15   to buoy – to encourage, to support
line 25   to traipse – to walk slowly
line 39   to repeal – to abolish, to annul
line 55   to squeeze – here: to put sb under pressure
line 59   ravages (pl) – damage, destruction
line 79   to keep in bondage – to keep under control

Autor: Bernd Wick, Neckartenzlingen
Textquellen: 1. By Jon Swain, Copyright Guardian News & Media Ltd 2016; 2. from Barack Obama's first speech to a Joint Session of Congress, February 24, 2009; 3. (Task II.2 d, quote) From: "Helen Mirren: Royal Family won me over (but I'm a working class dame at heart)" by Anita Singh, thetelegraph.co.uk, © Copyright of Telegraph Media Group Limited 2012; 4. Confucius; 5. Barack Obama, December 4, 2013
Bildquellen: 1. www.CartoonStock.com (Madden, Chris), Bath; 2. www.CartoonStock.com (Greenberg, Steve), Bath; 3. www.CartoonStock.com (Kamensky, Marian), Bath

I Comprehension (content 10 VP)

Tick the correct statement(s) or give a short answer. Use a quotation from the text to support each correct statement/solution: give the line numbers plus the first and last three words of the quotation. If the quotation is less than six words, write down the full quotation.

1. True/False

    On election night, Donald Trump's supporters were happy and relieved,   True ☐   False ☐
    but also surprised at the outcome of the elections.

    line(s) _____

    line(s) _____ 1 VP

2. Short answer

    Explain in your **own** words what John Vass wants to express by saying: "And today we made our voices heard." (line 12)

    _____

    _____

    _____ 1 VP

3. True/False

    Only elderly, white, non-college-educated men voted for Donald Trump.   True ☐   False ☐

    line(s) _____ 1 VP

4. Short answer

    Explain the intention behind Robin Speece's choice of the words "socialism" and "the end of the American dream" (ll. 44–46). What effect is created?

    _____

    _____

    _____ 2 VP

5. Tick the two correct boxes.

    All over Youngstown the negative effects of the economic crisis can be clearly
    a) ☐ tasted   b) ☐ smelt   c) ☐ seen   d) ☐ heard

    as they are
    a) ☐ omnivore.   b) ☐ omniscient.   c) ☐ omnipresent.   d) ☐ omnipotent.

    line(s) _____ 1 VP

6. Tick the correct boxes.

    Match the names of the Presidents with the free trade agreements and indicate whether they were/are in
    favour (pro) or against (con) the respective free trade agreement.   2 VP

	NAFTA		TTP	
	Pro	Con	Pro	Con
George W. Bush				
Bill Clinton				
Donald Trump				

**Autor:** Bernd Wick, Neckartenzlingen
Textquellen: 1. By Jon Swain, Copyright Guardian News & Media Ltd 2016; 2. from Barack Obama's first speech to a Joint Session of Congress,
February 24, 2009; 3. (Task II.2 d, quote) From: "Helen Mirren: Royal Family won me over (but I'm a working class dame at heart)" by Anita Singh,
thetelegraph.co.uk, © Copyright of Telegraph Media Group Limited 2012; 4. Confucius; 5. Barack Obama, December 4, 2013
Bildquellen: 1. www.CartoonStock.com (Madden, Chris), Bath; 2. www.CartoonStock.com (Greenberg, Steve), Bath; 3. www.CartoonStock.com
(Kamensky, Marian), Bath

7. Matching

Match the names of Donald Trump's supporters with their reasons for voting for him. Write the letters A–D in the appropriate column. You must use all the letters.   2 VP

Mrs Smith	Mrs Speece	Mr Jasinski

A is against neglecting the working class
B is in favour of reducing unemployment
C is against compulsory healthcare insurance
D is in favour of pro-life legislation

II.1 Analysis (content 10 VP, language 15 VP)

Describe and interpret the cartoon and relate its message to the text. Write about 200–300 words.

"Look - an uneducated white working class male. The sort of idiotic Brexit-voting, Trump-loving bigot who's full of intolerance and prejudice."

II.2 Composition (content 10 VP, language 15 VP)

*Choose **one** of the following tasks and write about 200–300 words.*

a) *Comment on how much the (factual/perceived) economic standing of voters has influenced the outcome of the 2016 Presidential elections.*

b) *Assess the advantages and disadvantages of the American political system, in particular the US electoral system, with regard to presidential elections.*

c) *"In a global economy where the most valuable skill you can sell is your knowledge, a good education is no longer just a pathway to opportunity – it is a pre-requisite" (Barack Obama, 2009). Discuss the statement.*

d) *"I'm not in favour of the concept of monarchy, but I do see the good in it if there's a good person in the role." (Dame Helen Mirren, British actress, 2012). Discuss the statement.*

Autor: Bernd Wick, Neckartenzlingen
Textquellen: 1. By Jon Swain, Copyright Guardian News & Media Ltd 2016; 2. from Barack Obama's first speech to a Joint Session of Congress, February 24, 2009; 3. (Task II.2 d, quote) From: "Helen Mirren: Royal Family won me over (but I'm a working class dame at heart)" by Anita Singh, thetelegraph.co.uk, © Copyright of Telegraph Media Group Limited 2012; 4. Confucius; 5. Barack Obama, December 4, 2013
Bildquellen: 1. www.CartoonStock.com (Madden, Chris), Bath; 2. www.CartoonStock.com (Greenberg, Steve), Bath; 3. www.CartoonStock.com (Kamensky, Marian), Bath

Speaking (Oral exam): Class in America

Partner A

Describe and interpret the cartoon and relate its message to the given quote.

Discuss the extent to which the USA is a class society. Some people argue that the American Dream does not exist anymore. Come to an agreement on whether this claim is justified.

"In a country well governed, poverty is something to be ashamed of. In a country badly governed, wealth is something to be ashamed of."

Confucius

Partner B

Describe and interpret the cartoon and relate its message to the given quote.

Discuss the extent to which the USA is a class society. Some people argue that the American Dream does not exist anymore. Come to an agreement on whether this claim is justified.

"The idea that so many children are born into poverty in the wealthiest nation on Earth is heartbreaking enough. But the idea that a child may never be able to escape that poverty because she lacks a decent education or health care, or a community that views her future as their own, that should offend all of us and it should compel us to action. We are a better country than this."

Barack Obama, 2013

Autor: Bernd Wick, Neckartenzlingen
Textquellen: 1. By Jon Swain, Copyright Guardian News & Media Ltd 2016; 2. from Barack Obama's first speech to a Joint Session of Congress, February 24, 2009; 3. (Task II.2 d, quote) From: "Helen Mirren: Royal Family won me over (but I'm a working class dame at heart)" by Anita Singh, thetelegraph.co.uk, © Copyright of Telegraph Media Group Limited 2012; 4. Confucius; 5. Barack Obama, December 4, 2013
Bildquellen: 1. www.CartoonStock.com (Madden, Chris), Bath; 2. www.CartoonStock.com (Greenberg, Steve), Bath; 3. www.CartoonStock.com (Kamensky, Marian), Bath

Erwartungshorizont
I   Comprehension (content 10 VP)

Tick the correct statement(s) or give a short answer. Use a quotation from the text to support each correct statement/solution: give the line numbers plus the first and last three words of the quotation. If the quotation is less than six words, write down the full quotation.

1. True/False   True ☑
    line(s) 1–2   "A ferocious roar … battleground state fell."
    line(s) 26–28   "… fearing the worst … chance of victory, …"

2. Short answer
    He wants to express that journalists and pollsters didn't (want to) know / realize that many people from the working class supported Donald Trump; but now this fact has been revealed by Trump's victory which was brought about by the votes of the working class.

3. True/False   False ☑
    line(s) 22–24   "… the turnout for Trump … and education levels."

4. Short answer
    Effect = exaggeration: Speece wants to portray Hillary Clinton as a socialist, which is regarded an insult in the US; the American Dream stands for opportunity and freedom, whereas Americans consider socialism to be the very opposite of freedom.

5. Tick the two correct boxes.   c) ☑ seen   c) ☑ omnipresent
    line(s) 60–65   "Signs of decay … dirty and faded."

6. Tick the correct boxes.

| | NAFTA | | TTP | |
	Pro	Con	Pro	Con
George W. Bush	x			
Bill Clinton	x			
Donald Trump		x		x

7. Matching

Mrs Smith	Mrs Speece	Mr Jasinski
B, D	C	A

II.1 Analysis (content 10 VP, language 15 VP)
Describe and interpret the cartoon and relate its message to the text. Write about 200–300 words.

- **Description:** On the right there are a white man and a white woman (possibly a married couple) who are looking/staring at a young white man. On the left there is the young white man (quite chubby/ overweight, with a cigarette hanging from his lip, no special haircut or outfit) who is strolling down the street, minding his own business. The caption (spoken by the man next to the woman, addressing her) reads: "Look – an uneducated white working-class male. The sort of idiotic Brexit-voting, Trump-loving bigot who's full of intolerance and prejudice."

- **Irony:** The man behaves (and speaks) exactly like the people he doesn't like because of their political opinion; he himself seems to be "a bigot who's full of intolerance and prejudice".

- **Message:** People should be tolerant of other (political) opinions. More general: we should not do (to other people) what we don't want other people to do (to us).

- **Message and text:** The text (newspaper article) is objective/neutral/unbiased. The author provides examples of real people who tell their personal story, which makes the article convincing. Furthermore, the author provides a lot of numbers, percentages, and facts (about former Presidents, trade agreements, etc.). This underlines the fact that the author is very knowledgeable about the topic and has done thorough research. The newspaper article is written in a factual style, the language used by the author is neutral. The author tries to explain the reasons why (certain) people voted for Donald Trump (without adding his own opinion or judgement).

Autor: Bernd Wick, Neckartenzlingen
Textquellen: 1. By Jon Swain, Copyright Guardian News & Media Ltd 2016; 2. from Barack Obama's first speech to a Joint Session of Congress, February 24, 2009; 3. (Task II.2 d, quote) From: "Helen Mirren: Royal Family won me over (but I'm a working class dame at heart)" by Anita Singh, thetelegraph.co.uk, © Copyright of Telegraph Media Group Limited 2012; 4. Confucius; 5. Barack Obama, December 4, 2013
Bildquellen: 1. www.CartoonStock.com (Madden, Chris), Bath; 2. www.CartoonStock.com (Greenberg, Steve), Bath; 3. www.CartoonStock.com (Kamensky, Marian), Bath

II.2 Composition (content 10 VP, language 15 VP)
*Choose **one** of the following tasks and write about 200–300 words.*

a) *Comment on how much the (factual/perceived) economic standing of voters has influenced the outcome of the 2016 Presidential elections.*

People who voted for Donald Trump because of their (factual/perceived) economic standing
- many people who once worked in the industrial sector, e.g. automobile manufacturing, coal and steel industries (in a region that was once referred to as the 'Manufacturing Belt' or 'Steel Belt') lost their job (→ deindustrialisation) and now live in the so-called 'Rust Belt' (→ members of the white working class)
- many people who are afraid of losing their job because of globalisation (and its effects on the US economy)
- many people who live in the (rural) region referred to as "America's Heartland," "Middle America," or "Fly-over country"
- many people who "felt forgotten" and left behind (economically) by the political establishment

People who voted for Donald Trump because of other reasons
- many people who didn't want Hillary Clinton (→ she has been part of the political establishment for a long time → her husband was President before her → "political dynasty")
- many people who didn't feel represented by any of the other candidates
- many people who are against illegal immigration, especially from Mexico/Latin America
- many people who are members/supporters of the NRA
- many people who are supporters of the pro-life movement (who are against abortion)

People who voted for Hillary Clinton
- many members of ethnic minorities (in general: low income)
- many members of the intellectual/cultural elites, e.g. many Hollywood celebrities (rich)
- many young(er) people (regardless of their economic standing)
- many people who support LGBT rights (regardless of their economic standing)

It can be assumed that the (factual/perceived) economic standing of voters has definitely influenced the outcome of the 2016 Presidential elections, but other reasons were important as well.

b) *Assess the advantages and disadvantages of the American political system, in particular the US electoral system, with regard to presidential elections.*

American political system: positive aspects
- the American Constitution (1787) is the oldest written constitution still in place
- US democracy is now the oldest/longest lasting in the world
- separation of powers: system of checks and balances
- (since 'The Great Compromise of 1787') there is a balance between the interests of the 50 states and the nation as a whole: Congress (a bicameral parliament) consists of the Senate (100 Senators who represent the 50 states) and the House of Representatives (435 representatives who represent 435 congressional districts)

US electoral system/Presidential elections: advantages
- the President can only do two terms → very democratic, provides for transfer of power
- the Presidential candidates (of the two big parties) are chosen by voters in primary elections and by party delegates in caucuses/state conventions → very democratic choice of candidates, provides for participation of the citizens
- the system of the Electoral College gives smaller states (with fewer inhabitants) "a political voice"

Autor: Bernd Wick, Neckartenzlingen
Textquellen: 1. By Jon Swain, Copyright Guardian News & Media Ltd 2016; 2. from Barack Obama's first speech to a Joint Session of Congress, February 24, 2009; 3. (Task II.2 d, quote) From: "Helen Mirren: Royal Family won me over (but I'm a working class dame at heart)" by Anita Singh, thetelegraph.co.uk, © Copyright of Telegraph Media Group Limited 2012; 4. Confucius; 5. Barack Obama, December 4, 2013
Bildquellen: 1. www.CartoonStock.com (Madden, Chris), Bath; 2. www.CartoonStock.com (Greenberg, Steve), Bath; 3. www.CartoonStock.com (Kamensky, Marian), Bath

US electoral system/Presidential elections: disadvantages

- the winner of the popular vote might not win the election; examples: Al Gore in 2000, Hillary Clinton in 2016
- what matters is the number of states a Presidential candidate wins
- the candidate who wins the majority (of the 538 Presidential electors) in the Electoral College becomes President
- the US electoral system is a majority vote; some people consider this to be unfair → many votes are disregarded, (the candidates of) smaller parties stand no chance
- some people believe that the Electoral College is an old-fashioned system

c) *"In a global economy where the most valuable skill you can sell is your knowledge, a good education is no longer just a pathway to opportunity – it is a pre-requisite"* (Barack Obama, 2009). *Discuss the statement.*

On the one hand, Obama is right:

- individual/personal knowledge becomes more and more important in an increasingly globalised world with a global economy/international trade, international communication/exchange of ideas and information, technological progress, digitalisation (widespread use of electronic devices, IT, internet, websites, e-mail, social networks, etc.)
- that means: a good education is "a pre-requisite" for finding a job/for being successful in an increasingly complicated world; people need e.g. (more) language skills, IT skills, etc.

On the other hand:

- not everybody (on the planet) has the chance to get a good education, especially in poor countries/ developing countries which often have a deficient/no school system
- people have different gifts and talents; not everybody can become an IT expert/software developer, etc.
- not every well-educated person might get a good job/might be successful
- mankind/political leaders must find a way to let everybody participate and profit from globalisation (the global economy, etc.)

d) *"I'm not in favour of the concept of monarchy, but I do see the good in it if there's a good person in the role."* (Dame Helen Mirren, British actress, 2012). *Discuss the statement.*

Pro (British) monarchy ("if there's a good person in the role")

- it's a cultural institution, it's part of a long historical tradition
- it's an institution that provides continuity and political stability (governments come and go)
- it's a symbol of national identity (and shared values)
- it's a symbol of national unity; (Presidential) election campaigns might divide public opinion
- a monarch can have an independent mind/does not depend on public opinion – like politicians who want to be (re)elected

Contra (British) monarchy

- there might be an unsuitable/(politically) untalented person in the role
- it's old-fashioned
- it's undemocratic
- it's way too expensive: too much pomp and circumstance
- a monarch might be out touch with reality, might not know anything about the concerns of the ordinary citizens

Autor: Bernd Wick, Neckartenzlingen
Textquellen: 1. By Jon Swain, Copyright Guardian News & Media Ltd 2016; 2. from Barack Obama's first speech to a Joint Session of Congress, February 24, 2009; 3. (Task II.2 d, quote) From: "Helen Mirren: Royal Family won me over (but I'm a working class dame at heart)" by Anita Singh, thetelegraph.co.uk, © Copyright of Telegraph Media Group Limited 2012; 4. Confucius; 5. Barack Obama, December 4, 2013
Bildquellen: 1. www.CartoonStock.com (Madden, Chris), Bath; 2. www.CartoonStock.com (Greenberg, Steve), Bath; 3. www.CartoonStock.com (Kamensky, Marian), Bath

Speaking (Oral exam): Class in America
Describe and interpret the cartoon and relate its message to the given quote.

Partner A
- **Description:**
  - in the top left-hand corner/in the background there is an old man (white hair; wearing something like a bathrobe) sitting on an oversized/very big money bag; he is sitting there in what appears to be a very comfortable posture with his arms spread out left and right; the words "tax break" are written on the money bag; the money bag is positioned on a (metal) platform that is attached to a kind of metal rod/screw; the words "concentration of wealth" are written on the platform
  - in the bottom right-hand corner/in the foreground there is a woman (wearing a skirt/dress) standing and looking at the old man; in her left hand she is holding a bag (made of cloth); the words "jobless benefits" are written on the bag; she is standing on a (metal) platform that is attached to a kind of metal rod/screw; the words "increase in poverty" are written on the platform
  - it's difficult to tell for sure, but the whole setup looks like/resembles some kind of balance (a pair of scales) with the two metal platforms as the two pans (dishes); here it symbolises the <u>im</u>-balance between rich and poor
  - the speech bubble spoken by the old man reads: "You have nothing to complain about … your side is growing too."
- **Irony:** the sentence spoken by the old man is very sarcastic; he is right by saying that the number of poor people is increasing ("your side is growing too"), but that is a very negative development for society as a whole; and of course the woman (as an individual) does have a lot to complain about: poverty and social injustice
- **Message:** the old man symbolises the rich (the upper class) who profit from tax breaks; the woman symbolises the poor (the lower class) who only receive jobless benefits; the speech bubble refers to the fact that the number of rich people as well as the number of poor people has been growing/is still growing
- **Message and quote:** the message of the cartoon matches the quote by Confucius: both criticise poverty/social injustice; the quote even establishes a connection between bad governance and the (disproportionate/excessive) accumulation of wealth

Partner B
- **Description:** in the centre there is a man with glasses and a moustache walking up a steep hill; he is in a stooping posture, bent forward; at the top there is a giant foot stepping on the man, the sole is touching the man's head and back; the man – in turn – is stepping (with his left foot) on a miniature version of himself; the miniature version of himself – in turn – is stepping on an even smaller miniature version of the man, etc.; there is no speech bubble or caption;
- **Irony:** the cartoon makes use of the idea of the matryoshka doll: the same figure is used/appears in different sizes
- **Message:** a man who lives a hard life (walks up a steep hill in a stooping posture) is caught in a very hierarchical system; he lives in a society with a pecking order (here: stepping on one another); he is oppressed/exploited (stepped upon from above) and he in turn oppresses/exploits others (steps on others below him)
- **Message and quote:** the message of the cartoon matches the quote by Obama: both criticise social injustice; the quote even establishes a connection between the gap between the rich and the poor and the resulting differences in chances in life; alluding that – if no support (education, health care, etc.) is provided by the government – poverty leads to (more) poverty → vicious circle

Autor: Bernd Wick, Neckartenzlingen
Textquellen: 1. By Jon Swain, Copyright Guardian News & Media Ltd 2016; 2. from Barack Obama's first speech to a Joint Session of Congress, February 24, 2009; 3. (Task II.2 d, quote) From: "Helen Mirren: Royal Family won me over (but I'm a working class dame at heart)" by Anita Singh, thetelegraph.co.uk, © Copyright of Telegraph Media Group Limited 2012; 4. Confucius; 5. Barack Obama, December 4, 2013
Bildquellen: 1. www.CartoonStock.com (Madden, Chris), Bath; 2. www.CartoonStock.com (Greenberg, Steve), Bath; 3. www.CartoonStock.com (Kamensky, Marian), Bath

Discuss the extent to which the USA is a class society. Some people argue that the American Dream does not exist anymore. Come to an agreement on whether this claim is justified.

Partner A and B

The American Dream does not exist anymore:

- increasing inequality/disparity between rich and poor
- increasing poverty
- growing wealth gap
- disappearance of the middle class
- increasing fragmentation of society: loss of (one common) American identity
- rifts in US society between: country – city, Republicans – Democrats, etc.
- many social problems: police violence, race riots, very high crime rate, high murder rate

The American Dream still exists:

- the US economy has recovered since the global financial crisis and depression in 2008
- today: low unemployment rate
- pull effects/many people from around the world still immigrate to America (for many different reasons)
- enduring appeal/attractiveness of the American way of life
- the US is the country with the highest number of millionaires and billionaires
- the US is still the leading nation in many/most fields of science and modern technology, IT, etc.
- most Nobel Prizes (360) have been won by Americans so far
- top US universities attract scholars and scientists from all around the world

Autor: Bernd Wick, Neckartenzlingen
Textquellen: 1. By Jon Swain, Copyright Guardian News & Media Ltd 2016; 2. from Barack Obama's first speech to a Joint Session of Congress, February 24, 2009; 3. (Task II.2 d, quote) From: "Helen Mirren: Royal Family won me over (but I'm a working class dame at heart)" by Anita Singh, thetelegraph.co.uk, © Copyright of Telegraph Media Group Limited 2012; 4. Confucius; 5. Barack Obama, December 4, 2013
Bildquellen: 1. www.CartoonStock.com (Madden, Chris), Bath; 2. www.CartoonStock.com (Greenberg, Steve), Bath; 3. www.CartoonStock.com (Kamensky, Marian), Bath

Große Mehrheit der Zuwanderer liebt Deutschland

Mitfiebern mit der Nationalelf: In Berlin-Neukölln zeigte sich bereits bei der Fußball-WM 2010 an einem Imbiss gelebte Integration. Viele Zuwanderer lieben Deutschland fast so stark wie Einheimische,
5 belegt eine aktuelle Studie. Integrationsministerin Özoguz sieht die Abkehr eines völkischen Verständnisses des „Deutschseins". Menschen mit und ohne Migrationshintergrund fühlen sich Studien zufolge ähnlich stark zur deutschen Gesellschaft
10 zugehörig. Bei beiden Gruppen liegt demnach das Zugehörigkeitsgefühl bei über 85 Prozent. Bei Zuwanderern christlichen Glaubens ist es höher als bei Muslimen. Das geht aus zwei Studien hervor, die am Dienstag von der Integrationsbeauftragten der
15 Bundesregierung, Aydan Özoguz (SPD), in Berlin vorgestellt wurden – eine Auswertung des Sachverständigenrats deutscher Stiftungen für Integration und Migration (SVR) und eine Erhebung des Berliner Instituts für empirische Integrations- und
20 Migrationsforschung.

Bei der Identifikation mit Deutschland sind demnach die Unterschiede gering. Der Studie zufolge stimmten rund 82 Prozent der Menschen mit Migrationsgeschichte der Aussage „Ich liebe
25 Deutschland" zu. Unter den Deutschen ohne ausländische Wurzeln liegt die Zustimmung nur unwesentlich höher (85,6 Prozent). Entscheidend für das Gefühl der Zugehörigkeit und des „Deutschseins" sind den Ergebnissen zufolge das Beherrschen der
30 deutschen Sprache, die deutsche Staatsangehörigkeit und ein fester Arbeitsplatz. Weniger wichtig seien Abstammung und Geburtsort.

Unterschiede finden sich jedoch bei den Herkunftsgruppen sowie bei Christen und Muslimen.
35 So sind den Studien zufolge vor allem türkischstämmige Zuwanderer pessimistischer. Hier fühlten sich 26 Prozent nicht zugehörig. Muslime, vor allem aus der ersten Zuwanderergene-ration, fühlten sich deutlich weniger zugehörig (knapp 70 Prozent)
40 als Zuwanderer christlichen Glaubens (etwa 91 Prozent).

Der Sachverständigenrat deutscher Stiftungen für Integration und Migration (SVR) erklärte, „exklusive Kriterien" für die Zugehörigkeit zur Gesellschaft

45 würden von Zuwanderern, die schon länger in Deutschland lebten, nicht mehr als so wichtig angesehen wie in den ersten Jahren nach ihrer Ankunft. Wie eine SVR-Umfrage zeigt, glaubt mehr als die Hälfte der Migranten (55,4 Prozent), die erst
50 maximal fünf Jahre in Deutschland leben, um zur Gesellschaft dazuzugehören, sei es wichtig, in Deutschland geboren zu sein. Unter den Zuwanderern, die schon zwischen elf und 15 Jahre in Deutschland leben, vertreten nur noch 33,8 Prozent
55 diese Meinung.

Integrationsministerin Özoguz will „weiter an diesem neuen deutschen Wir arbeiten und sicherstellen, dass sich keine Gruppe ausgeschlossen fühlt". Özoguz sagte, die
60 Studienergebnisse belegten die Abkehr von einem völkischen Verständnis des „Deutschseins". Trotz kultureller und religiöser Unterschiede gebe es eine „gefühlte Einheit" der Bevölkerung mit Deutschland. „Auf dieser Grundlage können und müssen wir weiter
65 an diesem neuen deutschen Wir arbeiten und sicherstellen, dass sich keine Gruppe ausgeschlossen fühlt", fügte sie hinzu.

„Wir sollten kein Integrationsverständnis weiterführen, das sich an 16 Millionen Einwanderer
70 richtet, wir brauchen vielmehr ein Integrationsverständnis für 81 Millionen Bürger", appellierte Özoguz mit Blick auf die Ergebnisse. Dafür brauche es unter anderem eine stärkere rechtliche und gesellschaftliche Partizipation, etwa
75 durch die doppelte Staatsbürgerschaft. Zur Wahrheit gehöre jedoch, dass viele Menschen seit Jahrzehnten Teil der Gesellschaft seien, aber politisch und rechtlich nicht dazugehörten.

Die Sonderauswertung des SVR fußt den
80 Angaben zufolge auf dem repräsentativen Integrationsbarometer 2016, für das im vergangenen Jahr knapp 5400 Menschen mit und ohne Migrationshintergrund befragt wurden. Für die Studie des Berliner Instituts für empirische Integrations- und
85 Migrationsforschung wurden 2014 insgesamt 8250 Menschen mit und ohne Migrationshintergrund befragt. Für einzelne Fragen wurden kleinere Stichproben genommen.

(530 Wörter)

Die Welt, 28.06.2016

I Mediation (content 10 VP, language 15 VP)
Your e-mail friend in the US is doing a project in his social science class on the question how much immigrants in Germany feel that they belong and how politicians have responded. Summarise the findings for him/her as presented in the previous article.

II Composition (content 10 VP, language 15 VP)
*Choose **one** of the tasks below and write at least 300 words.*

a) *Both, Walt and the Hmong family live in exile. Discuss.*

b) *"Like father, like son". Discuss the significance of this proverb with regard to the movie.*

Autorin: Susanne Pongratz, Stuttgart
Textquelle: KNA/dpa/nago www.welt.de, © WeltN24, 2016

Erwartungshorizont

I Mediation (content 10 VP, language 15 VP)

Your e-mail friend in the US is doing a project in his social science class on the question how much immigrants in Germany feel that they belong and how politicians have responded. Summarise the findings for him/her as presented in the following article.

Immigrants' sense of belonging:
- based on two studies
- Germans' and immigrants' identification with Germany almost the same
- Christian immigrants feel they belong more than Muslim immigrants; Turkish more pessimistic
- important for a sense of belonging is mastering the German language, German citizenship and a permanent job
- less important are origins and birth place
- increases with duration of their stay in Germany

Politicians' response:
- study proves that a sense of belonging does not depend on "a national German feeling"
- more efforts needed to make sure immigrants feel they belong and not excluded
- all 81 million citizens in Germany should feel that they belong
- advocate dual citizenship
- immigrants socially integrated but politically and legally separated

II Composition (content 10 VP, language 15 VP)

*Choose **one** of the tasks below and write at least 300 words.*

a) Both Walt and his Hmong neighbours are "displaced" persons – the Hmong family has left their homeland and settled in the US; Sue's and Thao's grandmother and mother still live in exile as they do not speak the language and have to rely on their (grand)children to communicate with their American neighbours. Walt also lives in exile, ironically at home, as he is the only white male left in the neighbourhood. He insists on his property which he is not willing to leave and have trespassed. However, he would not acknowledge that he lives in exile because he claims that this is where he belongs. But his insistence on the integrity of his territory contradicts his actual feeling of not belonging to the neighbourhood anymore. Walt's and the Hmongs' common sense of not belonging is actually the underlying reason why they do connect after all and overcome their feeling of being exiled. This is expressed at the very end when Thao attends the funeral service for Walt in his traditional Hmong clothes yet drives in the Gran Torino in the final scene.

b)
- **This proverb is not true for Walt and his sons:** they are estranged because Walt's sons do not share his patriotic values – they drive and sell Japanese cars rather than American cars, they are more materialistic than he is and they do not take a real interest in him; they do not really belong to each other and this might be partly the case because they have moved up on the social ladder (they live in a bigger house, daughter wants to go to college).
- **True for Walt and his 'adopted' son Thao:** Walt teaches Thao the American way of life by initiating him into a man's world i.e. speaking like a (working class) man, fixing things and taking out a girl. Thao willingly follows his commands and as the end of the movie suggests has been a docile pupil and become a "son".

Autorin: Susanne Pongratz, Stuttgart
Textquelle: KNA/dpa/nago www.welt.de, © WeltN24, 2016

I   Listening comprehension (content 10 VP)

Listen to the radio report twice. First read the annotations, then do the tasks below.

Annotations

Kat Chow – the name of the person telling her dad's story
cringe inducing – causing embarrassment
chink – a very offensive word for somebody from China

True or false? Tick the correct box.   3 VP

1. If you use different language it does not mean that people look   True ☐   False ☐
   at things differently.
2. Kat Chow's father still has an accent.   True ☐   False ☐
3. Kat Chow tells her father that he should hold onto the word 'Oriental'. True ☐   False ☐

Tick the one correct solution.   1 VP

4. Kat Chow's father's restaurant …
   ☐ was special as an Asian restaurant.
   ☐ attracted non-Asian customers.
   ☐ fulfilled his American dream.
   ☐ was financially successful.

Fill in the gaps.   2 VP

5. When using the word 'Oriental', …

   Kat Chow's father thought that the word was _____ .

   Kat Chow thinks that word _____ .

Tick the two correct solutions.   2 VP

6. When Kat Chow was a child, …
   ☐ she did not like interacting with white children.
   ☐ she was treated disrespectfully by her white friend.
   ☐ she knew that her friend's parents did not like her.
   ☐ her father did not mind being called 'Oriental'.
   ☐ the term 'Asian' was not popular among intellectuals.

True or false? Tick the correct box.   2 VP

7. Kat Chow loved working in the Chinese restaurant.   True ☐   False ☐
8. When meeting the white customer Kat Chow felt accepted as   True ☐   False ☐
   an American.

II   Analysis (content 10 VP, language 15 VP)
*Choose **one** of the following tasks and write at least 300 words.*

a) Walt says about Thao: "This kid does not have a chance." Explain this quote in the context of the movie and analyse how Walt deals with this observation.

b) Walt belongs to the past. Explain.

Erwartungshorizont

Transkript

My 'Oriental' father: On the words we use to describe ourselves

KELLY MCEVERS, HOST	President Obama has signed a bill that replaces the term Oriental with Asian-American in federal laws. Changing words is one thing. Changing minds is another thing. Kat Chow of NPR's Code Switch team has this story about her dad and how he chooses to describe himself.
KAT CHOW, BYLINE	My dad came to the U.S. in 1969 from Hong Kong. He speaks English lilted with Taishanese, and he still uses the word Oriental. It's his go-to term for anything Asian. This place used to be an Oriental restaurant, he'll say, as we drive by a boarded-up takeout joint. We use Asian or Asian-American now, I'll tell him. The term's been outdated for a long time. He just shrugs. I'm Oriental, he'll say.

My dad used to own one of those so-called Oriental restaurants in a tiny Connecticut suburb. It was his version of the American dream. He named it Lotus Garden. He wanted it to pull in a Chinese crowd, but it never did. It was a place where white people would go for egg drop soup. It looked like every other Asian restaurant catering to non-Asians - red faux leather booths, paintings of fish in ponds. And it would eventually go bankrupt.

In a way, my dad's oriental restaurant mirrored the word itself. It became something white people experienced as foreign, even if that's not what he intended. The restaurant is long gone, and my dad still calls himself Oriental. I have to remind myself he doesn't see the word how I do - cringe inducing. It makes me think of caricatures of grinning Asian men with ponytails and buck teeth. I worry that's kind of how my dad's neighbours see him. And here's why.

When I was 9 or 10, I was playing with a white girl my age. Out of nowhere, she hissed, shut up, you chink. It only occurred to me a couple of years ago that she may have heard her parents use it to describe my family. The word chink was always meant to cut, but there was a time - my dad's - when Oriental wasn't. When he learned English, Oriental was OK. By the time I was born, scholars and activists used words like Asian or Asian-American instead. There was a change in attitude, but not everybody got the memo.

When I was 16, I worked in a Chinese restaurant owned by a Cantonese couple. Every night, the staff would retreat to the back for family meal, one of my favourite parts of working there. It was the most Chinese people I'd ever been around not counting family, and that's why one memory stands out.

I was greeting customers at the front when a woman - white and middle-aged - said to be me, oh, your English is so good. And I said, I'd hope so; I was born here. She hadn't said your English is so good for an Oriental, but she might as well have. I felt Oriental - foreign, other. All the relief I'd had of being around people who looked like me evaporated. I did want to be seen as part of this group but on my own terms, not in the box this woman was trying to tuck me into.

That's one reason why I wanted my dad to stop using oriental. It was my worry that as long as he used it, it would be OK for others to feel that way about him. But even if my dad never says that word again and my generation of Asian-Americans don't use it, we can't dislodge it from everyone else's minds. We can think that by using this word and not that or dressing differently or having different tastes, our parents can make things better for themselves and, by extension, us. But all that wishing won't matter if the rest of the world won't bend.

MCEVERS	That's Kat Chow of NPR's Code Switch team.

Autorin: Susanne Pongratz, Stuttgart
Textquelle: © 2016 National Public Radio, Inc.

Solutions

I Listening comprehension (content 10 VP)

1. True ☑
2. True ☑
3. False ☑
4. ☑ attracted non-Asian customers.
5. When using the word 'oriental', Kat Chow's father thought that the word was <u>something positive/something he identified with</u> (1VP). Kat Chow thinks that word <u>misrepresents Asians/embarrasses her</u> (1 VP).
6. ☑ she was treated disrespectfully by her white friend.
   ☑ her father did not mind being called 'Oriental'.
7. True ☑
8. False ☑

II Analysis (content 10 VP, language 15 VP)
*Choose **one** of the tasks below and write at least 300 words.*

a)
- realistic assessment of Thao's situation vis à vis the Hmong gang members; they harass him and, as it turns out, even hurt him because his loyalties are with Walt and not with them
- Walt cares for him by teaching him values like working hard, finding a girl (and starting a family eventually) and thus entering mainstream America; this way he wants to protect Thao from the gang

b)
- Walt's sons think that he still lives in the 1950s and that he has not adapted to the present
- he cherishes things from the past like the Gran Torino which stands for hard work and the pride of the working class doing manual work and being loyal to American products
- he cannot accept cars being built by or bought from foreign manufacturers
- he cannot accept foreigners who are not willing to adapt to American culture and values

Autorin: Susanne Pongratz, Stuttgart
Textquelle: © 2016 National Public Radio, Inc.

How has the Confederate flag lasted so long in Mississippi?

Last June, the racially motivated shooting of nine African-American churchgoers in Charleston, South Carolina plunged the country into a debate over the relevancy and potential dangers of the Confederate
5 flag. The flag, which had been featured in photographs with the shooter, was removed from South Carolina statehouse grounds less than a month later. In the months that followed, the flag was thrust into the national spotlight as a symbol of contentious race
10 relations in the US. Municipalities around the country voted on whether to fly it, students were suspended from school for wearing clothes bearing the Confederate symbol, and social media users urged others to tear down privately owned flags on homes
15 and vehicles.

A year later, much of the commotion has died down, though the flag is still subject to heated debate. The debate is especially alive and well in Mississippi, the last remaining state to feature the Confederate symbol
20 on its state flag. Some cities, such as Macon and Columbus, have voted or issued executive orders to remove the flag, whereas others, including Petal and Gautier, have voted to keep it.

Earlier this week, opponents of the flag held a rally in
25 front of the US Capitol in an effort to draw attention to a federal lawsuit arguing that the flag incites racial violence and infringes upon 14th Amendment protections for black Mississippians. The lawsuit was filed after the state Legislature failed to act on bills
30 proposed following the Charleston mass shooting. "This is about America making a decision about who it is," rally co-organizer Aunjanue Ellis, who lives in McComb, Miss., told CNN. Mississippi House Speaker Philip Gunn, a Republican, took an anti-flag stand
35 shortly after the Charleston shooting occurred. "We must always remember our past, but that does not mean we must let it define us," Mr. Gunn said in a statement. "I believe our state's flag has become a point of offense that needs to be removed."
40 Twenty-one pieces of legislation were put forth by lawmakers following Gunn's statement, some in support of the flag and some in opposition to it. Anti-flag proposals included replacing the current flag with the historical magnolia flag, which was used by
45 Mississippi prior to 1894, or appointing a commission to design a new flag. Pro-flag lawmakers suggested requiring that the state flag be flown on government property, and also proposed withholding public funds

from public colleges and universities that have ceased to fly the flag since the Charleston shooting, such as
50 the University of Mississippi and the University of Southern Mississippi. Despite a plethora of wide-ranging proposals, none of the legislation made it out of committee.

This isn't the first time the question of whether to keep
55 the current state flag has come up. In a 2001 referendum, Mississippians voted on whether to keep the Confederate emblem on the flag or replace it with 20 white stars to represent Mississippi's status as the 20th state. Sixty-five percent voted in favor of keeping
60 the current flag. "If the citizens of our state want to revisit that decision, and I am sure at some point we may, it will best be decided by the people of Mississippi, not by outsiders or media elites or politicians in a back room," said Lt. Gov. Tate Reeves
65 last year. Similar sentiments have been expressed by Secretary of State Delbert Hosemann and Gov. Phil Bryant, who said in October that he'd like to see the Legislature put the issue on the ballot in 2016.

In the meantime, citizens on both sides of the debate
70 are collecting signatures for potential ballot referendums. "It's been our state flag since 1894. The flag means a lot to people," said Wallace Mason, a member of the Mississippi Division of the Sons of Confederate Veterans and one of the leaders working
75 toward Intiative 58, a referendum on a constitutional amendment to keep the current flag. "It's gone through a lot of history in Mississippi and it stands for the history of Mississippi," Mr. Mason told the Sun Herald, a newspaper in South Mississippi. "It doesn't stand for
80 any issues that have been brought up against it."

On the opposite side of things is One Mississippi Flag for All, a group that's collecting signatures for Initiative 55, a ballot referendum that would remove the Confederate flag. "I think that the momentum for
85 support for changing the flag is growing," said spokeswoman Lea Campbell to the Sun Herald. "I think people are starting to realize that it is harmful to the perception of what those outside of Mississippi think of Mississippi; harmful to economic development;
90 and harmful to racial progress and reconciliation." While both groups are optimistic, the soonest one of these initiatives could reach a statewide ballot is 2018.

(798 words)

Gretel Kauffman, *The Christian Science Monitor*, 2016

Autor: Bärbel Hafner-Wünning, Ebersbach an der Fils
Textquelle: From *Christian Science Monitor*, 19th September 2016 © 2016 Christian Science Monitor. All rights reserved. Used by permission and protected by the Copyright Laws of the United States. The printing, copying, redistribution, or retransmission of this Content without express written permission is prohibited.

I Comprehension (content 10 VP)

For true/false- and multiple-choice-tasks, give a quote from the text to support each correct statement: the line number(s) plus the first three and the last three words of the quote.

Tick the correct box.

1. In 2015, a violent attack on churchgoers in South Carolina triggered a debate on …
   ☐ potential symbols of racism.
   ☐ the design of the state's own flag.
   ☐ whether to continue flying flags on churches.
   ☐ the history of racial violence in the United States.

   Quote: _____ 1 VP

2. Subsequently, a dispute about the meaning of the Confederate flag   True ☐ False ☐
   began among the Southern states.

   Quote: _____ 1 VP

Complete the sentence.

3. Much of the debate has now focused on Mississippi, because _____ 1 VP

Tick the correct box.

4. Mississippi law makers have modeled new laws about their flag on   True ☐ False ☐
   national legislature introduced in the nation's capital.

   Quote: _____ 1 VP

Complete the sentence.

5. Angered by educational facilities which have stopped flying the Mississippi flag, legislators have

   proposed _____ 1 VP

Fill in the grid.

6. Throughout the text, both opponents and supporters of the Confederate flag are quoted.
   Match the people with the opinions. There is one extra opinion.   5 VP

Aunjanue Ellis	Philip Gunn	Tate Reeves	Wallace Mason	Lea Campbell

   A   The majority of Mississippians feel the need to replace the flag.
   B   Outsiders should have no say in the future of the state's flag.
   C   There are people who see the Mississippi flag as an insult.
   D   The current flag impedes the state's advancement.
   E   The Confederate flag is a purely historic symbol.
   F   The American identity is at stake here.

Autor: Bärbel Hafner-Wünning, Ebersbach an der Fils
Textquelle: From *Christian Science Monitor*, 19th September 2016 © 2016 Christian Science Monitor. All rights reserved. Used by permission and protected by the Copyright Laws of the United States. The printing, copying, redistribution, or retransmission of this Content without express written permission is prohibited.

II.1 Analysis (content 10 VP, language 15 VP)

Analyse the Confederate flag as an ambiguous symbol of belonging.

II.2 Composition (content 10 VP, language 15 VP)

*Choose **one** of the following tasks.*

a) *"We must always remember our past, but that does not mean we must let it define us."*
   (ll. 35–37, Philip Gunn, Mississippi House Speaker)
   Assess whether this statement applies to Larry Ott as well.

b) *Comment on the economic situation of the rural American South with reference to the town of Chabot.*

Autor: Bärbel Hafner-Wünning, Ebersbach an der Fils
Textquelle: From *Christian Science Monitor*, 19th September 2016 © 2016 Christian Science Monitor. All rights reserved. Used by permission and protected by the Copyright Laws of the United States. The printing, copying, redistribution, or retransmission of this Content without express written permission is prohibited.

Klett

Erwartungshorizont

I   Comprehension (content 10 VP)

1. In 2015, a violent attack on churchgoers in South Carolina triggered a debate on …
   ☑ potential symbols of racism.
   Quote: ll. 1–5 "Last June, the … the Confederate flag." or ll. 8–10 "the flag was … in the US."

2. Subsequently, a dispute about the meaning of the Confederate flag began among the Southern states.
   False ☑
   Quote: ll. 1-5 "Last June, the … the Confederate flag." or ll. 8–9 "the flag was … the national spotlight" or ll. 10–11 "Municipalities around the … to fly it"

3. Much of the debate has now focused on Mississippi, because it is the only state still featuring the Confederate symbol in its flag.

4. Mississippi law makers have modelled new laws about their flag on national legislature introduced in the nation's capital.
   False ☑
   Quote: ll. 29–30 "state Legislature failed … Charleston mass shooting."

5. Angered by educational facilities which have stopped flying the Mississippi flag, legislators have proposed to cut their funds/stop funding them.

6. Match the people with the opinions. There is one extra opinion.

Aunjanue Ellis	Philip Gunn	Tate Reeves	Wallace Mason	Lea Campbell
F	C	B	E	D

Extra opinion: A

II.1 Analysis (content 10 VP, language 15 VP)

- symbol: object/person that stands for something else, usually a concrete object/person representing an abstract feeling/idea
- ambiguous: doubtful, uncertain, obscure or capable of being understood in two or more possible ways
- belonging: the feeling of being part of sth

In the text, the flag is associated with:

negative contexts	positive or neutral contexts
- featured in photos with racist shooter (→ symbol of racist hatred) - symbol of contentious race relations in the US - citizens (black Mississippians) feel offended by it - flag is harmful to the state (the way outsiders perceive Mississippi) and thus hinders economic progress and racial reconciliation	- worn on clothes and used to decorate homes and cars (→ symbol of Southern pride) - part of the Mississippi state flag, as such it stands for the history of the state
- due to white supremacists claiming the Confederate flag as a banner for their nefarious purposes in the past, this flag symbolizes exclusion and discrimination for many Mississippians (→ a symbol for not belonging to the white majority/ruling class)	- Southerners use the flag to show patriotism and a strong bond with the South as a whole and their state in particular (→ a symbol to show their strong bond/sense of belonging to the South and what it stands for)

II.2   Composition (content 10 VP, language 15 VP)
*Choose **one** of the following tasks.*

Individual answers expected.

Autor: Bärbel Hafner-Wünning, Ebersbach an der Fils
Textquelle: From *Christian Science Monitor*, 19th September 2016 © 2016 Christian Science Monitor. All rights reserved. Used by permission and protected by the Copyright Laws of the United States. The printing, copying, redistribution, or retransmission of this Content without express written permission is prohibited.

The new president will inherit a profoundly divided United States

The new president of the United States is inheriting a deeply divided America, after an election season that dramatically heightened racial tensions, breathed new life into "alt-right" and white supremacist movements,
5 and saw deadly acts of racial violence both on and off the campaign trail.

In the American South, in a state that has been deeply divided by racial issues for generations, people say it's not something political leaders alone can fix,
10 and that all citizens will need to work to repair a badly divided country.

"I pray and hope that the country will come together as one," said Robert Johnson, standing outside his polling station in Memphis, Tenn., on Tuesday
15 afternoon, having cast his ballot after a long night shift. "I hope we take this as a lesson to realize how far apart we are and come together as one nation, instead of a divided nation. There's a lot we can do together if we work together, rather than just nag one another."
20 A swell in racial violence began to appear in the United States as early as the summer of 2015 and it has continued – and escalated – against the backdrop of the contentious presidential campaign.

The country was rocked by a series of shootings
25 of unarmed black men by police, leading to protests, and in some cases, riots. A peaceful Black Lives Matter protest of fatal police shootings of black men in Baton Rouge and Minnesota held in Dallas in July ended with the ambush murders of five police
30 officers and the injury of seven others, by a black man who professed wanting to kill white people, especially police.

Three more officers were killed in Baton Rouge days later in what appeared to be a racially-motivated attack.
35 Last week, in Iowa, a white man killed two police officers in ambush shootings after disputes with authorities over waving a Confederate flag in front of black people at a high school.

Closer to the campaign, incidents were both
40 anecdotal and documented, and were plentiful. A homeless Latino man was beaten and urinated on in Boston by men who made comments about Donald Trump. A black Muslim woman was assaulted in Washington by a woman who said she was voting for
45 Mr. Trump. There were reports of students in Wisconsin and Indiana chanting "Build that wall!" during games against teams with Hispanic players. A Republican Party headquarters in North Carolina was firebombed with the words "Nazi Republicans leave town or else." A
50 church in Mississippi was burned and the words "Vote Trump" were spray-painted on the side. Here in Tennessee, a truck belonging to a transgender veteran was spray-painted with Mr. Trump's name and set on fire east of Nashville on Saturday. In Memphis the next
55 day, a black man filmed a racist tirade by another driver, who again invoked Mr. Trump.

Lecia Brooks, outreach director for the Southern Poverty Law Center, which monitors hate groups in the United States, said her organization has seen marked and increasing racial polarization in the country in the
60 past year, which she attributed in large part to statements made by Mr. Trump and the Trump campaign during the long election season. "This kind of rhetoric has served to, I think, polarize the nation even more deeply along racial lines," she said. "It's
65 kind of this pulling apart." The result is what has been called "the Trump effect," where things that would previously have been unacceptable became part of mainstream conversation during the campaign. Hillary Clinton accused her opponent of both inciting violence
70 and "taking hate groups mainstream" and has described the election as being a choice between unity and division in the country. At a rally and concert in Philadelphia on Monday night, she said she deeply regretted how angry the tone of the campaign had
75 become and she called on people to come together, saying: "We have to bridge the divides in our country."

In Nashville, Brent Leatherwood, executive director of the Tennessee Republican Party, said that in the days after the election, people across the country will
80 need to "sit down and break bread" with those who may not look like them or live where they do, and stop seeing people as others, but as fellow Americans. "The responsibility is bigger than any one person tasked with leading our nation," he said. "I think the
85 citizens of our nation are tasked with doing that themselves." He said one of the key lessons for any elected official is "to listen first," and that will be vital for the new president going forward. "There are Americans out there facing big issues ... and they feel
90 like no one is listening to them," he said. "That's not a Republican or Democrat issue. That's an American issue."

Greg Henderson, who lives in a suburb outside Memphis, said he has personally seen an obvious
95 escalation in racism since the election, and believes it is actually a backlash to the presidency of Barack Obama. "For some reason, white males thought they lost eight years with Obama. They think they've lost some rights somehow," said Mr. Henderson. "I don't
100 know what white America thinks they lost. I haven't seen anything that they lost. I think people are taking steps forward, and maybe people taking steps forward and catching up to them feels like losing."

At the Ernest Withers Museum on Beale Street,
105 employee Veleska Lipford said she sees the history of racism in America and the struggle of the civil-rights movement on the walls around her every day, violence that included the assassination of Martin Luther King Jr. outside a downtown motel in 1968. She said she
110 was increasingly starting to recognize the same kinds of scenes and sentiments outside museum doors.

Autor: Bärbel Hafner-Wünning, Ebersbach an der Fils
Textquelle: © Copyright 2017 The Globe and Mail Inc. All Rights Reserved.globeandmail.com and The Globe and Mail are divisions of The Globe and Mail Inc., The Globe and Mail Centre 351 King Street East, Suite 1600 Toronto, ON M5A 0N19 Phillip Crawley, Publisher

"So many people died for it, and it's so sad because we are repeating some of this today," she
115 said. But as Election Day wound down in Memphis on Tuesday, Mauricio Calvo was among those expressing hope the country could repair some of the fractures of the recent months. While comments about Mexicans and immigrants hit home for Mr. Calvo and others in
120 the Hispanic community, he said the election clearly exposed divides in many areas: between urban and rural, white and non-white, Christian and non-Christian. And, he added, part of the new president's work will be to reach out to all segments of the
125 community. He echoed the idea that individual citizens will also need to take action in their own lives to help their country.

"It has for sure divided the country, and no matter what happens, it's going to take a while for the country to heal," said Mr. Calvo, executive director of Latino 130 Memphis, a community and advocacy group. He was born in Mexico, but has been in the United States for 23 years and his children are American-born. With his red, white and blue "I Voted Today!" sticker worn proudly over his heart, Robert Johnson said he hopes 135 the new president will realize they represent the whole country and will work for the interests of all. "The bottom line to everything is hate. Can we ever just get over hate?" he asked. As he pulled away from the polling station, he rolled down his car window and 140 added: "And respect. We need to respect one another. Respect will take care of hate."

(1280 words)

Jana G. Pruden, *The Globe and Mail*,
8 November 2016

I   Comprehension (content 10 VP)

For true/false- and multiple-choice-tasks, give a quote from the text to support each correct statement: the line number(s) plus the first three and the last three words of the quote.

Tick the correct box.

1. Author Jana G. Pruden characterises the 2016 presidential campaign by …
   ☐ challenging the candidates' programs.
   ☐ condemning its focus on racial violence.
   ☐ criticising the role of white supremacists.
   ☐ enumerating the negative side-effects.

   Quote: _____ 1 VP

2. In the American South, voters like Robert Johnson see   True ☐   False ☐
   reconciliation as a combined effort of leaders and citizens.

   Quote: _____ 1 VP

3. When giving an account of the racially charged atmosphere in the US, Jana G. Pruden …
   ☐ accuses South Carolina Republicans of blatant racism.
   ☐ highlights police brutality against Latinos.
   ☐ lists racially motivated crimes happening at campaign rallies.
   ☐ names both black and white perpetrators.

   Quote: _____ 1 VP

Give a short answer.

4. Explain what the article calls the so-called "Trump effect" in your own words by naming both cause and effect.

   _____ 2 VP

Fill in the grid.

5. Throughout the article, several opinions are given on the division of the country.
   Match the people with the opinions. There is one extra opinion.   5 VP

Brent Leatherwood	Greg Henderson	Veleska Lipford	Mauricio Calvo	Robert Johnson

A   Current racism has taken root during the previous presidency.
B   A leader should apply himself to the needs of his entire nation.
C   The election makes voters decide between partition and consent.
D   Americans need to see what joins them, not what separates them.
E   The division of the country is not restricted to matters of ethnicity.
F   The mistakes that were made in the past are now being reproduced.

II.1 Analysis (content 10 VP, language 15 VP)
Compare the exclusion experienced by the "Americans" who feel "no one is listening to them" (ll. 90–91) to the exclusion felt by Larry Ott and Wallace Stringfellow in Crooked Letter, Crooked Letter.

II.2 Composition (content 10 VP, language 15 VP)
a) *Comment on how symbols create identity in the American context.*

b) *Assess the role guilt plays for Silas Jones by considering the relationships to his mother and to Larry Ott.*

Autor: Bärbel Hafner-Wünning, Ebersbach an der Fils
Textquelle: © Copyright 2017 The Globe and Mail Inc. All Rights Reserved.globeandmail.com and The Globe and Mail are divisions of The Globe and Mail Inc., The Globe and Mail Centre 351 King Street East, Suite 1600 Toronto, ON M5A 0N19 Phillip Crawley, Publisher

Klett

Erwartungshorizont

Kürzungsvorschlag: Die Zeilen 39–56 (150 Wörter) können weggelassen werden, ohne eine Änderung beim Aufgabenapparat vornehmen zu müssen.

I Comprehension (content 10 VP)

1. Author Jana G. Pruden characterises the 2016 presidential campaign by …
   ☑ enumerating the negative side-effects.
   Quote: ll. 2–6 "after an election … the campaign trail."

2. In the American South, voters like Robert Johnson see reconciliation as a combined effort of leaders and citizens.
   True ☑
   Quote: ll. 9–11 "it's not something … badly divided country."

3. When giving an account of the racially charged atmosphere in the US, Janet Pruden …
   ☑ names both black and white perpetrators.
   Quote: ll. 29–36 "with the ambush … in ambush shootings"

4. Due to the content of its campaign slogans/speeches (1 VP), the Trump campaign made topics which had previously been objectionable suitable for mainstream conversation (1VP).

5. Match the people with the opinions. There is one extra opinion.

Brent Leatherwood	Greg Henderson	Veleska Lipford	Mauricio Calvo	Robert Johnson
D	A	F	E	B

Extra opinion: C

II.1 Analysis (content 10 VP, language 15 VP)

"Americans"	Larry Ott	Wallace Stringfellow
• there are Americans who feel left out • during the Obama presidency, white males felt disadvantaged • however: according to Greg Henderson, "white America" hasn't lost anything, but others (non-whites) have caught up • some whites may feel as if the others' gain is their loss	• there are Americans who feel left out • during the Obama presidency, white males felt disadvantaged • however: according to Greg Henderson, "white America" hasn't lost anything, but others (non-whites) have caught up • some whites may feel as if the others' gain is their loss	• grows up/lives on the fringes of society (poverty, isolation, no steady job) • feels drawn to another outcast (Larry) and wishes to emulate him • is ultimately rejected by Larry (and thus has nothing to lose)
→ this frustration has led to an increase in racism and racial violence in recent years	→ this has led Larry to bully others (name-calling: Jackie, Silas), act against his good sense (goes along with Cindy's scheme), accept a dubious friend (Wallace)	→ leads Wallace to kill Tina Rutherford (to copy Cindy's murder), attempt to kill Larry, attack a police officer (Silas)
in each case, the feeling of exclusion (and possibly helplessness) leads to violent reactions; however, Larry is only violent as a young boy: later, his exclusion leads to desperate attempts at acceptance; in adulthood, his exclusion leads to resignation and retraction, ultimately severing his ties with the community		

II.2 Composition (content 10 VP, language 15 VP)
Individual answers expected.

Autor: Bärbel Hafner-Wünning, Ebersbach an der Fils
Textquelle: © Copyright 2017 The Globe and Mail Inc. All Rights Reserved.globeandmail.com and The Globe and Mail are divisions of The Globe and Mail Inc., The Globe and Mail Centre 351 King Street East, Suite 1600 Toronto, ON M5A 0N19 Phillip Crawley, Publisher